an insight and guide to
JORDAN

Other books by the Author
The Gulf States and Oman
1977

an insight and guide to
JORDAN

Christine Osborne

Photographs by the Author

Longman

Longman Group Limited,
Longman House,
Burnt Mill,
Harlow, Essex.

First published 1981
Reprinted 1985

ISBN 0 582 78307 0

British Library Cataloguing in Publication
Data
Osborne, Christine
An insight and guide to Jordan.
1. Jordan – Description and travel –
Guide-books
I Title
915.695'0444   DS154

ISBN 0 582 78307 0

Printed and bound in Great Britain by
William Clowes Limited, Beccles and
London.

DEDICATION

To Aileen Aitken

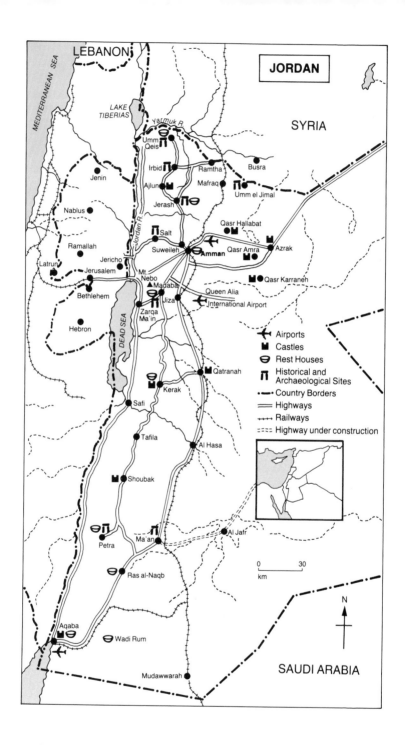

Contents

Contents

Foreword by Queen Nour

For me, writing an introduction for a book about Jordan is not a very satisfying task. It is almost frustrating. There is so much to write about our country, and yet tradition deems introductions short and general in nature.

Only about sixty years old as a modern state, yet its people are the inheritors of several civilizations that span thousands of years of history. Situated on one of the great crossroads of the world on the bridgehead between Asia and Africa, indigenous and invading civilizations left indelible markings of their legacies across the country. In Jordan it is almost impossible to sink a shovel into the ground without turning up some vestige of the past.

Archaeological excavations have shown significant traces of the Stone, Copper, Bronze and Iron Ages. Later, the Ammonites, Edomites, the Nabataeans, Greeks, Romans, Byzantines and down to our own day Arabs left visible evidence of their existence throughout the country.

The fabulous Nabataean Petra, a city carved in the rose-red rock stands today as a stunning witness to a remarkable civilization that defied the might of Rome between 300 BC and AD 500.

The amphitheatres in Amman and Jerash are exquisite examples of glorious Roman architecture. Jerash and Umm Qeis are today regarded as two of the most well preserved Roman cities in the world, complete with colonnaded cobbled streets, baths, theatres, forums and temples. Byzantium is immortalised by abundant tableaux of mosaics depicting the people's way of life. The famous mosaic map of Jerusalem at the Greek Orthodox Church in Madaba is possibly the oldest map of the city of Jerusalem in existence. The Crusaders left two castles almost intact. One in Kerak (Crac de Moab) and the other in Shaubak (Monreale); both in the southern part of the country. Early evidence of the indigenous Arabs and Islam is seen in several fortifications like the Rabad castle built in the northern part of the country to defend the Arab heartland against the invading forces of Byzantium and later the Crusaders. The Desert Castles were built by the Ummayad Princes in the seventh century mainly for hunting and recreational purposes.

But all this is Jordan's past. What of Jordan's present? Modern Jordan is something of a miracle. Less than sixty years old as a modern state it has been through four wars in three decades. The inflow of refugees tripled the size of its population within a period of twenty-five years.

Eighty per cent desert and without oil, Jordan defied tremendous odds and has become a modern state with a network of good roads, a thriving industrial and agricultural sector. The schools are packed with students; with more than 60,000 seeking higher education in local and foreign universities.

Jordanians have one of the highest standards of education in the area. Because of its central location Jordan is fast becoming an international centre for business, making it an ideal route to the lucrative markets of the Gulf and Arabia.

Jordan offers a moderate climate, warm and sunny for almost seven months between April and October.

Jordanians are probably the kindest and most hospitable people in the Middle East, who have retained the finest qualities of their Arab heritage and remain open-minded and receptive to the trends of a changing modern world.

Above all Jordan is blessed with a wise and enlightened leadership. Under HM King Hussein, Jordan has become an example of stability and moderation in an area undergoing a fast political, economic and social evolution.

We want the people of the world to see our country, to enjoy its history, heritage and culture. Also to appreciate its present and its aspiration for a peaceful and better future.

We also want the visitor to meet and get to know our people. Such contacts undoubtedly lead to better understanding among the peoples of the world.

Author's Foreword

A fresh May morning dawns in Amman with the promise of heat. Although it is still only six o'clock, birds twitter in a cypress outside my window and from a distant hill comes the faint hum as the first bulldozer of the day begins work.

Shortly, when the souq opens, I will drive downtown for last-minute buys of spices and a gold chain that I have admired over many visits to Jordan.

At midday ALIA, The Royal Jordanian Airline, will fly me to London, a strange feeling, having become involved with a country, to leave, with the last word written.

I leave behind several people whom I would like to thank, but there are also others who helped, perhaps only briefly, or even unknowingly, towards the completion of this book and photographs.

Michael Hamarneh, Under Secretary, Ministry of Information, and Abdel Rahman El Bahri, Marketing Director, Ministry of Tourism, who was extremely helpful. Ali Ghandour, Chairman of ALIA, The Royal Jordanian Airline and Norma Qarrain, ALIA, Director Customer Relations. Maher Abu Jafar, Reserves Manager, Royal Society for the Conservation of Nature in Jordan and Dr. Dawud Al-Eisawi, Faculty of Science, University of Jordan. Peter Salah, Information Adviser to Prime Minister, Adnan Haboo, UNDP, Hotel Training Centre, Amman; and Barbara van Daelen for use of the under-water photograph in the colour section.

In East Jerusalem, Raji E. Khoury, Chief Executive Officer of Shepherd's Tours & Travels was particularly kind and helpful.

In England I would like to thank Emma Bodossian of ALIA for liaising between London and Amman.

In Australia, Katherine Kouvaras kindly read the manuscript.

My mother was always patient and encouraging during my comings and goings between Lake Macquarie, London and Amman. Were she and my driver, Adeb Debebneh to meet, they would no doubt find plenty to talk about.

Adeb, who was never late, has my special thanks.

Christine Osborne
1984

The publishers are grateful to GEO Projects, s.a.r.l., P.O. Box 113, Beirut, Lebanon for source material used for the map of Amman on Page 20. The following works have also been referred to: *Guide to Jordan*, The Franciscan Fathers, and *This is Jerusalem*, Herbert Bishko, Heritage Publishing Ltd.

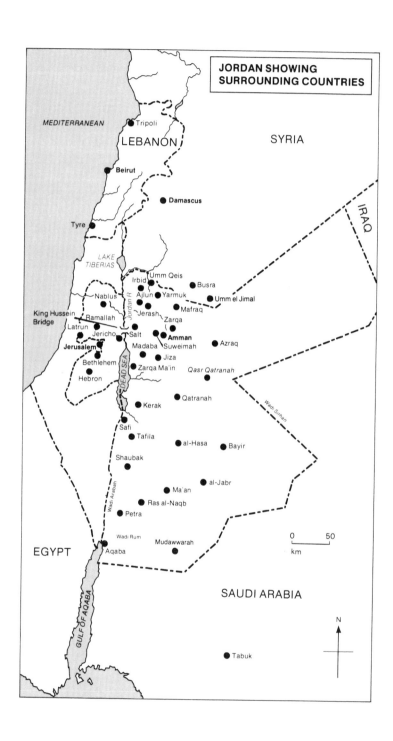

JORDAN SHOWING SURROUNDING COUNTRIES

MEDITERRANEAN

LEBANON

SYRIA

Tripoli

Beirut

Damascus

IRAQ

Tyre

LAKE TIBERIAS

Umm Qeis

Irbid   Busra

Ajlun   Yarmuk   Umm el Jimal

Nablus   Mafraq

Jordan R.

Jerash

Zarqa

King Hussein Bridge

Ramallah

Latrun   Jericho   Salt   **Amman**   Azraq

Jerusalem   Madaba   Suweimah

Bethlehem   Zarqa Ma'in   Jiza

Hebron   Qasr Qatranah

DEAD SEA   Qatranah

Kerak

Safi

Tafila

al-Hasa   Bayir

Shaubak

al-Jabr

Ma'an

Wadi Araba

Ras al-Naqb

Petra

Wadi Sirhan

Wadi Rum   Mudawwarah

EGYPT   Aqaba

SAUDI ARABIA

GULF OF AQABA

0   50
km

N

Tabuk

Chapter One

Location and Area

On a map of the Middle East, the Hashemite Kingdom of
Jordan resembles a clenched fist being struck against Israel
which has occupied the West Bank of the River Jordan
since 1967. Including the occupied territories, Jordan has
a total area of 96,188 square kilometres. It shares borders
with Syria, Iraq and Saudi Arabia; 27 kilometres of coastline at the head of the Gulf of Aqaba save it from being
landlocked.

Jordan is divided into distinct physiographic regions:
the western depression (Jordan Valley and Dead Sea
trench), the high plateau (including the eastern escarpment, or East Bank Uplands) and the eastern desert zone.

The western depression is an extension of the Great Rift
Valley, caused by a subsidence in the surface of the earth
20–30 million years ago. The fault, which begins in
Malawi, in Central Africa, cuts up through East Africa and
the Red Sea, through Jordan, as far north as Lebanon
where it is known as the Plain of Bekaa. Since its formation, the valley has remained unstable. Subsequent
movements have triggered off earth tremors, and the
severe earthquake in Amman in 1927 contributed to a
further sinking. The country's main watercourse, the
River Jordan, flows through the valley to the Dead Sea,
which occupies the central part of the depression. To the
south, Wadi Arabah forms a ridge between the Dead Sea
and the Gulf of Aqaba.

Jordanian landscape: desert surrounds the pine-clad jebels

Rising to a height of 1,865 metres is the eastern escarpment, or East Bank Uplands, the western perimeter of the
high plateau of central Jordan. Three vast chasms, Wadis
Zerqa, Mujib and Hasa, divide the range into four administrative districts which correspond roughly with the kingdoms of the Old Testament: Ajlun (Gilead), Balqa (part of
the Moabite and the Ammonite kingdoms), Kerak (the
Land of Moab) and Ma'an (the Land of Edom and later part
of the Nabataean Kingdom). The Jordanian capital of
Amman lies on the eastern side of the hills as they gradually flatten into steppes. Farther east a semi-desert pebble
terrain covers two-thirds of the total area of the plateau.

The area known as the Eastern Desert is not uniform;
the north and east at Umm el-Jimal and Azraq is lava and
basalt country, a continuation of the basalt outcrop of
Jebel Druze, in Syria. The southern desert is also marked
by soaring granite and sandstone outcrops expressed at
Wadi Rum and Petra.

Scattered oases are a characteristic of the eastern desert in Jordan. The most important, Azraq, is the only permanent body of water in 50,000 square kilometres. A shallow depression known as Wadi Sirhan extends for 322 kilometres south-east of Azraq. It also has extensive supplies of subterranean water yet to be utilised, and the remains of ancient dams (either Roman, or Ummayad) indicate the likelihood of ancient cultivation. Wadi Sirhan forms part of Jordan's eastern border with Saudi Arabia.

Jordan experiences a generally arid climate which ranges from a true desert heat to a more temperate, Mediterranean variety in the north. During summer, temperatures reach 40 °C in the eastern desert; the Dead Sea depression also experiences high readings, with a correspondingly high humidity. Amman, situated at a height of 750 metres (918m on the jebels or hills), is fortunate in that it enjoys a big range between day and night temperatures which can vary by as much as 20 °C even in mid-summer.

The normally brief winter, from November to February, brings northern Jordan an annual average rainfall of 600 millimetres. The eastern desert zone receives less than 100 millimetres, while Aqaba has a very low average of 31 millimetres.

During this period, the desert experiences frosts, and snow flurries occur in the eastern escarpment. The exceptional winter weather in 1980 brought blizzard conditions to the high areas of Jordan, including Amman, when conditions were the most severe since weather records were started in 1923.

Jordan also received an abundant rainfall in winter 1980. Many areas had 150 per cent of their average seasonal rainfall, but the probability of such an exceptional rainfall is remote.

Spring, from April until May, is the most pleasant time to visit Jordan when the normally barren land is covered with grasses and wild flowers. The most common of these are wild mustard, purple thistles, red poppies and anemones, convolvulus, hollyhocks, blue anchusa and the black iris of Jordan. Jordan has over 500 species of native wild flowers. Generally speaking, mid-summer is too hot for comfortable sightseeing and a characteristic haze often restricts visibility, especially in the western depression and Wadi Rum.

The table shows the approximate period of man's occupation of Jordan and the regions which have yielded evidence of civilisation:

Approximate dates	*Findings*
PALAEOLITHIC c.200,000– 8,000 BC	Flintstone weapons and tools from the regions of Aqaba, Wadi Rum, Ma'an and Jafar. Also Azraq, Khanasereh and Jerash. Designs chipped and scratched in the rock-face around Kilwa, in the Jabal Tubaiq area, which possibly represent a hunting scene.
NEOLOTHIC c.8,000–4,500 BC	Pre-pottery settlements around Jericho. Remains of large brick dwellings with early courtyard concept of design. Villages with finely built houses and workshops near el-Beidha. Also the remains of settlements at Abu Suwan, near Jerash, Wadi el-Yabis in the Jordan Valley, and Kilwa in the desert. Later this period is characterised by elaborate irrigation systems from Jericho which indicate an economy based on farming. At Jericho, a temple with representations of religious deities and plastered human skulls. A pottery Neolithic Culture in Yarmuk.
CHALCOLITHIC c.4,500–3,000 BC	Mud and brick dwellings from Ghassual with imaginatively decorated wall frescoes of probable religious significance. Flintstone tools and pottery. Other sites from this period occur in the area between Jerash and Amman. South-east of Amman are signs of inhabited caves at Sahab. Dolmens, huge stone slabs covered by a larger slab, of probable cultic or funereal significance in many areas.
BRONZE AGE c.3,000–1,200 BC	Early Bronze Age pottery from Irbid and the Dead Sea area. Early shaft tomb from Bab edh-Dhra' and the remains of a fortified town having a stone wall 13 metres thick. Burnished pottery from a site south-west of Lake Tiberias. Dolmens from Early to Middle Age Bronze periods. Traces of urban life from the Middle Bronze

4

Approximate dates	Findings (Cont'd)
	Age in tombs in Amman, Sahab, Na'ur and Irbid. Pottery sherds and a late Bronze Age temple on the site of Amman Airport. Scarabs, weapons and pottery of Mycenaean and Cypriot origin indicating trade. In Dothan, tombs have yielded late Bronze Age pottery, oil-lamps, jugs and chalices.
IRON AGE c.1,200–400 BC	The Balu'ah stele from the Moabite period. The Mesha stele, inscribed with urban achievements of the time. Basalt stone with bas-relief from Kerak. Early Iron Age tombs from Madaba and Mount Nebo. Seals from a tomb in Amman and an Ammonite inscription on Tell Siran, near Amman, describing the achievements of King Ammanidab in the sixth and seventh centuries. Male and female sculptures from Khirbet el-Hajjar. Tombs from the Sahab Tell. Slag heaps in Wadi Arabah indicating primitive mining of metals and copper. (Deut. 8:9.) Domestic vessels, jugs, goblets, lamps, etc. Anklets, bracelets, rings, a scarab and a seal among artifacts from the Baqah valley, 19 km, N.W. of Amman.
NABATAEAN PERIOD c.400 BC–AD 160	Monumental temples and sandstone reliefs at Petra. Inscriptions at Wadi Rum. Pottery at Rabba. Cisterns and inscriptions at Umm el-Jimal.
ROMAN PERIOD AD 63–324	Remains of the Decapolis cities, notably monumental ruins of Jerash. Theatre, nymphaeum, and other ruins in Amman and Umm Qeis. Recent discovery of Roman temple relics near Pella. Herod's fortress at Machaerus in the eastern escarpment. Roman milestones by the King's Highway near Kerak. Vestiges of irrigation canals elsewhere. Remains of a Roman fortress at Lajjun.
BYZANTINE PERIOD AD 324–636	Christian churches in Madaba, Jerash and Umm el-Jimal.
ISLAMIC PERIOD AD 630–1099	Religious and secular buildings. Desert castles or hunting-lodges and baths.
CRUSADER PERIOD AD 1099–1268	Fortresses at Kerak, Shaubak, Tafila, Aqaba, Wadi Musa. Arab fortress at Ajlun. Castle at Azraq.
MAMELUKE PERIOD AD 1263–1516	Restoration of above fortresses.
OTTOMAN PERIOD AD 1516–1918	Castle ruins at Qatranah and north of Ma'an. Baths at Qatranah.

Most historians concede that the fertile Jordan Valley was where primitive man first ceased a hunting and gathering existence and began cultivating his own food. This is confirmed by the discovery of rough agricultural implements near Jericho, indicating the dawn of civilisation in this region about 8–7,000 BC. Since then, the valley's strategic position between the Arabian peninsula and the Mediterranean Sea has attracted a stream of travellers and invaders.

The Canaanites are generally credited with being the original settlers; by the late second millennium, they had established a flourishing urban civilisation in the valley. About this time, the Phoenician coast was settled by a former sea-faring people from the Aegean Sea, the Philistines, who subsequently named it Palestine.

Tribal migrations from Mesopotamia continued throughout the Middle Bronze Age. Most relative to Jordan were the Ammonites, whose capital was Rabbath-Ammon (on the site of modern Amman), the Amorites, who settled in the north between the rivers Zerqa and Yarmuk and also around Hisban, the Moabites who moved into the eastern escarpment around Madaba, and the Edomites, who staked out a kingdom in the southern hills of the escarpment, extending to the edge of the desert.

Among many other tribes were the Israelites, who were closely related to the Aramaeans. One tribal patriach, Abraham, settled his family and flocks at Hebron, but prolonged famine led them to leave in search of new pasture. Their Old Testament story is well known: after being enslaved in the pyramid building projects of ancient Egypt, they wandered for forty years in the Negev Desert, led by Moses.

Finally reaching the Edomite Hills, their passage was blocked by the Edomites, so Moses led them on a detour to the east of the escarpment (Num. 20:16–21). When the Ammonites also refused to allow them to cross their territory, the Israelites attacked the weaker Moabites and broke through to the hills overlooking the Jordan Valley.

One of the most famous passages in the Bible depicts Moses pointing out Palestine from the summit of Mount Nebo.

On his death Joshua led the twelve tribes. Descending the escarpment and crossing the River Jordan whose flow miraculously stopped, they sacked Jericho and other valley towns, and marched on Jerusalem. Following bitter fighting against the Philistines, the Israelites claimed Jerusalem as their own capital, in 1,000 BC.

Under David, the Israelite forces then launched a series of retaliatory raids on the kingdoms of the eastern escarpment, the Edomites being particularly singled out for attack. A decisive victory over the Israelites was won by the Moabite King, Mesha, who engraved details of the battle on the now famous 'Mesha stele', but within several years, all of Palestine, Syria and Jordan came under Assyrian influence, in the early seventh century BC. Following a revival of Judah, or southern Palestine, Jerusalem was conquered by Nebuchadnezzar, in 587 BC. When Cyrus the Great took the throne of Persia in 539 BC he extended his empire to include Syria and Palestine, and under his rule many Jews were allowed to return to Palestine.

Lying about forty kilometres east of Jerusalem, the Jordan Valley was seen as a convenient corridor for the armies of Alexander the Great pushing towards Egypt. As a result of his campaigns, Hellenistic influence pervaded for the following 300 years. Disputes over territorial settlements after Alexander's death were not resolved until the country came under Seleucid rule, in 198 BC. A century later, under Antioch, the Seleucids invaded Egypt and attacked Jerusalem. The heirs of Antioch enlarged their territory, gaining control over Jordan to the Mediterranean, but Seleucid superiority effectively ended when Roman legions conquered Damascus and finally Jerusalem, in 63 BC.

Herod was recognised as King of Judaeah by the Roman

Senate and during his long reign, from 37 BC to AD 4, the region enjoyed a period of peace and prosperity. Unrest following his death saw Palestine made a 'Province of Judaeah', administered by the 10th Roman Legion.

Where other invaders had failed, the Romans also succeeded in subduing the Nabataean civilisation centred on Petra: in AD 106 the prosperous city was incorporated into the Roman Province of Arabia.

At the time of Nabataean expansion, a federation of cities known as the *Decapolis* came into being in northern Jordan. Modelled on Greek cities, with three – Pella, Dion and Gerasa – probably even founded by Greek soldiers, all, except one, were situated east of the River Jordan. The cities were never a fixed number as they joined and withdrew from the Decapolis, but historians believe the original members were probably the following: Seythopolis (Beisan), Pella (Tabaqat el-Fahl), Dion (Husn), Gadara (Umm Qeis), Hippos (Fiq), Raphana (al-Rafah), Gerasa (Jerash), Philadelphia (Amman), Kamatha (Qanawat) and Damascus. Busra, in southern Syria, was also a probable member of the league, originally set up for trading purposes, but organised into a military alliance by the Romans against the Jews and pillaging Bedouin tribes.

Jordan flourished under the Romans who built new towns, encouraged the arts and eventually put a stop to tribal feuding. Their occupation of the region lasted until the fourth century when the Emperor Constantine embraced the faith of Jesus Christ. Christianity flourished under Byzantine rule, but it ended abruptly in AD 614 when, aided by the Jews, Persian forces swept in, massacring and looting in a destructive period lasting twenty years.

As a result of this, the weakened Byzantine Empire could not prevent the forces of Islam penetrating the country from Arabia. The new religion of the Prophet Mohammed swept across the Middle East and in AD 636 Moslem armies defeated the Byzantines at the Battle of

Yarmuk. By AD 640 all Syria, Jordan and Palestine came under Moslem control.

For three decades after the Prophet's death in AD 632, the Arab Empire remained a theocracy, but slowly it became a secular empire. Islam's first rulers, the Ummayad Caliphs, made Damascus their capital in the eighth century, but Jordan remained important owing to its strategic position on the caravan routes. Desert people, the Ummayads also visited it on hunting-trips, a legacy of which are the splendid fortresses still seen today (see Chapter 6). Yet another reason for establishing a foothold in northern Jordan was to secure the support of local tribes.

Coming out of a secret hiding place at al-Humayah, north of Aqaba, a rival family, the Abbasids, transferred the Second Caliphate to Baghdad. The resultant economic and cultural boom in Mesopotamia saw many cities of the Decapolis period begin to decline, while about this time, in the late eleventh century AD, the Pope began urging Christians to rally against Islam and recapture the holy places for Christianity. A series of largely unsuccessful Holy Wars followed, with the only victory in the First Crusade of 1099. In 1187, Jerusalem was recaptured by the famous Moslem warrior, Saladin ibn Ayyub.

Early in the thirteenth century AD the Mongol rulers of central Asia combined with the powerful Mamelukes of Egypt in attacking Jerusalem. Following a dispute, the Mongols withdrew and the Mamelukes captured the remaining relics of Crusader occupation. By the end of the century, the Christian invaders were in flight.

The fourteenth century heralded a new invasion, that of pillaging armies of Tamerlane; then, a century later, the long-suffering country was occupied by the Turks.

During the subsequent 400 years of Ottoman domination, the region sank into a state of economic stagnation and moral despair. The Turks' only contribution during this period was the construction of the Hejaz Railway through Jordan from Damascus to Mecca, at the cost of thousands of trees that once clothed the eastern escarpment.

The history of modern Jordan began with the mutual desire of the Arabs and the Western powers to rid the area of the Turks.

In 1914, the Sharif Hussein, ruler of Hejaz (the region which formerly included the holy cities of Mecca and Medina and extended as far north as Ma'an), was approached to petition the Turks for self-rule. When this failed, the Sharif, who was the great-grandfather of King Hussein, assumed leadership of the Arab Nationalist movement. After assurances of support were received from Britain and other allies, what is known as the Arab Revolt was launched in June 1916.

Three months of desert warfare saw the collapse of all the Ottoman garrisons except Medina and when Faisal, the third son of the Sharif, recaptured Aqaba, the Turks capitulated.

In October 1918, Faisal set up an Arab government in Damascus; but in July 1920 the allies expelled him to Iraq, and the British, with the French, divided Syria, Palestine and Trans-Jordan into respective spheres of influence.

Arab reaction was profound, especially when it was learnt that the Balfour Declaration favoured the creation, in the Arab homeland, of a Jewish State and that the Palestinians were to suffer the consequences.

Rallying Arab nationalism, the Sharif's second son, Abdullah, marched to Ma'an with the intention of liberating the country for the Arabs. Arriving in Amman in March 1921, he established the Emirate of Trans-Jordan. Following discussion in Jerusalem with Winston Churchill, the Emir Abdullah secured British recognition of the new emirate, but as the Sykes-Picot agreement provided for Trans-Jordan to become a British mandate, a British adviser was installed.

On 25 May 1923, Britain formally recognised the independence of Trans-Jordan under the Emir Abdullah, who ruled until 1939. In that year a cabinet responsible to the

Emir was established, and a twenty-member legislative assembly elected. Jordan's Arab Legion then made a notable contribution in assisting Britain to subdue a pro-German *coup* in Iraq during World War II, and it also fought against the Vichy French in Syria.

When the British Mandate ended on 25 May 1946, the Emir Abdullah was proclaimed king of the now fully independent and sovereign state.

When Britain relinquished its Palestine mandate in 1948, Jordan's Arab Legion and a combined force from the League of Arab States attacked the illegal State of Israel. Thousands of Palestinians fled from the war zone, leaving their houses and land to the Zionists but Jordan, despite its meagre resources, accepted the refugees and accorded them citizenship.

In 1949, United Nations intervention halted the fighting and an armistice line drawn across Palestine gave the Jews the coastal plain and the Arabs the barren hills of Judaea, leaving them without a Mediterranean access. Jerusalem

Phosphate mining at Al-Hasa

was divided, with most of the holy sites in East Jerusalem made the responsibility of the Arabs.

In April 1950, Central Arab Palestine (the West Bank) voted to join Trans-Jordan and the two were united as one state, hereafter known as the Hashemite Kingdom of Jordan.

In July 1951, King Abdullah was assassinated on his way to pray at Jerusalem's al-Aqsa Mosque. His eldest son, Prince Talal, was proclaimed king, but due to ill health he was succeeded by Prince Hussein, then only seventeen. Hussein formally ascended to the Hashemite throne on 25 May 1953.

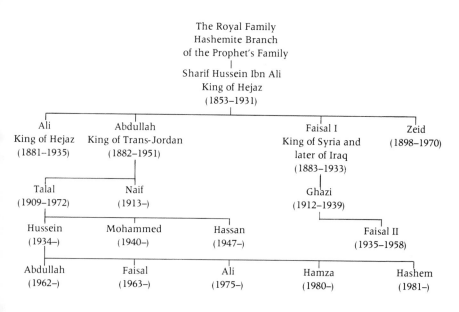

The constitution of the Hashemite Kingdom of Jordan declares it a hereditary monarchy under the king, who is vested with power of its legislative, executive and judiciary. Legislative power resides in the National Assembly and consists of the Senate and House of Deputies which is elected by universal suffrage (those over eighteen). Although the monarchy is hereditary, the king may choose his heir—provided he has royal blood of the

Hashemites. In 1965, King Hussein selected his younger brother, Prince Hassan, as Jordan's Crown Prince.

For administrative purposes, the country is divided into governorates: Amman, Balqa, Irbid, Kerak and Ma'an. Headed by a governor, or *muhafez*, each governorate is further divided into administrative areas, each about the size of a London borough.

According to the Housing and Population Census of November 1979, Jordan has a total population of 2,152,273.

The major population centres are:

Amman: 648,587 (rising to 1 million during the working week)

Zarqa:	215,687
Irbid:	112,954
Salt:	32,866
Kerak:	11,805
Ma'an:	11,308
Aqaba:	30,800

The average growth rate is 0.537 in Amman and 0.0615 in the expanding port of Aqaba.

Of Jordan's total population, 1,200,000 are Palestinian. A total of 444,000 are registered with the United Nations Relief and Works Agency. They live in ten relief camps, of which the biggest is Al-Baq'a with 160,000 people (13 kilometres north of Amman, on the road to Jerash). Al-Wehdat and al-Hussein camps in central Amman house about 75,000 refugees.

The decentralisation of Amman is a government priority with a major scheme to attract the optimum population – about 150,000 – back to the Jordan Valley.

There are estimated to be some 40,000 Bedouin living in Jordan, although many are considered a transitory population passing through from Syria to Iraq and Saudi Arabia, in search of grazing. The re-settlement of the Bedouin and the improvement of their living standards is also part of the government five-year plan involving the construction of schools, clinics, houses and the creation of jobs.

Studies carried out among several thousand Bedouin families in 1976/7 by the University of Jordan revealed discrepancies between their general condition and that of townspeople, which was to be anticipated.

In 1976, general poor health resulted in the life expectancy of a Bedouin being about fifty years.

The general health of men was found to be better than that of women, as a result of priority feeding of male infants and better nutrition afforded later in life through the Armed Forces. Only 13 per cent of boys were wasted, compared with 20 per cent of girls. A diet grossly lacking in protein was the main factor for their poor state of health.

The survey also showed the educational level of the Bedouin to be well below the national average, which has a 70 per cent literacy rate. A historic problem has been that parents do not wish their children to attend school as they become economically active at an early age, herding goats and performing useful domestic chores.

A government priority is to establish schools in all Bedouin re-settlement villages. Adult education programmes are also being initiated in order to explain to parents the ultimate viability of their children being educated. The overall programme depends on the Bedouin becoming sedentary where such facilities as houses, schools and clinics are available. Linked with the re-settlement of the Jordan Valley is the availability of water for cultivation.

History shows that the original Jordanians are descended from several hundred tribes who have lived there for centuries. A majority migrated from Mesopotamia, others came from the Hejaz, Palestine, Egypt and Yemen, or trekked south from Syria and Lebanon. Preponderantly Arab, they are Sunni Moslems who follow the orthodox branch of Islam.

The non-Arab Sunni Moslem minority known as the Circassians who settled in Jordan in the late nineteenth century trace their origins to two Indo-European Moslem tribes. Following Russia's invasion of the Caucasus, beginning in the tenth century, many Circassians migrated south. In 1878 the first settlers arrived in Amman, also in Jerash, Na'ur and Wadi Sir.

Jordan's Circassian community numbers some 25,000 and consists of several groups, or tribes, known as Adigah. Another tribe, the Shishan, or Chechen identify with them except for language. Chechen communities are found in Azraq, Zarqa, Ruseifa and Suweilih; they number about 5,000. Two seats in parliament are always allotted to Circassians from each community, who use Arabic as a common language.

Circassians occupy many influential posts in the government and the army, although a majority are agricultural workers and urban landlords. They are credited with helping to re-build Amman.

Other minorities in Jordan are the Turcomans and Bahias, the latter having migrated from Iran in 1910.

About 12 per cent of Jordan's population is Christian including Greek Orthodox, Protestant and Roman Catholic, who trace their origins from early Christian converts in the area, and from the West Bank towns where Christianity was born.

Jordan also has a small Armenian community.

Since the civil war in Lebanon, many Lebanese have settled in Amman where they are involved in finance, real estate and shops – mainly the fashion, hairdressing and restaurant trades.

There is a fast-growing foreign community, mainly American, living in Amman.

Jordan has an economy traditionally based on agriculture and grazing. Cereals, fruits and vegetables were historically exported through the port of Haifa, but when this was included in the State of Israel in 1948, Jordan not only lost its European export market, but had suddenly to divert its produce domestically to cope with the demand of thousands of refugees.

Having survived the traumatic years following the partition of Palestine, Jordan appeared to face certain economic ruin in 1967, when Israel occupied 32,000 hectares of the West Bank of the River Jordan.

As a result of the Six-Day War, Jordan lost 40 per cent of its gross national product. Gone was 30 per cent of its cereal land, 45 per cent of its vegetable production and 60 per cent of its fruit-growing area. With the seizure of the West Bank went 90 per cent of Jordan's revenue from tourism, 48 per cent of its industrial ventures and 53 per cent of commercial enterprises.

The closure that year of the Suez Canal and domestic problems concerning the Palestinians in 1970–71 further added to the depressed state of the economy; as well, there was a natural reluctance to invest in Jordan during the unstable mid-seventies. Concurrently, the booming Arab oil states lured thousands of skilled and unskilled workers to the Gulf. As a result of which, Jordan is now a labour importer, (an estimated 60,000 foreigners, mainly Egyptians, Syrians and Pakistanis, work in the country). However it is these annual remittances estimated at JD180.4 million,[1] from the estimated 300,000 expatriate Jordanians that are responsible for the country's robust economic state.

Expatriate earnings, massive loans from the Arab states (mainly from Kuwait, Saudi Arabia and Abu Dhabi) and the country's sustained period of economic stability see the government, private sector and overseas investors seeking to develop projects which should ultimately lead to Jordan's self-sufficiency – a quite remarkable fact when it is considered that thirteen years ago people were predicting it would collapse.

Credit is being channelled into four major areas of development: mining, industry, agriculture and tourism. The bulk of investment is in mining and manufacturing, primarily in the production of phosphates, potash, chemical fertilisers, refined petroleum products and cement.

[1] Source: Central Bank of Jordan, January 1980. $US 1 = JD 0.3058.

The Central Bank of Jordan Statistical Bulletin, published in August 1979, gives the following details:

Principal Industries		*Production*	
	Unit	1975	1978
Phosphates (dry)	000 tons	1352.2	2320.2
Cement	000 tons	572.2	553.0
Petroleum Products	000 tons	828.2	1396.6
Electricity	mill. kWh	374.4	571.5
Iron	tons	31304	65289
Textiles	000 yards	952.6	1140.9
Fodder	tons	41456	51841
Pharmaceuticals:			
Liquid	000 litres	358.9	496.7
Other	tons	113.4	142.8
Cigarettes	mill. cig.	1856.0	2628.0
Paper	tons	4190.0	4620.0
Leather:			
Sole	tons	531.4	197.9
Upper	000 sq. ft.	2215.4	2807.9
Spirits	000 litres	5502.0	5654.1
Liquid Batteries	000 batts	44.4	44.3
Detergents	tons	4202.6	7147.2

Begun in 1955, phosphate production at Ruseifa and Al Hasa is Jordan's oldest industry, now valued at some $90 million. Diammonium phosphate for domestic consumption will soon come on-stream at the Jordanian Fertiliser Company on the Gulf of Aqaba.

The biggest project, the Arab Potash Company at Ghour al-Safi processes potash by solar evaporation of Dead Sea water. Output, largely for export, will bring an estimated $660 million in revenues annually.

Al-Hasma region is believed to be rich in copper, manganese and iron deposits, while Jordan has large quantities of shale-oil at al-Lajjun, near Kerak.

Most of Jordan's oil is purchased as crude at market

prices from Saudi Arabia, for processing at the Zarqa oil refinery. Although shale-oil is costly to process – it must be extracted from rock by heat and pressure – in Jordan's case the straightforward method of furnace-roasting is seen as a viable possibility. The deposits, estimated at 10 billion tons by the Jordanian Natural Resources Authority, are considered to be potentially valuable with consistently rising oil prices.

At present, foodstuffs are Jordan's major export, contributing to 20 per cent of the GNP. The main crops are wheat, olives, grapes, barley, melons, aubergines, tomatoes, lettuce, citrus fruits and tobacco. Vegetables and fresh fruits are exported by refrigerated road-haulers to ready markets in the Arab Gulf States. Jordan is also self-sufficient in eggs.

The modernisation of farming methods, the re-seeding of former grasslands, controlled grazing, the use of contour ploughing and chemical fertilisers are part of the plan to increase yield.

The linchpin in the government's agricultural policy is the careful husbandry of the Jordan Valley by an autonomous body known as the Jordan Valley Authority founded in 1972.

Agricultural expansion is aimed at extending irrigation in the valley through the construction of dams and the extension of existing canals. Linked with these plans is the organisation of infrastructure in the region, and the resettlement of thousands more farmers who fled as a result of the Six-Day War.

Tourism is the fourth aspect of Jordan's broad development plan.

Transporting visitors to tourist sites quickly and providing facilities in the form of hotels and rest-houses is central to planning by the Ministry of Tourism and Antiquities. $160 million is also being invested in the leisure industry by the private sector.

The most visible evidence of development is the number of new hotels in Amman, which is seen as a base from which to visit the kingdom. By the late 1980s, all Jordan's tourist attractions should offer first-class accommodation and restaurants.

An ambitious plan exists to create an ultra-modern resort area, involving the construction of an inland canal complex at Aqaba, complete with marinas, hotels, apartments, shopping malls and a golf course.

Among many other projects is the building of a modern spa resort, one of the first in the Middle East, for the hot springs at Zarqa Ma'in, and a ferry service for sightseeing on the Dead Sea.

Keeping abreast of the news in Amman: a Roman pillar provides a convenient seat

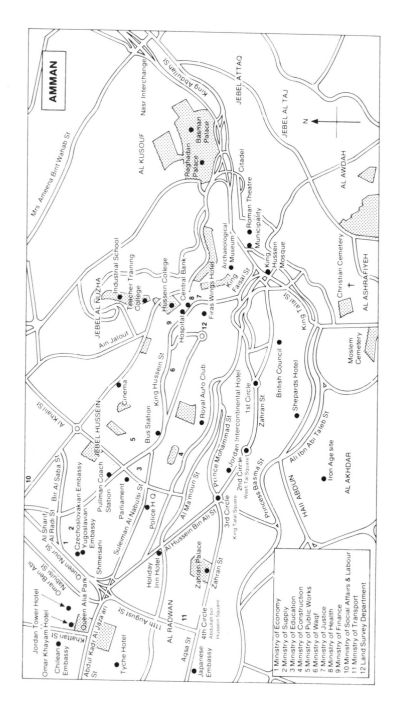

AMMAN

N

King Abdullah St
Nasr Interchange
JEBEL ATTAQ
JEBEL AL TAJ
AL AWDAH
Mrs Ameena Bint Wahab St
AL KUSOUF
Raghadan Palace
Basman Palace
Citadel
Roman Theatre
Municipality
King Hussein Mosque
Archaeological Museum
King Faisal St
Christian Cemetery
AL ASHRAFIYEH
Industrial School
Teacher Training College
Hussein College
Central Bank
JEBEL AL NUZHA
Firas Wings Hotel
8
7
9
Hospital
12
Moslem Cemetery
Ain Jalouf
6
King Talal St
King Hussein St
Cinema
Royal Auto Club
British Council
JEBEL HUSSEIN
Bus Station
5
Jordan Intercontinental Hotel
1st Circle
Shepards Hotel
Al Khalil St
Prince Mohammad St
Zahran St
10
Bir Al Saba St
Czechoslovakian Embassy
Yugoslavian Embassy
Pullman Coach Station
Parliament
3
Police H Q
Suleiman Al Nabulsi St
4
Al Mamoun St
Jordan Intercontinental Hotel
2nd Circle
Wasfi Tal Square
King Talal Square
Princess Basma St
Ali Ibn Abi Taleb St
Iron Age site
AL AKHDAR
HAII ABDUN
Al Sharif
Al Radi St
1 2
Shmeisani
Holiday Inn Hotel
Al Hussein Bin Ali St
3rd Circle
Zabdeh Palace
Zahran St
AL RADWAN
Queen Nour St
Nablus St
Omar Ben Abi
Khattab St
Jordan Tower Hotel
Omar Khayam Hotel
Chilean Embassy
Queen Alia Park
Abdul Kad'l Al Jaza an
Tyche Hotel
11th August St
4th Circle
Abdullah Ibn Hussein Square
11
Aqsa St
Japanese Embassy

1 Ministry of Economy
2 Ministry of Supply
3 Ministry of Education
4 Ministry of Construction
5 Ministry of Public Works
6 Ministry of Waqf
7 Ministry of Justice
8 Ministry of Health
9 Ministry of Finance
10 Ministry of Social Affairs & Labour
11 Ministry of Transport
12 Land Survey Department

20

Chapter Two

Amman: the Gateway to Jordan

Although the Hashemite Kingdom of Jordan is comparatively young, dating from the union, in 1950, of Trans-Jordan and Central Palestine, its capital, Amman, was settled in the Bronze Age. This is shown by the discovery of tombs and potsherds around the Seil Amman, a small stream that still flows through the valley, or *wadi*. As with much of the history of Jordan and Palestine, one learns from the Bible that modern Amman occupies the site of ancient Rabbath-Ammon, capital of the Ammonite Kingdom in the second millennium before Christ (Deut. 3:11; 2 Sam. 12:26, 17:27; Jer. 49:2).

Following their migration from Mesopotamia, the Ammonites, together with other tribes, had staked out an independent kingdom in the eastern escarpment to the north of Wadi Mujib. It was this situation which the Israelites found, much later, on their exodus from Egypt. They subsequently attacked their enemies, forcing their way through the Kingdom of Moab to the south of Rabbath-Ammon.

It is recorded that after the Israelites' conquest of Palestine, they turned their vengeance on the old escarpment kingdoms, besieging Rabbath-Ammon and finally subduing the city by cutting off its water supply from the Seil Amman. The Ammonites henceforth became vassals of the Kingdom of Judaeah, regaining a measure of independence only in the ninth century BC. However by this time they faced Assyrian expansion, but on the Assyrian defeat at Nineveh in 612 BC, they became subject to Babylon and then to Persia.

There is no further biblical reference to Rabbath-Ammon which is not heard of again until the Kingdom was absorbed into the Greek empire of Alexander the Great. Initially it was ruled by the Ptolemies of Egypt, then under Ptolemy II, the city became completely Hellenised, being re-built and re-named Philadelphia.

In 218 BC Philadelphia was recaptured by the Seleucids, but weakened by dynastic disputes in the first century BC, Philadelphia was absorbed into the Nabataean kingdom. By the end of this century Roman legions had pushed east as far as Philadelphia, and under Herod the Great it was taken for Rome.

Contrasts in downtown Amman with a Roman theatre nestling in the hillside like a shell

Under Roman administration Philadelphia joined the Decapolis, a federation of some ten cities holding the monopoly of ancient trade. On the profits of trade between the states, or *polis*, the Romans constructed civic buildings, temples and theatres in Philadelphia. Although the city was the farthest east in the Roman empire, it is said that the legions felt at home there, surrounded by hills and with a climate similar to their native Rome.

Philadelphia's strategic position – on the Trajan Road between Busra[1] and Petra – helped to fill the coffers, and when the Nabataean empire was annexed as the Roman Province of Arabia in AD 106, the city grew even more prosperous. Recognising its importance, the early Byzantine rulers made it the seat of the Christian bishopric of Petra and Philadelphia.

In AD 635 Amman was taken by Arab forces of the Ummayad dynasty in Damascus, but when their successors, the Abbasids, moved the second caliphate to Baghdad, trade moved east and Amman, like the other cities in the Decapolis, began to decline. Nothing is heard of the city for the next thousand years: when Circassian settlers arrived in 1878, they began laying the foundations of modern Amman.

Following his victory over the Turks and with the aim of ridding Jordan of foreign domination, the Emir Abdullah entered Amman in March 1921. He chose the city as the seat of government for the new Emirate of Trans-Jordan which was recognised by the Anglo-Jordanian Treaty signed in May 1923. When the British Mandate ended on 25 May 1946, Amman became capital of the Hashemite Kingdom of Jordan.

At the time it was a logical choice. The town had water, it occupied a naturally defensive position and it was situated on the historic crossroads of the Levant. In the 1920s, no one could have foreseen the tragic events of 1948 which caused thousands of Palestinian refugees to settle in Amman, placing severe strains on the city's infrastructure.

[1] A Roman city in Syria

As a result of this settlement, and more recently because of the shift of business from war-torn Beirut, Amman has overflowed from the valley and sprung up on the surrounding hills, giving the city its characteristic roller-coaster appearance.

To understand the lay-out, visitors are recommended to start a tour in downtown Amman, the site of the first settlement, by the small stream which flows into the River Zarqa. Upon visiting the Roman heritage of Philadelphia, they should see the bazaar district surrounding the King Hussein Mosque then work uptown, to modern Amman on the northern hills, or jebels.

Streets run off the jebels into downtown Amman

Downtown Amman is squeezed into a small area at the foot of Jebel Qala'a, one of seven major hills on which the city is built. The focal point is an Ottoman-style mosque built in 1924 on the site of the original mosque, dating from the early Islamic period.

Two great roads were the basis of the Roman plan of Philadelphia. The main one, known as the *Decumanus Maximus*, followed the course of the valley, or wadi, to meet with the Trajan Road to Petra. Nothing remains of this road, although the public works department frequently finds pieces of broken columns when laying sewage pipes and telephone cables.

Fenced off from traffic on a corner of Saqf el Seil Street are the ruins of a large Nymphaeum, dating from the second or third century AD. Although restoration work has been carried out the present surroundings make it hard to imagine the once opulent shrine where Roman citizens took their marriage-vows.

Remains of the Roman nymphaeum in downtown Amman

Walking east from the Nymphaeum one reaches the Roman theatre, resembling a fossilised snail-shell sunk in the hillside. The most impressive vestige of Roman Philadelphia, it is inscribed to Antonius Pius V. The theatre used to seat five to six thousand spectators, and is still used for summer concerts and performances by Jordanian folklore troupes.

On the east side of the theatre is a smaller theatre, known as the Odeon, also built in the early second century AD. Situated in this historic corner of Amman is the old Philadelphia Hotel which will be demolished and replaced by public gardens. The theatres and the *Decumanus Maximus* comprised the cultural and commercial centre of ancient Amman.

A road behind the King Hussein Mosque winds up Jebel Qala'a, or Citadel Hill, to the Amman Archaeological Museum. The building is situated on the summit of three terraces of varying heights which display further remains

Roman amphitheatre echoes to folk-music

of the Roman occupation of Amman: a fortified temple and a Byzantine church. There are also remarkable remains of an Ummayad castle.

Massive walls, now crumbling, used to enclose the Temple of Hercules overlooking King Abdullah Street in downtown Amman. Archaeologists date the temple from the reign of Marcus Aurelius in AD 2. It is known to have enshrined a marble statue of the god, estimated from fragments picked up on the site to have stood some 9 metres in height. The remains of a Byzantine gate are seen in the west wall surrounding the temple where children play hide-and-seek among the fallen stones.

Walking past the museum brings one to the great castle dating from Ummayad times, designed in the shape of a Greek cross and entered from the south gate where the door jambs are still to be seen. The room leading off was possibly an audience hall and displays elaborate geometric and floral sculpturing in the stonework.

A street of now fallen columns lead out of the north gate of the castle, or *qasr*. In one of the ruined buildings on the left is an Ummayad latrine. Outside the castle to the left of the museum are the overgrown ruins of what was probably the Ummayad town where Bedouin graze their goats overlooking Amman, probably unaware of its historic significance.

Surmounted by these once stately buildings, Jebel Qala'a must have been an imposing sight during Roman times. From the summit visitors enjoy an impressive view of modern Amman: east over the Roman theatre and north to Raghadan where the royal residences and the King's working palaces are guarded by soldiers resplendent in red and black Circassian uniforms. To the south, one looks across downtown Amman towards Jebel Ashrafiyeh crowned by a distinctive zebra-striped mosque.

Redolent with all the sights and smells of a Middle Eastern city, the bazaar district is the pulse of downtown Amman.

They shop in pairs, or groups, carrying their purchases on their heads ...

Busiest is King Talal Street, a melting-pot of peoples drawn to Jordan from all over the Arab world. Standing out in the sea of pedestrians passing the King Hussein Mosque are Palestinian women wearing the embroidered robes of Bethlehem and Hebron. They shop in pairs, or groups, carrying their purchases on their heads.

28

Abu Darwish Mosque, Jebel Ashrafiyeh, Amman

Nowhere else in the Middle East displays such variety in head-wear as downtown Amman. The most common is the Arab *kuffiyah*, but there are tall black hats worn by bearded Greek prelates, sheikhs in red tarbushes, labourers from Aswan, their heads wrapped in woollen head-scarves, turbanned Yemenis, men from Hunza recognised

29

by the rolled beret of the Northern Areas of Pakistan, traffic policemen in white, spiked helmets, Korean engineers sporting blue jockey-caps, hitch-hikers, their heads protected by floppy terry-towelling hats and, inevitably, groups of American visitors wearing fresh, cream panamas.

Pervading the streets is the pungent scent of cardamom, the aromatic capsule of various plants of the ginger family which the Bedouin have drunk in their coffee since time immemorial. More bewitching odours drift from shops selling all manner of spices from Zanzibar to the East Indies – sacks of sumak, cumin, tumeric, coriander, cinnamon and cloves. The cost for an ounce? Not more than 50 pence. The owner twists it into a cornet of yesterday's *Al Rai* newspaper.

Opposite the Nymphaeum a rancid odour emanates from a dairy shop which sells blocks of white cheese, tins of black and green olives and plastic pots of yoghurt. The owner invites one to try a shiny black olive, then he breaks off a piece of the salty goat's-milk cheese and finally he insists one tastes a spoonful of the rich, creamy *labaneh*.

Others shops sell baskets of fresh and roasted nuts – almonds, walnuts, hazelnuts, pistachios, peanuts, pumpkin-seeds and salted water-melon seeds. The friendly proprietor presses some pumpkin-seeds into one's palm. As elsewhere there is no charge and after a polite chat he bids one a pleasant stay in Amman.

If cardamom is an omnipresent aroma, so is the haunting smell of fresh bread and biscuits. In a nearby bakery more than a dozen different kinds are baked and toasted in roaring clay ovens. Some are comma-shaped and finger-size, others are round, twisted, dusted with poppy seeds, or stuffed with dates. One is a crusty bread flavoured with thyme, nearly a metre long.

I best like *ka'ik*, another variety of bread baked in a ring with a soft centre and a crisp crust sprinkled with sesame seeds. Wherever throngs of people pass, someone is always to be found selling *ka'ik*. I was told one man had sat at the top of the steps near the gold market for twenty years. He arrived precisely at seven each morning, carrying a shallow box of bread on his head, a stool dangling from his shoulder and a bag in his hand. The bag contained oven-baked eggs, which are eaten with a pinch of salt, pepper and sumak (see Chapter 8) sprinkled on the bread – a delicious snack costing about 100 fils.

Often rising in the dark, manual workers do not eat before leaving home, but work stops about nine for the 'poor man's breakfast' of *foule* – mashed chick peas and onion rings drenched in lemon juice and oil. At this hour, about 300 men are served in a small café in an alley below al-Bader Hotel.

Rich smells of caramelising sugar issue from an alley near the Arab Bank where a shop is baking syrup-drenched *knaffeh* (see Chapter 7). The hard-working owner cooks over 200 kilos of the sweet daily. Each time a fresh batch is ready, scores of hungry young men seem to appear from nowhere – a ticket for a plate of *knaffeh* costs 100 fils at the door with a queue often stretching down to King Hussein Street.

At the round intersection with King Hussein Street and Prince Mohammed Street is a coffee house known as the 'Central Café' which is reached by climbing up a dark flight of stairs. This café is the bastion of local male society in downtown Amman. Men gather here to gossip and to play *tric-trac*, that age-old Middle Eastern game believed to have first been played some 5,000 years ago in Ur, in southern Mesopotamia. One can have tea or coffee with a *nargila*, or 'hubble-bubble' pipe, either inside, or sitting outside on a balcony overlooking Basman Street.

In alleys leading off King Faisal Street, workmen sit on upturned crates, smacking the counters down with all the panache of a professional soccer player kicking a goal. While young Jordanian boys may be more attuned to soccer, the older generation continues to follow backgammon as passionately as ever. A mother-of-pearl *tric-trac* board is an attractive souvenir of Amman.

While there are many craft shops in uptown Amman, tourists will probably have more pleasure buying in the bazaar shops in Souq Balabseh and Souq Asfour. The Bukarian Market opposite al-Hussein Mosque sells perfume, olive wood carvings and chrome trinkets.

Then at the entrance of the mosque is another tiny shop selling not only Arabian perfumes but also famous brands made under licence from France. For a moment here, the fragrance of rose, musk and sandalwood outstrips the insistent odour of cardamom. When buying in the bazaar one must bargain, and no matter how ferocious the shop-keeper may seem, he loves the cut and thrust of a good haggle!

It is not possible to bargain in the gold souq where prices are pegged to the fluctuating world market for gold. In downtown Amman there are some forty goldsmiths, mainly Palestinians, who can tell the current going rate at any hour of the day or night.

In their small shops off King Hussein Street, thousands of pounds of gold glitters on black velvet trays: earrings, bangles, pendants, coins (many showing St George slaying the Dragon), and charms in the design of hearts, camels, fish, squash racquets, Qurans and maps of Palestine. Solid ounce blocks are popular with visitors from the Arab oil states. Western tourists normally procrastinate, while a 'runner' fetches coffee or tea. Once again, there is no charge, even if one spends an hour just looking, which after all is half the fun of browsing through a Middle Eastern bazaar.

Uptown Amman is a world apart from historic Philadelphia. If tourists were suddenly to be dropped on Jebel Amman or Hussein they would wonder where they were! Streets are immaculately clean with clipped floral roundabouts, one sees people with blow-waved hair wearing the latest in European fashion and Gucci shoes; and instead of the haunting songs of Fairouz, shops are blasting western disco-music.

Driving up from downtown Amman one reaches the first roundabout, or Circle, on Jebel Amman. Off the First Circle runs Abu Bakr al-Siddiq Street, known more simply as Rainbow Street – a local 'Bond Street' where one can buy anything from Danish furniture to Japanese hi-fi. People who know Beirut will be reminded here of Hamra.

Located on the right of a steep lane descending from the Second Circle is an interesting craft shop, the Jordanian Crafts Development Centre – *El Eidi* – in English meaning 'the hands'. A private enterprise, it aims to stimulate local craftsmen and women in order to preserve local cottage industries such as weaving, pottery and embroidery.

Travelling higher up the hill, on the right, before the road pierces the Third Circle (also known as King Talal Square), is the Jordan Inter-Continental Hotel, the first five-star hotel built in Amman and still the most popular for businessmen and conferences.

From the east wing of the Inter-Continental, the view of Amman across Jebel Weibdeh is not unlike a gigantic rock-garden, folded hills sprinkled with buff-coloured houses looking as though they are quarried from the rock, rather than built on it. In *Arabia Through the Looking Glass*, Jonathan Raban writes: 'If one squinted for a moment, there were no houses at all, just a pastel-coloured abstract of rocky outcrops and crevices'.

Vegetation thrives, despite the rugged terrain, though much of it is stunted and twisted from the effort of pushing through the ground. Cedars, *henas* (the local eucalyptus) and tall pandanus grass provide shade for patios, and over garden walls, jasmine bushes drop flowers on to the pavement.

Beyond the Third Circle houses almost like mini-palaces line Zahran Street. Extravagantly designed, almost Mexican-style villas are a feature of the newest uptown residential district of Haii Abdoun where many Lebanese have settled. Adjacent Shmeisani is also experiencing a boom in construction, this time in hotels, rising among the apartment blocks. Building in uptown Amman tends to follow a pattern: first a hotel goes up, followed by ancillary shops such as a pharmacy, travel agent and bookshop.

Uptown Amman is essentially a city composed of self-sufficient villages. Although shopping is cheaper downtown, there is no parking, and in an effort to improve Amman's baffling traffic-jams, many streets running off the jebels have been made one-way; so that unable to park, or to turn round, residents must drive all the way downtown in order to come up again!

Of several sporting clubs in Amman, the biggest is a combined sports and culture complex located on Queen Alia Street. Al-Hussein Sports City, also called al-Hussein Youth City, reflects the government's concern with the people's welfare in providing a 25,000-seat stadium for soccer matches and track events, three swimming-pools, a gymnasium and squash, volleyball, basketball and badminton courts. The vast Palace of Culture is always packed for any art or fashion exhibitions. Jordanians are proud of their rich cultural heritage and Amman's newest acquisition is the Royal Cultural Centre which doubles for theatre, concerts and conferences. Behind the centre within al-Hussein Sports City is a large public park with the National Monument to the Unknown Soldier. The 30,000 trees planted in the gardens are safe from vandalism which is unheard of in the Middle East.

To witness middle-class Jordanians enjoying a day off, the park should be visited early on a Friday afternoon. Elderly citizens are seen seated round the remnants of a picnic, fathers are proudly walking with babies on their shoulders while older children kick a ball under the pines. Significantly, women are segregated. They sit together on park benches discussing the week's domestic events. The scene is reminiscent of a family outing on Sunday, in London's Regent's Park.

Many wealthy people in uptown Amman have their

own swimming pools. Alternatively they relax around the palm-lined pool at the luxury hotels. During spring and summer, Friday race-meetings are an attraction. They are supervised by the Royal Racing Club, near Attuneib, off the new airport highway.

A popular leisurely Friday drive is to a historic site, rarely visited by tourists, known as Qasr el-Abd, which lies eighteen kilometres east of Amman. A ruined Tobiade palace dating from 200–175 BC, the castle may not be as impressive as Amman's amphitheatre, but it is unique. According to Monsieur François Larché who is reconstructing the design of the palace for the French Institute of Architecture in the Middle East (in co-operation with the Jordanian Ministry of Antiquities), Qasr el-Abd is the only extant Hellenistic palace in the entire Middle East.

Monsieur Larché, who has studied the site for several years, refers people interested in the history of Qasr el-Abd to the writings of the Roman historian, Flavius Josephus.

Following a rift within the Tobiade family, who governed the Jordan Valley from Amman in the second century BC, one tribal branch, led by Prince Hyrcanos, migrated to the area in Wadi Sir, and began to construct a palace-fort known as Qasr el-Abd.

At first the tribe lived in caves in the cliffs; then, little by little, they built themselves houses around the stream flowing through the wadi.

Using slave labour, probably local Bedouin, Hyrcanos then began constructing a white and rose-coloured limestone palace on an artificial island surrounded by a moat.

Building was interrupted by the Seleucid conquest of Jordan in 2 BC; then the Romans confiscated it as state property, which was probably fortunate since it was never divided up. When the Byzantines occupied the region they discovered an intact, though incomplete, building within which they built a small fortress for their own defence.

Situated near the Jordan fault, the palace was probably

damaged by successive earthquakes, certainly by the major earthquake in AD 747. The site lay abandoned for nearly 1,000 years; not until 1961–62 was it excavated, by an American archaeologist, Dr Paul Lapp, who is credited with the discovery of the first of several bas-reliefs of panthers.

Tourists should try to visit Qasr el-Abd. The drive through Wadi Sir is charming; the road twists and turns through a quiet, conservative corner of Jordan where farmers wear the traditional costume of black jacket and baggy cream trousers. Especially after winter rains, the cliffs sprout white hollyhocks and those with sharp eyes will spot the mauve rock rose, *Cistus villosus.* Rounding a shoulder of rock beyond the one shop in the local village of Araq el-Amir, one confronts the eastern wall of Qasr el-Abd, standing in front of the base of a cliff.

Monsieur Larché's patient digging and numbering of the large stones (some weighed 20 tonnes) has resulted in the building fitting accurately the ancient description by Flavius Josephus.

The plan is probably Oriental, but the decorations of Qasr el-Abd are decidedly Greek. Swirling floral capitals are scattered about, probably demonstrating the Egyptian influence which followed the Hellenisation of Alexandria.

Hyrcanos was evidently proud of his palace, for to approach the main entrance from the west, visitors were obliged to circumambulate the moat. The moat in fact was never filled and when the Seleucid occupation interrupted construction of Qasr el-Abd, Hyrcanos committed suicide.

What is seen today is the partly erected east wall of the palace featuring the splendid lion fountain. Altogether eight lions, eight lionesses, two panthers and four eagles have been discovered carved in rocks which were probably rolled into position by teams of slaves using ramps and wheels to trundle them along the floor of the wadi.

Traces of primitive saws and unfinished columns are to be seen in the nearby quarry. Byzantine occupation is witnessed by crosses on some of the capitals and others

Qasr el-Abd, lion fountain on the East wall

carved in the rocks. A two-level structure, the palace measured 40 metres by 20 metres, and probably rose to a height of 18 metres. The monumental gate from the east wall lies about 100 metres away, in a citrus fruit grove.

It is a good idea to take a picnic lunch, and photographers will find the morning sun provides backlighting for the palace. There are fine views over the valley, once enjoyed by the present monarch's grandfather, King Abdullah, a frequent visitor to Qasr el-Abd.

Concerning photography in Amman, morning is also the best time to photograph the bazaar and the King Hussein Mosque. Permission should be sought before photographing any pedestrians: Palestinian women should not be photographed. So as not to attract attention, or offend custom, western women should dress discreetly in downtown Amman, keeping sleeveless dresses and shorts for Aqaba.

Chapter Three

The King's Highway to Petra

Hidden inside soaring outcrops at the southern end of the eastern escarpment is Petra, the 'rose red' city, carved almost entirely from rock. So many tourists endeavour to see Petra in a day trip from Amman, but in doing so, they miss one of the marvels of the Middle East. To explore Petra's monuments carved by former Arab nomads, one must penetrate deeper into the city than merely as far as the Treasury. This temple, though arguably the most inspired, is only the start of Petra, from where many tours short of time return to Amman. I have visited Petra on several occasions and each time I discover something new – another altar, or temple, or perhaps the same monument bathed in a different light. The journey from Amman to Petra also follows a fascinating route past biblical towns and Crusader castles in the east bank escarpment. In order to explore Petra thoroughly and to be able to stop at these historic sites, one should plan an absence from Amman of at least two nights. Petra has rest-house accommodation and the new Petra hotel overlooks the weird sandstone shapes in the valley, some 30 minutes' stroll from the ancient city.

The road trip to Petra follows the King's Highway which is, with the Desert Highway and the Dead Sea–Wadi Arabah Highway, one of the three great roads linking northern Jordan and the Gulf of Aqaba.

Na'ur is the first significant town after Amman; the

الطريق السلطاني الطريق الصحراوي

DESERT KINGS
HIGHWAY HIGHWAY

Travellers' choice to Aqaba

original Circassian settlement dates from 1878. The
white-washed houses, set amidst vine-yards (Judg. 2:33;
Isa. 16:8–10) makes it seem more like a village in rural
Greece: bells toll in the Greek Orthodox Church and
women, dressed in black, sprinkle water on the clean,
though dusty streets. There are even cats, a rare sight in

Adeb, the author's driver, left. His Christian family lives in Na'ur

the Middle East, sitting slit-eyed on sunny balconies covered in bougainvillea. I visited the home of my driver in Na'ur. Like most of the villagers, the Debebneh family are Christians, and have lived there for five years. Refreshed by coffee made by their daughter, and a pomegranate picked in the garden by the youngest of five sons, I thus began my own journey down the King's Highway.

A few kilometres south of Na'ur is the modern village of Hisban, significant in that it occupies the site of the biblical Heshbon, capital of the Amorite kingdom, one of the most northern of the ancient states in the eastern escarpment. Walking about, one can see the remains of a wall which archaeologists date from the late Iron Age. Tombs have yielded Mameluke and Byzantine pottery and the Roman, or Byzantine cisterns, temples and the ruins of a

hammam, or bath-house, indicate many centuries of civilisation beneath present-day Hisban.

Forty minutes' drive from Amman is Madaba, the biblical Medba, a border town between the Ammonite and the
Moabite kingdoms in the eastern escarpment. The town is
mentioned on the famous 'Mesha Stele', a basalt rock on
which its ruler, King Mesha, carved a record of his battles,
and other achievements, against the invading Israelites.
(Isa. 15 and 16.)

A provincial town under the Greeks, it became a
bishopric under the Byzantines from which period date its
famous mosaics, to be seen in some fourteen churches and
numerous houses in and around the hill-top settlement.

The Persian invasion of AD 614 destroyed much of
Madaba. The following century it was razed by an earthquake, remaining abandoned until resettled by Christians
from Kerak in the early nineteenth century. While removing the rubble to dig foundations for their houses,
these settlers discovered the beautiful mosaics which had
remained hidden for so long.

It seems that Madaba must have been a veritable school
of that delicate art, for dozens of mosaics exist in private
homes, notably houses in Mitri el-Masaraweh, Aziz
Shawaihat and Misa'ad el-Tual; but the most important is
the remarkable map of Palestine which can be seen in the
Greek Orthodox Church in central Madaba. (The church is
locked, but visitors should knock hard for a guide to come
with the keys.)

During the construction of the church in 1896, workmen broke the original mosaic which measured 25 by 6
metres, but the remaining piece is still a vivid depiction of
sixth-century Palestine. The centre shows a plan of
Jerusalem with many of its important buildings such as
the Church of the Holy Sepulchre. Jericho is also depicted,
surrounded, as it still is, by lush palm groves, while at the
mouth of the River Jordan fish swim desperately away
from the current sweeping them into the Dead Sea.

In the town a small museum displays other mosaics and

a collection of Roman and Byzantine jewellery and pottery. Nearby are two shops where craftsmen weave traditional Madaba rugs considered the finest in Jordan – a mark of prestige in local households and a good buy for tourists.

The rest of Madaba has little of interest to the visitor except perhaps for the occasional appearance of a timeless figure riding a donkey.

The countryside between Amman and Madaba is especially rich in wild flowers. Besides common species such as *Anchusa strigosa* are the delicate mauve rock rose *Cistus Villosus*, bushes of feathery flowered *Capparis Spinosa* and clumps of Jordan's national flower, the black iris.

On the edge of the escarpment, eleven kilometres from Madaba, is Mount Nebo, the alleged site of the tomb of Moses, the greatest prophet in the Old Testament.

Traditionally there is supposed to have been a memorial to Moses in the vicinity of Mount Nebo first recorded in the diary of a Roman pilgrim called Egeria in the fourth century AD. After struggling up the mountain on a donkey, she writes of finding herself in a monastery inhabited by holy men, probably Coptic priests, who assured her that 'Holy Moses was buried here by angels' (Deut. 34:6). Other Christian pilgrims report a similar chapel, or monastery on Mount Nebo, and the Franciscans, who have been excavating the area since 1933, are convinced it is the site of the tomb.

What tourists see today is a sixth-century Byzantine church resting upon the well-identified remains of an early chapel. When the floor of the building was uncovered in 1976, it revealed one of the most perfect early Christian mosaics ever found: a work of high artistry depicting diverse figures such as a pig-tailed slave leading an ostrich on a leash, a curious spotted camel, and hunters tracking an elephant and a lion. The Asiatic lion is known to have been widespread in Palestine and Jordan, but it is interesting to consider whether elephants ever lived in the semi-tropical region around Jericho, in the Jordan Valley.

Four kilometres south-east of Mount Nebo is another beautifully preserved mosaic in a church on the summit of Khirbet el-Mukhaiyat. This mosaic is patterned with lyrical scenes of mythical creatures, lions and a bull cavorting round an altar. Archaeologists believe el-Mukhaiyat is the site of the biblical town of Nebo which was, like Madaba, a flourishing Byzantine settlement.

Dhiban, the ancient Moabite capital 65 kilometres from Amman, is where the 'Mesha stele', an inscribed basalt slab, was found in 1868. Although it was broken, a member of the French consulate had fortunately made an impression of it before leaving. He returned to collect the fragments and sent them to Europe for experts to piece together. The original stele is now exhibited in the Louvre Museum in Paris, and copies may be seen in the British Museum and the Archaeological Museum in Amman.

Twenty kilometres south of Dhiban the highway descends into Wadi Mujib, one of the most cavernous valleys in the Middle East. About halfway down is a point to pull off the road and enjoy a spectacular panorama. On the opposite side, as the highway begins its steep climb up to the town of Kerak, are two Roman mileposts.

Kerak is known for its lofty Crusader-built castle, the most important of the fortresses built in 'Oultre Jordain' (the areas to the east of the River Jordan) whose signal fires could be seen in the knights' headquarters in Jerusalem.

Following the recapture of the Holy City in the First Crusade, the highest-ranking noblemen staked out for themselves six independent states, the main four being the Kingdom of Jordan, the Princedom of Antioch and the Counties of Tripoli and Edessa. Christian forces had also secured the coastal plains of Palestine, but beyond the east bank escarpment, 'Oultre Jordain' lay open to attack. To strengthen this flank, the Crusaders advanced east, building a series of forts between the Dead Sea and Aqaba, at Kerak, Shoubak, Tafila, Petra, Aqaba and on the Ile de Graye. The location of each castle was measured by the distance that a horseman could ride in a day: at night, they relayed news to each other by means of bonfires.

Kerak, or the 'Crac de Moabites', was built by order of the King of Jerusalem, Baldwin 1, who had led the First Crusade with his brother, Godfrey de Bouillon. Not only was the construction of the castle on the edge of a precipice a mammoth task, but it also presented a considerable job to maintain and defend, plus the need to feed and equip its soldiers.

In order to isolate the castle completely, a moat was sunk across an isthmus connecting with its battlements and it was from this high wall that Moslem captives were hurled to their deaths.

Kerak soon prospered from road-tolls imposed on travellers using the King's Highway and, guarded by sentries watching from the parapets, the inhabitants were able to cultivate food in the nearby valleys. Although the soldiers risked attack on longer journeys, no-one overtly challenged the Latin kingdom of the Christian knights until the rise to power of the Moslem warrior, Saladin Yusuf ibn Ayyub.

Born in 1138, a Kurd of Tekrit in Armenia, Saladin learned soldiery at the court of Damascus, gaining respect for his courage and integrity on the battlefield. Seizing a weakness in the knights' defence, in 1174 he launched a *jihad*, or Holy War, to expel them not only from Jerusalem, but from the entire Near East.

In Jerusalem, Baldwin III had died leaving only a thirteen-year-old leper heir who at first endeavoured to rule acting solely on the advice of an old family friend – Miles de Plancy, the Lord of Kerak.

When dissension flared over land rights, the Count of Tripoli was appointed Regent. Matters were still unresolved when de Plancy was murdered, and division grew within the Crusader ranks. Despite repeated requests reinforcements failed to arrive from Europe and the now fatally ill king elected to call a truce with Saladin.

Under the agreement, pilgrims of both religions were to

be allowed freedom of passage to their respective holy sites in Jerusalem and Mecca and all Christian captives in Aleppo were to be released. Among those freed was the former Count of Antioch, Reynald de Chatillon who, on learning of the death of de Plancy, travelled to Kerak and wooed Stephanie, his wealthy widow.

Reynald became progressively motivated by greed, and in 1181 he broke the truce by plundering a rich caravan in which Saladin's sister was travelling from Damascus to Mecca. This act of treachery provoked renewed Moslem attacks on Christian strongholds, and Saladin succeeded in capturing a thousand Christian pilgrims in revenge. Following an abortive effort to take Kerak, the Moslem warrior spent the next four years in harrassing other Crusader strongholds and raising a huge army to attack Jerusalem.

Crossing the River Jordan on 1 July 1187 with an army numbering between 20–30,000 men he inflicted terrible losses among Crusader ranks. When Jerusalem fell on 2 October, several knights were taken to Saladin's tent for interrogation. Recognising Reynald among them, Saladin rebuked him for his acts of treason and robbery, and receiving an insult in reply, is said to have unsheathed his long sword and struck off the Crusader's head. With a small force of knights, the widow Stephanie managed to hold the castle for a further twelve months until famine forced them to capitulate.

The Third Crusade, led by King Richard 'the Lion-Heart', attempted to regain Jerusalem, but like the Fourth Crusade in AD 1200–1204 it was a failure, and the knights began their final retreat from Jordan and the Holy Land. Kerak then became an Arab stronghold, fought over by successive dynasties until in 1894 the Turks captured it from two powerful tribes, the Beni Hemeida and the Majali of Hebron. Following allied successes in World War 1, Kerak became a British administrative centre.

The main street of Kerak leads into the castle which, despite its ruinous state, is a fine example of medieval architecture. One can explore the underground dungeons, dark and draughty with a pallid vegetation creeping over the crumbling stones. A soaring flight of stairs leads to the upper storey, now roofless, sunk with deep cisterns. The wells, over 20 metres deep, are unmarked and one should watch one's step. At this height, I found myself looking down on an eagle wheeling after prey. As I watched, an air-current lifted the bird level with the castle ramparts; then it planed out over the wadi.

A famous story told about Kerak is that of the night of Baldwin's sister's wedding to the seventeen year-old step-son of Reynald and Stephanie de Plancy. Suddenly, above the merry-making, there echoed the sound of cannon fire smashing into the castle as Saladin launched a surprise attack. The Governor of Kerak is said to have got up from the banquet table and arranged for a meal to be sent down to the Moslem warrior, with a message telling him of the celebrations. Saladin is reported to have acknowledged the gesture by enquiring as to the position of the nuptial chamber, so that his men might avoid firing at it.

A final view of the 'Crac de Moabites' is from the King's Highway as it leads into Wadi Hasa, the second great valley scouring the escarpment. On either side of the wadi terraced fields descend like stairways. In April and May, still unploughed, many fields are covered with *Phlomis nichnitis*, a dark yellow bush interspread with purple thistles and the taller spindly mauve heads of wild garlic; while later in the year some fields are green with cabbages and okra and others are yellow with the stubble of the wheat harvest.

Just over halfway to Petra one reaches Tafila, a small town situated on the side of a mountain overlooking a valley cultivated with figs, olives and apple orchards. The Crusader castle here is too ruinous to warrant more than a glance before continuing the next 60 kilometres to Shaubak.

Known as the 'Crac de Monreal', Shaubak Castle was the first of seven built by Baldwin I in 1115 to control the route between Syria, Egypt and the Hejaz. Like Kerak, it was beseiged on several occasions by Saladin who eventually cut down the Christian flag in 1189.

During the thirteenth and fourteenth centuries the Mamelukes carried out restoration work on the castle, but without subsequent maintenance it has fallen into decay. The best angle to view it is from the approach road, at which distance the old castle can maintain a façade of former grandeur.

Forty kilometres south of Shaubak lies Petra, which requires a totally different approach. It must be entered, walked over, climbed upon and explored as thoroughly as a doctor examining a person for broken bones. Although many monuments are broken and weathered, it is immensely impressive, a place where the mind soars out of time in an ecstasy of isolation. Petra is unique among the world's ancient cities in that it has not changed since its discovery in 1812. There is no subsequent building inside the city, no cars, nor even 'conveniences'.

Contrary to the widely held belief that there is only one access into Petra, through the famous chasm, or gorge, known as the *siq*, there exists a second, historic route to its old suburbs of el-Barid and el-Beidha. Visitors, however, enter Petra by riding on a horse, or by pony-trap, or by walking through the narrow *siq* which twists for 3 kilometres between the towering cliffs. I prefer to walk: for although the way is rocky, one can concentrate on Petra's history and the rich heritage left by its Nabataean inhabitants.

Staying overnight in the rest-house on a recent visit to Petra, I rose shortly after dawn. The guides were still asleep and in the wadi the horses waiting for the day's tourists were quietly chewing hay. Strolling down towards the *siq* I flushed a hare which sat up, startled, then bounded off behind the Box Tombs, which are carved from the side of the hill and appear to be isolated from it. (Archaeologists are uncertain of their use, whether as tombs, or as types of sacrificial altars.) Farther along the

The awesome chasm of the *siq* leading into Petra

path through the wadi I arrived at the Obelisk Tomb, standing high up in the cliff face – a stylised carving bearing a similarity to Pharaonic sculpture. (Unlike the ancient Pharaohs, the Nabataeans did not use slave labour in their building projects.) Admiring the conduits cut in the rocks, I saw a dazzling blue, long-legged lizard, later identified as a Blue Sinai lizard, a native of Petra. Then, after some fifteen minutes or so, I entered the twilight world of the *siq*, my footsteps awakening thousands of sparrows which flew out, chirruping, into the light.

Petra – the classic Greek word for 'rock' – is locked inside soaring sandstone outcrops separating the high plateau from the western depression of Wadi Arabah. To the north, the outcrops merge with the Moabite Hills, while in the south they widen until spreadeagled on either side of the Gulf of Aqaba. Primitive man and his herds no doubt drank at Ain Musa, the spring in the wadi leading down to Petra, (said to be the spring that gushed forth when Moses struck the rock), but actual settlement probably dates from when a passage was found through the apparently impenetrable rock barrier into Wadi Arabah.

Water and accessibility helped Petra to develop as a caravan staging-post for the major eastern trade routes out of Arabia: the frankincense route originating in the Hadramaut and, following the east coast of the Red Sea, the silks and spices route traversing central Arabia from the Gulf, and the wealthy route from Africa, via Egypt, bringing ivory, ostrich feathers, apes, animal hides and slaves.

The southern hills of the eastern escarpment were settled by the Edomites. Edom, meaning 'red' in Arabic, is an apt description of the rugged jebels; but Giorgio, the cook who accompanied Edward Lear, the writer and landscape artist, on his travels through the Near East, describes the scenery even more vividly: 'Oh Signore,' he is reported to have exclaimed on entering Petra with Lear, 'we have come into a world where everything is made of chocolate, ham, curry-powder and salmon!'

The Kingdom of Edom is considered to have been the wealthiest of the independent states in the escarpment. The Edomites grew prosperous on road-tolls from caravans passing Petra, and through their mastery of the art of primitive metalwork obtained from copper deposits in Wadi Arabah. The rich mines in the rift valley were the cause of constant fighting with the Israelites and when alliances with the other kingdoms did not hold, many of the Edomites were enslaved in the mines, the profits going to King Solomon.

A story sometimes told by Petra's guides relates how one of the Judaean kings had 10,000 Edomites flung to their deaths off the towering central rock of Umm el-Biyara. Whilst it is not unlikely that Edomite families found hiding on the rock were killed, most historians agree that the biblical 'thousands' is an error in translation.

Centuries of feuding ended when the Babylonians sacked Jerusalem and captured many Jews for work in building projects in Nineveh. Profiting from this, many Edomites moved down from the hills to settle in the more fertile area of Palestine, but they found themselves outnumbered after the Persian conquest of Babylonia allowed many Jews to return. Slowly they were incorporated into a Jewish community, so that by the first century Edom, as a separate kingdom, had begun to decline.

History first records the exploits of the Nabataeans about this time. Like others before them they were nomads, leading an itinerant existence in central and northern Jordan, grazing their herds and profiting from the age-old Bedouin occupation of pillaging caravans. When Persian imperialism began threatening these activities, the Nabataeans folded their tents and migrated south, to settle around the springs of el-Beidha and Wadi Musa. Their transition to a sedentary life was so gradual that the remaining Edomites did not feel threatened, even initiating the newcomers into some of the teachings of their own civilisation.

As former nomads, the Nabataeans had never applied themselves to the work and creative aspects of a settled existence; but history records that they were an adaptable people who possessed a flare for organisation and a genius for sculpting.

The Roman writer, Strabo, gives an idea of the

Nabataean character in his journals of about 54 BC.

Although he did not visit Petra, Strabo discussed it at length with a scholar who had lived there. He writes of the Nabataeans as being a temperate, industrious race who enjoyed a democratic form of society. Valleys are described as abundantly cultivated with fruits, and a penchant for cooking with sesame-seed oil is mentioned.

Two principal deities are known to have been worshipped by the Nabataeans – Dusares, who symbolised strength and is frequently represented as a carving of a solid block of stone; and al-Uzza, the deity of water and patron of fertility to whom it is believed the Nabataeans dedicated the great temple Qasr el-Bint.

It is normal that one of the most revered deities should have been associated with water, reflecting the obsession of desert peoples with even the smallest life-giving spring. The Edomites evolved a form of cistern conservation, but the Nabataeans went further. They displayed an extraordinary grasp of engineering by cutting conduits in the *siq* so that Petra, being on a lower gradient could receive water channelled down from Ain Musa. They also constructed a dam to trap run-off from the cliffs and laid earthenware pipes to convey water to the city centre. At the height of Petra's prosperity, it is estimated that the pipes coped with supplying the demands of a population of between 20–30,000.

Petra's most outstanding feature, its Nabataean architecture, is unquestionably eclectic displaying Greek, Egyptian and Roman influence. However, being situated at the convergence of trade routes, it was inevitable that local architecture became diluted. Syrian and Greek artisans who settled in Petra under King Aretas III undoubtedly influenced the notably Corinthinian-like appearance of the famous Treasury. Only the 'step pinnacle', or 'crow-step' pattern of architecture, is held to be uniquely Nabataean. The soft, crumbly sandstone precluded more detailed work, but the 'crow-step' carving is dramatically effective. No matter how small the tomb displaying this step pattern, it is never dwarfed by the mass of rock from which it is carved.

Besides having a genius for sculpting, the Nabataeans also proved to be talented potters, a craft probably taught them by the Edomites. Fragments of pottery picked up in Petra have been recognised as Nabataean by their wafer-thin, terracotta-coloured porcelain decorated with leaves in colours ranging from sepia to café-au-lait. Under King Aretas III the first coins were minted, a skill also inherited from the Edomites who became absorbed into a wholly Nabataean civilisation.

At that time there were no Arabic letters, inscriptions being made in Cufic, a crude form of writing which evolved in Cufa, a city south of Baghdad. The Nabataeans at first used the Aramaic of ancient Mesopotamia, but by the middle of the first century BC the script had assumed specialised characters. Graphologists generally agree that today's Arabic alphabet grew from this divergence of scripts. One of the best inscriptions in Petra is seen between the inner pilasters, or columns, adorning the façade of the Turkamaniyah Tomb.

Thus, from a simple tribal settlement evolved a flourishing urban society, the nucleus of an empire that once extended from Medain Salih in Saudi Arabia to Damascus. At the outset, the Nabataeans engaged in commerce, charging tolls from caravans; and in view of the volume of trade passing Petra, it is no wonder the city grew rich.

Eventually, passing merchants spread stories of the prosperous metropolis carved in rock in south-west Jordan, arousing the interest of the great powers seeking to dominate the region. The first to attack Petra, in 312 BC, were the Seleucid heirs of Alexander the Great. It was said that they were repulsed by a handful of Nabataeans defending the entrance to the *siq*. Following this experience, Petra continued to enjoy an independent existence for several centuries – the more they earned, the more the Nabataeans embellished the cliffs with monuments, also carving colossal tombs for their kings.

The city's initial contact with Rome came in 63 BC when King Aretas deflected an assault made by the forces of Pompey, but no state no matter how wealthy, or well fortified, had been able to withstand the might of Rome, and Petra was finally annexed in AD 106 by Roman legions who cut off its water supply.

Historians believe it is also possible that Rabel III, the last ruler of Petra, made an agreement which provided that if the kingdom were not attacked during his reign, it would subsequently pass to Rome on his demise. There is no record of a battle fought over Petra, and once incorporated into the Decapolis, it lost all previous status.

Already influenced by Greek culture, Petra adapted quickly to Roman rule. The change is apparent in its architecture with the appearance of baths, theatres and colonnaded streets. Again historians cite the Nabataeans' intelligence in recognising the superiority of Roman architecture and engineering; for instead of rejecting it, they incorporated it into their own designs with some of the finest monuments dating from its Roman period.

Due to increased competition from northern towns in the Decapolis, Petra begin to fade as a business centre by the fourth century AD and as sea travel took over from the traditional overland trade routes, the once prosperous city began to decline.

The rise of the Byzantine Empire did nothing to avert its stagnation, and by the time of the Islamic conquest Petra was a place of relatively minor importance, inhabited only by a few thousand Bedouin. It emerged briefly when the Crusaders built a small fortress there, but on their retreat from the Holy Land, a curtain fell; wind-blown sand began weathering its temples and Petra lay lost, virtually forgotten by the world for over a thousand years, until 1812.

The discoverer of Petra, Johann Ludwig Burckhardt, was a dedicated young Swiss explorer who went to great lengths to toughen himself for a rugged life, and to understand the Moslem world. The son of an army colonel, he developed an interest in Sir Joseph Banks's projects of discovery in Africa and the Near East.

Following a visit to England, Burckhardt volunteered for exploration work. After a short term in Malta, realising a commitment to Islam, he sailed to the eastern Mediterranean where he disembarked and joined a caravan travelling to Aleppo. After spending two years perfecting his Arabic and studying Moslem culture, Burckhardt set out, still on behalf of the British African Association to discover what he could of the Near East.

Disguised as an Arab pilgrim, Burckhardt visited Philadelphia, then travelled down the King's Highway to Wadi Musa where he struck camp. It was around the camp-fire here that Burckhardt listened to the Bedouin discussing a 'lost city' and he determined to see if it was the fabled Petra he had learned about from scholars.

At first he found it difficult to engage a guide, since although he appeared to be an Arab he did not belong to the local Lyathene tribe. Only when he announced his intention of sacrificing a lamb on the Temple of Aaron[1] did the Bedouin agree to show him their secret city; for although still uncertain about the stranger in their midst, no-one was able to object to such a noble act.

So at dawn, on 22 August 1812, Burckhardt set out following his Bedouin guide, making his way along the rocky bed of Wadi Musa. As the rising sun warmed the surrounding peaks, there could be heard creaking and echoing sounds with an eerie humming, as though lost spirits were trapped in the clefts of a giant necropolis. (I also heard this strange, unaccountable humming – a weird, disturbing sound similar to the buzz of long-distance telephone wires.)

'I was without protection ... where no traveller had ever before been seen', Burckhardt wrote in his journal.

Arriving at the *siq*, he must have felt as though he was walking down a corridor to the centre of the earth; but

---

[1] Aaron was the brother of Moses, and the Bedouin in Petra make an annual sacrifice in his memory.

suddenly, at the end of the gorge, came his first evocative glimpse of Petra, of the sumptuously carved façade of the Treasury, or Khazneh.

Coming into the light again, he continued to follow the direction of the wadi, stopping to sketch the tombs and other monuments until his guide became restless, saying they were the work of a magician and urging the explorer to make his sacrifice and leave.

Burckhardt completed other journeys in Arabia and Africa, but none ranks with his discovery of the Nabataean capital. His tomb is in the Moslem cemetery in Cairo, inscribed 'Ibrahim ibn Abdallah', the name Burckhardt adopted when travelling as an Arab. He died not by the bullet of a suspicious Bedouin, as one might guess, but from dysentry, on 17 October 1817.

News of the discovery of Petra prompted others to follow in Burckhardt's footsteps: the French academic, Leon de Laborde; the engraver Linant; the American biblical scholar the Reverend Edward Robinson; David Roberts, who specialised in water colour paintings of the Middle East, in particular of Egypt and the Holy Land and who made some splendid sketches of Petra in 1829; Henry Layard who discovered Ninevah; Edward Lear; and Charles Doughty, author of *Arabia Deserta* who evidently disliked the place, writing how '. . . the eye recoils from . . . the ghastly waste monuments of a sumptous barbaric art. . .'!

Doughty was the only person to take such an objection to Petra. Since the publication of the first paper on the city in 1905, Petra has received a steady stream of visitors. Happily a visit there today is just as exciting as it was in Burckhardt's time, without the danger from hostile Bedouin.

A great deal of controversy surrounds the present seventy Bedouin families living in Petra's caves and tombs. The government wants to resettle them near Wadi Musa, in order to provide them with the same services available to all Jordanian citizens. Accustomed to living in Petra, however, the Bedouin do not wish to move, claiming links with the ancient Nabataeans and therefore a right to stay.

Archaeologists express their concern lest the Bedouin damage Petra's unique monuments; but not having known another existence, they are naturally unable to appreciate their significance. Many tombs are blackened by their camp-fires. Also, needing to earn a little money, they are constantly digging for artifacts to sell, the irony being that on finding a statue, or a coin, they are unable to assess its worth and subsequently only ask a quarter of the real value.

A notice near the rest-house forbids the buying of antiques, a warning equally intended to safeguard visitors; for in Petra, as in any ancient city, the majority of the artifacts are fakes. Occasionally, whilst one is exploring the city, a child approaches offering to sell a tiny statue, or a small lamp, or some other object that could easily be concealed in the palm should they be confronted by a tourist policeman. It is impossible to tell whether they are genuine or not.

I saw only one person selling anything openly – a grizzled old Bedouin known as Sheikh Salameh, or Abu Saksouka (Father of the Beard), who lived in a cave near the Roman theatre. On an old case discarded by a tourist, he arranged a few oddments to tempt the passing trade: a silver bracelet, a terracotta vase, a broken *nargila* and a blackened coin. The only genuine thing was, in fact, the cheap silver bracelet: according to Sheikh Salami the others were copies, made to look antique in the Damascus *souq*.

The following monuments are by no means a complete tally of what is to be seen in Petra, but they represent some of the most significant and interesting features for a visitor spending two to three days there.

Sculpted for maximum effect at the end of the *siq* is the soaring Treasury, dating from AD 2. Solitary and uncluttered by other monuments, the rose-coloured stone seems at times almost to glow. One is made aware of its

First glimpse of Petra, the soaring 'treasury' of Khanzah

colossal size by seeing it in relation to the horses walking past the base. An urn on the top is damaged by bullets fired at it over the centuries by local Bedouin and passing travellers: tradition says a Pharaoh deposited treasure inside, but like everything in Petra, the urn is carved from solid rock.

57

The rock face from which the Treasury is carved shelters it from water run-off and wind-borne dust, so that it is one of the best preserved of Petra's monuments. Others, including the actual rocks, are greatly weathered, giving the city its peculiar appearance of 'melting ice-cream cornets'.

As Wadi Musa widens slightly after the journey through the *siq*, tombs and houses are seen cut out of the surrounding wall of rock, their Nabataean artistry being recognised by the typical 'crow step' pattern. Beyond the Treasury is the Roman theatre, carved in the second or third century AD to seat some 3,000 spectators.

On the right, cut into the side of Jebel Khubtha, is a group of Petra's most elaborate tombs, collectively known as the Royal Tombs.

Walking from south to north one passes the Urn Tomb, an imposing, elevated structure having a decidedly Roman influence, although it is Nabataean in architectural design. Chambers, or *loculi*, placed out of reach of scavenging animals and grave-robbers, indicate its use in funerary rites. The interior was remodelled as a church in AD 446 and the deep courtyard gives a grand panorama of the city. Next reached is the Silk Tomb or Rainbow Tomb. Although architecturally insignificant, it is noteworthy for the rippling colours, or marbling effect of the sandstone. A short distance away is the Corinthian Tomb, obviously inspired by the design of the Treasury with the Roman fondness for lofty columns, regrettably broken in an earthquake. Some historians consider it to be a copy of Nero's famous Golden Palace in Rome but, like the Urn Tomb, elevated niches reveal its use as a tomb. From this point a track leads into the valley, joins up with rock again, and reaches the final monument known as the Tomb of Sextus Florentinus, the Roman governor of Arabia in AD 127. An inscription on the tomb, erected by his son, quotes his wish to be buried in Petra – an expression of fondness, perhaps, for this rocky outpost in the Roman Empire.

Winding round the base of Jebel Khubtha, Wadi Musa

leads into the open site of central Petra, its long Colonnade Street running straight as a Roman javelin towards the monumental Tenemos Gate. The ruined state of the city's baths, market places, temples, palaces and a once elaborate nymphaeum, belie what Petra must have been like at the height of its prosperity. '... a bee-hive of activity, densely populated, with houses packed together on the surrounding hills ...' writes Iain Browning in his book *Petra*. The absence of any free-standing structures suggests they were destroyed in the same violent earthquake which wrecked Jerash, Jerusalem, Madaba and other towns in the mid-eighth century AD.

At the end of the Colonnade Street, the Tenemos Gate guards the way into the sacred precincts of the great Qasr bint Pharaon or Qasr el-Bint. Historians suppose it was dedicated to an important female deity, such as al-Uzza, or to the daughter of an Egyptian pharaoh. A huge building sculpted of flesh-coloured sandstone, it was evidently constructed so as to overlook Petra, which it still does, with the winged lion temple, the only free-standing buildings to have withstood the ravages of time. Of Roman design, but built in the late Nabataean era, it stands on the site of an older Nabataean civilisation where excavations have revealed the eroded base of a statue dedicated to the Nabataean king, Aretas IV (8 BC–AD 40). The name 'Aretas' used by the Nabataean kings, is a Hellenised version of the Arabic name Harith, or Harithat, beginning with the first king, Aretas I, in 169 BC.

To the west of the Qasr bint Pharaon is the sheer-sided rock on which the Crusaders constructed their fort. From this point at sunset, the Royal Tombs are not rose-pink, but rather a blood-red, making clear the meaning of Edom. In the west looms Umm el-Biyara, the rock from which the 10,000 Edomites were supposedly thrown to their deaths, a perilous climb even today, recommended only to young and agile tourists.

Most people avail themselves of one, or two walks: to Petra via the Treasury and Royal Tombs, returning by route of the High Places of Sacrifice, or via the Treasury and Royal Tombs through central Petra to the Monastery, or *Deir*.

The first follows a rough track leading upwards behind the Qasr el-Bint, reaching a flat ridge highlighted by a solitary pillar, with two fallen companions at its base. The Faroun Pillar seems unrelated to any building and its use is suggested to have been connected with a lunar cult. Attributing anything inexplicable to the pharaoh, or 'magician', the Bedouin call the pillar *Zinn Faroun*, the Phallus of the Pharaoh.

Nearby is the Katute Site, an interesting structure thought to have been the dwelling of a prosperous merchant who, for reasons unknown, vacated it some time after the Roman annexation of Petra. Was it as a result of the civic-conscious Romans dumping the town's rubbish near his doorstep? Yet to be excavated, the Rubbish Dump overflows into Wadi Farash, winding up the Atuf Ridge.

A series of tombs is carved here of which the most noteworthy are the Renaissance Tomb, so-called for its elegant, Italianate façade, the Tomb of the Roman Soldier, the burial site of someone of obvious rank, its interior greatly blackened by Bedouin camp-fires, and the Garden Tomb. Opposite the Tomb of the Roman Soldier is the Triclinium, where banquets were held to commemorate the dead. It has no façade, emphasis being on the lavish Roman interior of soaring fluted columns, worked in the mauve-veined sandstone.

It is a steep ascent from here to the High Places, nearly 350 metres above sea level. On the way up, the Lion Monument is passed – a startling carving, obviously destined as a drinking fountain, but for some reason never finished.

The Nabataeans leave the impression that they were compulsive sculptors, for everywhere evidence of their work is found in finished and half-finished carvings. One imagines them assiduously chipping away at the cliffs, then suddenly climbing down and instead of completing the project, beginning a new sculpture somewhere else.

The area on top of the ridge is divided into two sections, the southern half, or the Obelisk Ridge (whose two carved obelisks probably represent Dusares and al-Uzza) and the northern section, or the Place of Sacrifice.

Despite its exposed position, the High Place of Sacrifice remains in a remarkable state of preservation with the edges of the altars being as sharp as though they were cut only yesterday. Popular novels and the cinema depict blood sacrifices as brutal pagan orgies; but to the Nabataeans, a sacrifice was an expression of their faith, an occasion of joy to be able to offer something to their gods. The blood was sprinkled on their houses since they believed it afforded them divine protection.

There is an inscription in Medain Salih[1] in Saudi Arabia, recording the immolation of a young man which confirms that the Nabataeans practised human as well as animal sacrificial rituals. Adolescent girls and boys are also believed to have been sacrificed to the Goddess al-Uzza.

The altars cut with gutters for draining the blood, the ritual cleansing basins and the seats carved in the cliffs for the spectators, can all be seen by visitors who complete the climb up from Petra. The view alone makes the climb worthwhile.

The ancient city lies in a basin of hot-coloured hills, in the north flowing towards el-Beidha and in the south, peak upon peak sliced by valleys, one of which is the route to Wadi Arabah.

'... a place, this, impregnated with history and the resounding silence of forgotten rites,' writes Iain Browning, whose book, *Petra*, is for serious students of the Nabataean civilisation.

The second walk follows the trough of Wadi el-Deir, cutting in a northerly direction from the Qasr bint

---

[1] Medain Salih – often called the 'Petra of Arabia' – lies about 380 kilometres north-east of Jeddah at the southern extent of the Nabataean empire. It contains more than 100 tombs carved between 1 BC–AD 76.

Pharaon. Many of the tombs in this valley are inhabited by Bedouin who set the hills ringing with the weird call they use for herding goats; while at night their voices, often raised in family disputes, drift out from pin-prick fires in the towering cliffs.

It is important to pick the right time to see Petra's monuments at their best. Eleven in the morning is ideal for the Treasury, just as late afternoon is right for the Royal Tombs, when the setting sun also fires the Monastery – the question at this hour being whether to camp out, or to stumble back to the rest-house on a perilous, if not haunting journey through the *siq* at night.

On the first stage of the long climb leading up to the Monastery is a small *triclinium*, a place where funeral banquets were held to honour the dead. Of classic Roman architecture, it is known as the Lion Tomb, named after two lions, now badly eroded, adorning the façade.

Tourists ride or walk into ancient Petra

To the left is one of the numerous carved blocks dedicated to Dusares, symbolising strength. It is an appropriate spot since from here on the climb becomes tough, step after gruelling step as the gorge narrows, then widens round outcrops of rock. Finally, sweating and dizzy, one climbs the last stair on to the plateau where the first thing that catches the eye is a Bedouin selling refreshments.

While sipping an orangeade and admiring his enterprise in carrying his load all the way up the stairs, one can now turn one's full attention to the Monastery, a mountainous carving in a massive shoulder of rock.

Architecturally it resembles the Treasury, with the same high-columned façade and sober interior. Its very size, 50 metres wide and 45 metres high to the top of the urn, suggests that the Monastery was very sacred to the Nabataeans – a demonstration also of man's early achievements in the Middle East.

The two walks require two days. They do not include the long trek to el-Barid and el-Beidha, where excavations, now reaching 'Level Seven', have discovered Neolithic buildings which indicate some form of civilisation here, possibly pre-dating Jericho (9–7,000 BC).

Chapter Four

The Jordan Valley–Dead Sea Trench

The northern trajectory of the Great Rift Valley runs for a distance of some 356 kilometres through western Jordan. The depression, or trench, contains the Jordan Valley, the Dead Sea and the semi-desert ridge of Wadi Arabah which fills the southern end to the Gulf of Aqaba.

Overlooked by the high escarpments at the northern end of the trench is the Jordan Valley, extending from Lake Tiberias to the Dead Sea. The valley, or *ghor* in Arabic, experiences a Mediterranean type of climate with hot, dry summers and temperate winters. The rainfall averages between 380 millimetres in the north to 100 millimetres in the south, and humidity ranges from 28 per cent in summer to 84 per cent in winter.

Flowing through the valley is the River Jordan which receives water from the Zerqa and the Yarmuk, forming Jordan's north-west border with Syria. Combined with water from wadis, an estimated 1,880 million cubic metres is lost through evaporation and the remaining 1,250 million cubic metres flows into the Dead Sea.

In biblical times the Jordan Valley was the most fertile belt in the Levant, but centuries of habitation, over-grazing and the felling of its once dense forests eventually transformed the 'promised land' into eroded wasteland.

In the early 1950s, the Jordanian government began a programme to harness the valley for irrigation and to upgrade archaic farming methods. Responsibility for the project lies with the Jordan Valley Authority, formerly the Jordan Valley Commission, which was established in 1972 and is modelled on the Tennessee Valley Authority.

The key to opening the valley to greater productivity was the construction of the East Ghor Canal, which acts as a by-pass in bringing water from high up the River Yarmuk to irrigate the east bank. From this artery, now extending for more than 100 kilometres, dozens of small feeder canals supply farmland along the way.

The construction of a series of dams is equally important. Completed in 1977, the $35 million King Talal Dam irrigates over 6,000 hectares of new land. The dam was also built to supply Amman's drinking water, but the quality of the water has been spoiled by nitrates picked up in the dam's catchment area around the highly urbanised, industrialised town of Zerqa. Eutrophication has developed from algae becoming overfertilised and its excessive growth has reduced the oxygen level of the water. The authorities are seeking a reduction in this imbalance which also risks contaminating water for irrigation.

The biggest dam is to be the 350 million cubic metre Maqarin Dam, planned to utilise the enormous amount of surplus water in the River Yarmuk. The dam will not only store water for irrigation, thereby increasing irrigated farmland to over 30,000 hectares, but will also supply the expanding town of Irbid with drinking water, at present pumped from the eastern oasis of Azraq. The building of the Maqarin Dam will involve construction of a 980-metre tunnel under a mountain in order to divert water into the East Ghor Canal. Syrian co-operation is required for the project, since although the Yarmuk rises in Jordan, it has a confluence with the River Harir in Syria before flowing into the River Jordan.

The JVA is also responsible for a scheme to develop correspondingly the local infrastructure. Plans include the construction of 36 communities throughout the valley, 9 educational zones, hospitals, mosques, shops and community services. Land re-distribution calls for the division of large farms with compensation for the owners. Under the new scheme, the largest holding will be 20 hectares and the smallest 4 hectares. Long-term, low-interest loans are to be made available for farmers to purchase housing: training centres will also educate them to new farming techniques.

Encouraged by the good start made by the JVA, of the original 100,000 people who fled the valley in 1967, some 80,000 have returned and their labour sees the East Bank taking on new life.

The signs of success show everywhere, in the fields of swaying wheat and abundant crops and tomatoes, melons, cucumbers, aubergines, potatoes and other produce. The year-round sunshine in the valley means off-season crops, and the more recent use of plastic hot-houses, or clôches, has frequently trebled production of certain crops. The plastic sheeting is a locally manu-

Jordan Valley is the food bowl of Jordan

factured polyethylene costing an estimated $16–20,000 to cover a square hectare, but whose cost is recuperated by the increased production within two to three years. Clôches have increased the Jordan Valley tomato crop from 86,364 tonnes in 1977 to 211,338 in 1978. The cabbage crop increased over the same period from 6,300 tonnes to a record 27,433 tonnes. The cultivation of flowers is being considered with the ready markets in other Arab countries which import most of their blooms from Europe.

The potential for farming the Jordan Valley becomes apparent when it is seen that only half the area is under cultivation, yet it produces 50 per cent of the country's fruit and vegetables, plus 93 per cent of all Jordan's agricultural exports.

Apart from having a rural interest, the valley abounds in historic sites. The most interesting of these is a large tell or mound of archaeological significance, near the agricultural station of Deir Ala which archaeologists believe to be a settlement dating from the Middle Bronze Age about 1600 BC. Deir Ala is known to have been the site of a temple by the discovery there, in 1964, of a seventh-century tablet, inscribed in Aramaic, which tells of the prophet Bileam, meaning 'the bear'. From this and other discoveries, it is known that Deir Ala had an independent culture.

Another significant mound is Tell es-Sa'idiyeh which historians consider might be the biblical town of Zaretan (Josh. 3:16). Excavations have revealed a small fortified city on the site and several artifacts dating from the early Bronze Age.

At Tell el-Mazar, also Bronze Age, students and archaeologists from the University of Jordan and the Department of Antiquities are excavating to determine the inter-communal relationships of the ancient settlements.

To the north of Tell es-Sa'idiyeh is the village of Tabaqat el-Fahl which is built near the ruins of the Greco-Roman city of Pella founded by the armies of Alexander the Great, about 310 BC. In fact Pella is probably even older, since it appears under the name of Bikhil in documents recovered from Tell el-Arma dating from the fourteenth century before Christ. In February 1980, a team from the University of Sydney discovered relics of a Roman temple of which the foundations, walls and columns are still standing. The discovery, which also includes decorated marble slabs, was made on the ancient site of Pella.

The name of the River Jordan flows through the bible like the meandering course of the river itself: if measured as the crow flies, it is about 104 kilometres long; but in fact its loops and curls make it over 300 kilometres long.

To Christians, the Jordan has great spiritual significance as being the place of Christ's baptism; children of the British Royal family are traditionally baptised with its holy waters. Now, Israeli occupation of the West Bank has turned the sacred area into a military zone, making it impossible to reach the river, let alone bathe in it as Christians did on Epiphany Sundays. Also gone are the little stands, under the trees, selling flasks of holy water. Tourists who travel from Amman to Jerusalem across the King Hussein Bridge will glimpse the river from the bus – a narrow muddy stream, bordered by banks of tangled vegetation, trees and tall reeds.

Few records exist of people attempting to navigate the River Jordan to the Dead Sea – history's most famous inland sea, redolent with evocative names such as Herod the Great, Lot, and Sodom and Gomorrah.

The most valiant effort was made in 1835, when an Irishman called Costigan had a boat brought overland from the Mediterranean to Lake Tiberias, from where he sailed downstream to the southern shores of the Dead Sea. After eight days' searching for water and suffering from severe dehydration and sunburn, he managed to reach the northern shore from where his servant crawled to Jericho for help. Although taken by horse to Jerusalem, Costigan died of the effects, aged only thirty-three. The northern aspect of the Lisan peninsula is named in his memory, and the southern aspect after a Lieutenant Molyneaux who reached the sea in 1837, but who also died from the effort.

Fish live in the River Jordan despite the high levels of sodium and magnesium chloride. Any that are accidently swept into the Dead Sea (as depicted in the mosaic map of Palestine in Madaba) are soon to be seen, floating belly upwards.

One of the few places where one can actually drive below sea level, the Dead Sea is known by a variety of other names: Old Testament maps show it as the Sea of Arabah; the Sea of Zoar is another name[1]; and the Romans knew it as *lacus asphalitis*, or the Sea of Asphalt, because of the occasional blobs of asphalt that bob up to the surface.

Another name is the Sodomitish Sea after the alleged sexual excesses of the inhabitants of the settlements of Sodom and Gomorrah, on the southern shores. Genesis 19 relates how Abraham's nephew, Lot, lived in this vicinity and how, before destroying the towns, God warned Lot and his family to flee. As related in the Bible, Lot's wife, taking history's most famous backward glance, was cast into a pillar of salt. Hence the Sea of Lot is another name for the 920 square kilometre stretch of water.

Apart from a few houses at Suweimah on the plain at the foot of the escarpment, there are no modern settlements on the eastern shore of the Dead Sea. Of the remains of the five biblical cities (Sodom, Gomorrah, Admah, Zebouin and Zoar), there is no trace. Wearing heavy lead weights to stay submerged in the excessively buoyant water, divers have searched unsuccessfully for any signs of the ruins of the infamous cities. Should any relics remain, they may eventually be exposed when the Arab Potash Company drains areas of the sea at Safi: even then they will lie under centuries of foul-smelling ooze.

Limited by the Jordan Valley to the north and by Wadi

---

[1] 'Dead Sea' *Encyclopaedia Britannica*, p. 117.

Arabah to the south, the Dead Sea is about 76 kilometres long by about 15.7 kilometres across. It has a very narrow eastern shoreline rising abruptly to the Moab Hills; the Judaean Hills form the western aspect of the depression. The maximum depth of the sea is about 399 metres in the north-east corner; south of the Lisan Peninsula it averages about 2 metres deep.

Before the rupture in the earth's surface resulted in the rift depression, an extended Mediterranean Sea is thought to have covered the whole area of Palestine and Syria. During the early Pleistocene Period the sea rose to a height of 220 metres above its present level, when it was a vast inland sea stretching from Lake Hule (which the Israelis have since drained for cultivation) to 60 kilometres beyond its present limits, prevented from overflowing into the Gulf of Aqaba by the higher ridge of Wadi Arabah. With evaporation prevailing over precipitation, the Pleistocene Sea gradually shrank to its present form.

As well as the River Jordan, which contributes about 300 million cubic metres a year, several wadis flow into the Dead Sea. Springs also gush into it along the shore near Zara and numerous inlets bubble through the actual sea bed. Since there is no outflow, a balance is maintained by evaporation, although in summer, the excessive heat and the absence of rain cause the water level to fall between 3 and 5 metres below the winter level.

This natural balance between in-flow and evaporation was maintained for thousands, even millions of years until the late 1960s when man-made interference caused the Dead Sea to start shrinking. The reasons are that too much water is being withdrawn from the tributaries of the River Jordan for use in irrigation projects. The basins constructed in the southern end of the Sea by the Israeli and Jordanian potash extraction projects are also accelerating the normal rate of evaporation.

In the nineteenth century, camel caravans were able to cross the Dead Sea at its narrowest point in the Lisan Straits, but in the early part of this century the waters rose, making such a journey impossible. The result of the above experiments, coupled with a sustained drought in 1976–80 was that a 12–15-kilometre stretch of land appeared in the sea in the summer of 1979. Experts then predicted that the sea would fall a further 2–3 metres by 1988 and they forecast that the Dead Sea might even dry up within a thousand years if water is continually removed from its inflow. This may be so, but the excessive winter rains of 1980 dumped so much water in the Dead Sea basin that the level is now about 1.2 metres higher than the normal winter level. Proposed plans for canals, from the Mediterranean and the Gulf of Aqaba, to utilise the drop in the production of hydro-electricity would also raise the level of the Dead Sea.

The intense salinity – 25 per cent, compared with only 4–6 per cent in ordinary ocean water – is the most interesting aspect of the Dead Sea. Throughout the Early Pleistocene Epoch of the Pluvial Period, streams carrying thick sedimentary deposits of rock salts, clay, shale and gypsum ran into the sea. Similarly today, the higher than normal concentration of sodium chloride in the River Jordan, added to the minerals leached by wadis flowing off the escarpment, the seepage in the sea floor and the sulphurous springs along the shore, all contribute to its excessive mineral content. Dead Sea salts also contain magnesium, potassium and calcium chloride, magnesium bromide and calcium sulphate.

The amount of chemicals becomes apparent in an experiment involving a glass of the water: when the water has evaporated, the glass is seen to be two-thirds full of yellowish-white crystals. Minerals present in the sea water are also evident in the residue which collects in the basins built at the potash plant.

The best-known historical figure associated with the Dead Sea is Herod the Great, King of Judaeah in 40 BC. Suffering from rheumatism and other complaints, Herod is said to have sought relief by bathing frequently in the Dead Sea and in the mineral springs of Zarqa Ma'in. Growing weaker, he was carried there by litter from his fortress retreat at el-Mukawir, a small village overlooking the sea (where John the Baptist was reputedly beheaded after Salome's dance).

Although the water from Zarqa Ma'in flows into the Dead Sea, there is as yet no vehicle access from the shore. To reach the springs, one drives down the King's Highway to a turn off near Madaba, about 65 kilometres south of Amman. The road descends through ruggedly beautiful scenery in the eastern escarpment to a stream, lined with pink oleander, and a waterfall splashing off the cliffs. Zarqa Ma'in is fed by over sixty springs, some of them cold, but many are hot enough to cook in. The maximum temperature needed for spa water is 35 °C but Zarqa's springs range between 45–63 °C.

German standards classify a spa as mineral if the ratio of salts dissolved in the water does not amount to less than one thousand per million. Tests at Zarqa Ma'in show that dissolved salts in its springs constitute 2,000 units per million, placing it in the same medicinal category as the best spas in Europe. Further tests carried out by experts from Weisbaden show the springs to have a therapeutic value for many types of rheumatic disorders as well as ailments of the respiratory tract.

As a result of these studies, the government has announced its intention to develop Zarqa Ma'in as the most advanced spa resort in the Middle East. A first class hotel, chalets, camping facilities, restaurants, baths and tepidariums are planned.

Present facilities only cater for low income visitors, mainly nationals from Middle East countries who camp in tents along the stream. A local official said that people who visited Zarqa Ma'in regularly, over a six-week period, claim the springs are 90 per cent effective (but he added that it made no difference to them if they had already lost an arm or a leg!).

Westerners who visit Zarqa Ma'in like to bathe under its hot cascades, but locals prefer the privacy of a hot indoor pool sunk in the cliff face. Open to men during the morning and women in the afternoon, the baths are very popular with the Bedouin – especially the women, who suffer from back ailments resulting from their heavy manual work.

When the Dead Sea–Wadi Arabah Highway is completed, tourists will be able to drive to Aqaba via the spectacular coastline along the Dead Sea shores. In 1984, there still remained a rough section of road between Zarqa Ma'in and Safi, necessitating travel by landrover. Normally travelling alone with my driver, on this occasion I took a friend, so as to take the usual photograph of someone floating in the Dead Sea. Although she does not swim, she agreed to come knowing that the excessive mineral content of the Dead Sea makes it so buoyant that one cannot swim in it, but merely roll around on it, as though on a giant water-bed.

A bridge one day will ford the hot springs of Zarqa Ma'in flowing into the Dead Sea

To me, the Dead Sea is beautiful – yet repellent. On a hot day in the Jordan Valley, the shimmering blue water looks so inviting, but it is tepid and if not quickly washed off in freshwater, the salts may burn the skin. On a still day, the springs bubbling up from the sea-bed send currents rippling across the surface. At summer's end, when the water level has fallen, rocks along the shore stand encrusted in salt like strange, hot-weather icebergs.

Apart from a few scattered *henas,* reeds, and low shrubs, there is little vegetation on the shoreline. The Dead Sea is the only place in Jordan where there are no Bedouin tents. There is no grass for grazing their herds, but the Bedouin also hold the sea in awe. According to local superstition, birds do not dare to fly across the surface for fear of inhaling the poisonous fumes.

Of all beautiful birds to see, I glimpsed a sapphire blue king-fisher in Wadi Zarqa Ma'in. The Mountfort expedition to Jordan in 1963 (including Guy Mountfort and led by Sir Julian Huxley) recorded swallows, martins, fantail ravens and kestrels, planing off the escarpment. In former times the hills were inhabited by leopard, cheetah, ibex and mountain gazelle. A few gazelle still survive among the more inaccessible crags; the last surviving leopard was shot in 1964, in Ain-Taribi, on the western shores of the sea.

Between Zarqa Ma'in and Zara, eight kilometres south of Suweimah, a number of small springs flow into the sea. One forms a clear, deep pond where water-beetles slowly propel themselves among the reeds, and dragon-fly larvae crawl over the soft clay bottom. Like the fish in the River Jordan, they perish if washed into the sea where only the *Halobacterium halobium,* a halophilic, or salt-loving micro-organism, survives. Near Zara, tamarisks and date palms jut out from the escarpment: the spring-water also supports other shady trees, making it a pleasant spot for a picnic.

South of Zara, the new highway is being bulldozed across the Lisan Peninsula which sticks into the sea like a tongue, the meaning of the word. There is a branch road through Wadi Kerak to Kerak: in the depression, the highway continues in the direction of the massive potash complex at Ghour al-Safi, at the southern end of the Dead Sea.

Potash has been known since biblical times when it was used as a fertiliser, of which it is still the essential ingredient. The Arab Potash Company has made Jordan a major supplier of potash with production by the mid-eighties expected to reach the equivalent of 1.25 billion gallons per year. Twenty-five thousand acres of dykes are being laid along the southern shores of the sea. The coarse salts, already 97 per cent potassium chloride by natural evaporation, are pumped to a refinery where further re-crystallisation produces magnesium chloride and magnesium bromide.

Dykes built for potash extraction in the Dead Sea

Other minerals which are extracted from the Dead Sea are common salt, from brine, and asphaltite, either from rocks containing bitumen, or as portions that float on the water. The latter material is also used in the manufacture of skin salves. Prospecting for oil in the region of Mount Sodom and the Lisan Peninsula has so far been unsuccessful.

Safi experiences a severe summer climate with the evaporating sea water turning the air salty and sulphurous. Where it evaporates in the basins, the sea-bed has split into chunks of red and orange layers of mud. Salt pinnacles rear out of the remaining puddles which are a vivid burgundy colour from a halophilic algae, *Dunaliella*, which thrives in such conditions.

Wadi Arabah occupies the southern end of the Jordan Valley–Dead Sea trench. The valley is about 177 kilometres long by about 5–7 kilometres wide, limited in the east by the Edomite Hills which flatten into the isolated jebels surrounding Aqaba. A feature of the scenery in the wadi is a series of high, knife-edged dunes running parallel to the new highway between Aqaba and Safi. Two-thirds of Wadi Arabah is semi-desert, supporting scattered low shrubs, mainly *Haloxylon persicum*, a dark green segmented stemmed bush growing up to 2 metres in height. The valley has a true desert climate with a winter rainfall of less than 100 millimetres.

Jackal, rock hyrax, ibex, striped hyena, mountain gazelle and desert hare all lived in the regions. The Bedouin occasionally report sightings of gazelle and hare, and ibex possibly survive in the Edomite Hills.

The famous mines in Wadi Arabah are of historic interest, but although the highway has made some of the sites accessible, one requires an expert guide to locate them: to date there has been little excavation and the sites are unmarked.

Thirty-six kilometres south-east of the Dead Sea is Khirbet Nahas, where copper mines were worked during and after the prosperous reign of King Solomon. Eight-and-a-half kilometres south-south-east is a mound near Wadi Feinan, a great mining and smelting centre from the Bronze Age until the Arab conquest. A huge site, it lies 10 kilometres across the hills from Shaubak. Seven kilometres south-south-west of Petra is es-Sabrah, an extensive Nabataean mining and smelting centre. Thirty kilometres from the small village of el-Gharandal, on the other side of the valley, is Meneiyah, one of the richest copper mines in the wadi.

The existence of rich mineral deposits, with access to Petra and to Red Sea commerce, explains why Wadi Arabah was always considered an important area. The wealth accumulated by the Edomites, the rapid rise of the Nabataean civilisation and the prosperity enjoyed in Jerusalem, all stem from this relatively small southern end of the Jordan trench.

Apart from an interest in the dunes, there is no reason for tourists to stop in Wadi Arabah on a journey from Amman to Aqaba. El-Gharandal is a small Bedouin village of about fifty houses and tents and a cluster of date-palms. Where Wadi Firhan spills its water on the valley floor, many Bedouin cultivate small vegetable holdings. Near here, a red and green tiered oriental pagoda is a tribute to South Koreans who built the Dead Sea–Wadi Arabah Highway through some of the toughest country in Jordan.

Chapter Five

Aqaba and the Desert Highway

Jordan occupies seventeen kilometres of coast at the head of the Gulf of Aqaba, the narrow finger of the Red Sea extending for 161 kilometres from its entrance near Ras Mohammad, in the southern Sinai peninsula.

The gulf is part of the same depression, or rift, that runs from central Africa through the Red Sea to Lebanon. Physiographically it closely resembles the dry trench of Wadi Arabah, displaying the same abrupt escarpments which plunge to depths of 1,868 metres. The water temperature varies between 21° and 30°C: grass beds and coral reefs are the main marine vegetation.

Lying south of latitude 30°, Aqaba's historic importance relates to three main features: its strategic location at the head of the Red Sea, a plentiful supply of fresh water and the proximity of the rich mineral deposits in Wadi Arabah.

In biblical times it was known as *Ezion-Geber* (Deut. 2:8), a flourishing port from where King Solomon's ships, laden with copper, sailed for Ophir. In-bound goods from the African continent, Arabia and India were unloaded for transportation north, via the caravan route through Petra. Aqaba was the terminus of the great Roman road from Damascus, and for a time the town was the headquarters of the famous Tenth Roman Legion. During the twelfth century, the settlement became part of the Crusader kingdom of 'Oultre Jordain'. The knights built two fortresses there, one in Aqaba and a second on the Ile de Graye, a small islet lying 7 kilometres out in the Gulf (now in a military zone), from where they monitored shipping. After the Crusader withdrawal from the Levant, Aqaba lapsed into obscurity and is scarcely mentioned under Ottoman domination, when the town was administered as part of Hejaz.

In 1841, Britain granted Egypt the protection of Sinai and with it certain Red Sea garrison towns, including Aqaba. When sea travel overtook land travel as the most popular means of making the pilgrimage to Mecca, Egypt abandoned these rights to Turkey in 1906 and Aqaba was not heard of again until 1917, when Faisal and the British officer, T. E. Lawrence, captured it during the Arab revolt.

In 1925, despite protests from Saudi Arabia that it was historically part of the Hejaz, both Aqaba and Ma'an were incorporated in the new Emirate of Trans-Jordan. When the historic ports of Jaffa and Haifa were handed to the Jews, Trans-Jordan turned to developing its only coastal access, the meagre wedge of land along the Gulf of Aqaba.

A treaty signed with Saudi Arabia in 1965 finally settled the border question and the shortage of land in Aqaba. In return for some 6,000 square kilometres of desert in south-east Jordan, Saudi Arabia ceded 13 kilometres of its coastline on the Gulf of Aqaba. This additional territory has enabled Jordan to expand the port and urban areas, and to establish a local tourist industry in Aqaba.

The 'eighties see Aqaba growing into Jordan's fastest developing city. In the mid-'sixties, it was little more than a sleepy seaside settlement with a population of some 2,000 living in *pisé*, or packed mud houses among the palm-groves: a census in 1982 showed that the town had over 30,000 inhabitants.

Aqaba's burgeoning residential area is spreading north, into the head of Wadi Arabah, and where a score of wooden and corrugated iron shops once comprised the *souq*, tall commercial buildings have taken their place.

Shipping activity has increased five-fold in the past decade: 275 ships were registered in 1968 compared to over 2,000 today. The modern container terminal handles cargo bound for Syria, Saudi Arabia and Iraq, the latter via a desert road to Azraq, linked with the highway to Baghdad. The major export from Aqaba is phosphate, which arrives by rail from the mines at Al Hasa, 170 kilometres north.

Aqaba's Solar Energy Research Station, built in 1977, is the first in the world to apply the 'heatpipe' principle to the desalination of sea-water using solar heat. Expressed simply, the process works by the sun heating collecting surfaces to temperatures of 70°–80°C. Sea-water passing

Pioneering solar energy at Aqaba

through metal pipes within the collecting plates is heated, forming vapour, which on striking a cooler surface in the process, is condensed into fresh water. The station can produce 3 cubic litres of fresh drinking water daily from 5 cubic litres of sea water.

Aqaba lies on the lip of the Gulf at the base of rugged, red hills which make a dramatic backdrop to the town. In front are the tourist hotels lining a strip of golden sand between King Hussein's summer palace and a palm-fringed cove where fishermen moor their craft. A second row of hotels, shops and restaurants is built along Palace Street, a long, shrub-lined boulevard sweeping past the beach towards the town: all the hotels are within fifteen minutes' stroll from the shops.

Although Aqaba basks in balmy winter weather, summer temperatures can reach 50 °C and in this heat locals take their time over things, as do citizens of hot countries the world over. They work flexible hours, starting at six, or seven, then stopping by noon when nothing stirs during the fiery afternoon.

At four o'clock, traffic begins to crawl again and people fill the cafés for tea or coffee. Wealthier merchants are served on the pavement outside their office, or shop. The 'runner' is usually a Yemeni, or one of the many Indo-Pakistani expatriates working in Jordan. Work then continues until seven, or eight o'clock, when a breeze may bring the temperature down by one or two degrees.

A town plan of central Aqaba resembles a game of noughts and crosses, consisting of vertical streets crossed by horizontal streets, with banks, taxi-ranks, barber's, grocer's and souvenir shops filling the squares.

One of the most interesting craft shops I visited was Naif Store, an 'Aladdin's cave' overflowing with Bedouin artifacts such as antique jewellery, camel-hide saddle bags, rugs, *nargilas* and attractive amber worry-beads. The owner, a Palestinian who speaks good English, also has an interesting museum in his house in Abu Mahfouz Street, Upper Aqaba.

Traders in Aqaba. A cup of coffee before returning to work

Other shops sell hand-embroidered Bedouin shirts and dresses from Wadi Rum, plus high-priced, yet proverbial gold jewellery. In a shop in Old Port Street, one can watch the art of filling bottles with patterns of multi-coloured sand, a local innovation that requires a steady hand. Aqaba has a small *souq* for fruits and vegetables and supermarkets sell tinned meats, cheeses and wines.

The art of filling bottles with coloured sand

The head of the Gulf of Aqaba has few species of edible fish. According to marine scientists, the cause of this is the low plankton level due to a small amount of nutrients which in turn reduces the concentration of other organisms normally feeding on plankton, the result being a low economic value in fish.

Another more deadly reason is that wind-borne dust from the phosphate loading terminal has killed sections of adjacent coral reef, with a subsequent diminishing of reef fish. Attracted to other work, fishermen have also turned their backs on the sea. Although it is often difficult to find fresh fish in local restaurants, there is a small enterprise supplying the market with fish caught in waters further south, off Saudi Arabia. Saudi Arabian law does not grant fishing rights to Jordanians. However, since these fisherman are Lebanese, they have been able to circumvent the rule, staying out from five to seven days, and catching mainly bream and cod. Their boats have been painted luminous orange to avoid collision with shipping plying the busy maritime lanes in the Gulf.

On Friday the port is idle as Aqaba takes a holiday with the rest of Jordan, and Amman residents converge on the sea by plane or car, travelling a distance of 335 kilometres via the Desert Highway. From dawn until dusk, crowds of bronzed people are to be seen water-skiing, wind-sailing, riding up and down the beach on camels and making tours of the coral reefs in glass-bottomed boats.

Diving is the most popular activity. Besides the infinite beauty of the fish and coral, the Gulf is unusual in having cool, vertical currents and strong winds which displace surface water, so that even on the hottest day, diving is cool and invigorating. Excellent visibility makes Aqaba a paradise for the underwater photographer. Scuba is essential for deep dives, but snorkelling is ideal in depths from three to ten metres off-shore.

Coral, a result of centuries of secretions by tiny coral polyps to form the beautiful calcareous skeletons seen today, was worn by the ancient Romans. Red coral was especially valued for amulets, being one of the few species not to fade when removed from the sea.

Other common species are *acropora*, or branch coral, *fungia*, a round, mushroom-like coral and *montipora*, whose skeleton has the form of a flat surface rolled into a scroll-like form dotted with small cavities. Much rarer is *archelia*, a black, tree-like coral growing only at great depths, the first piece of which was found by King Hussein, a keen diver. Spear-fishing and the collection of coral are now both banned, but a specimen of *archelia* is exhibited in the Naif Museum.

It is impossible to list the innumerable varieties of fish in the Gulf of Aqaba, but some more familiar are the anemone, or clownfish – a small orange fish with a white band on its head, which shares a symbiotic relationship with the sea anemone; the antiases – another orange fish swimming in schools among the gorgonian coral; the triggerfish – a burly, bluish-green fish named for its dorsal spine and having the distinctive buck-toothed appearance of all coral eaters; the parrotfish – one of the most brilliantly coloured of reef fish ranging from blue to rose with rainbow stripes around its eyes and mouth; and the pipefish – a quaint, cream and mottled brown fish jetting over the bottom on small, whirring fins.

On my last visit to Aqaba I snorkelled in an area where the indigo-coloured trench comes to within 50 metres of the aqua shallows. Festooned with a profusion of pink and white branch coral, every nook and cranny in the reef held a gaudy fish peering out inquisitively at my intrusion: a cheeky clownfish, swimming in the waving tentacles of a yellow sea anemone; sturgeon fish searching for sea urchins; and almost camouflaged in the waving sea grass, a mottled brown *hamour*, or cod.

At the base of the reef, a school of parrotfish crumbled coral and a pair of black and yellow batfish back-watered in a cave. Then, as I watched, from out of the soft, cherry-blossom fronds of a *Dendronephthya* swam a red and aqua-fringed nudibranch – a type of sea slug, which breathes through external gills and performs a sinuous dance as it swims. (Red Sea Arabs call it a 'Badia', as its movements resemble the undulations of the famed Egyptian belly-dancer.)

Surfacing, I scattered the ranks of miniature sapphire-blue fish rising and falling like clouds of butterflies; then, diving once again, I saw a spotted eagle ray trailing a metre-long tail. Below me a pair of flashing silver caranx circled each other in a fascinating courtship ritual, turning over and over before disappearing into the depths.

Diving down, I picked up a fat sea cucumber which exuded white streamer-like secretions that rolled up like a tangled ball of knitting wool.

Then suddenly I froze; for thirty metres away a white-tipped reef shark was zoning along the side of the escarpment. Holding on to a lump of coral, I debated whether to retreat to the shore, or to remain still (a difficult exercise when one is snorkelling), but on seeing me, the shark itself reacted; its body stiffened and a quick flick of its tail sent it on a torpedo-like trajectory into the trench.

Although sharks and barracuda are common in the Red Sea, it is rare to see them in the Gulf of Aqaba, their absence being attributed to the above-mentioned scarcity of the pelagic, or free-swimming species of fish on which they feed.

Attention is however drawn to two fish which favour the rocky shallows around the shoreline. One is a brown and white feathery finned fish known as the lionfish or chickenfish which is capable of giving a painful sting, and the other is the thirteen-spined stonefish, whose sting is fatal. On one occasion we caught a large lionfish off the beach in front of the Aqaba Hotel. There are no reports of anyone ever having seen the well-camouflaged stonefish, just as there is no record of anyone having stepped on one!

Taking everything into consideration, and having dived extensively in the Pacific and Indian Oceans as well as the Red Sea and the Mediterranean, I would say that Aqaba is a good spot to spend a diving holiday. In so many other places a boat is required to reach the reefs, but here one can dive straight off the shore and unlike the capricious winter climate of many resorts, winter sunshine is guaranteed with temperatures between November and March averaging 24 °C. Most visitors like the relaxed atmosphere and casual style of dress: while dressing discreetly so as not to offend Moslem custom, only simple clothes are needed with long skirts ideal for evening. Bikinis are permitted on the beach.

Dusk is a lovely hour to stroll along the beach as the jebel turns mauve in the setting sun and a tern skims the water's edge for fish. Farther out in the Gulf a late wind-

Aqaba basks in balmy winter sunshine

sailor endeavours to catch the breeze blowing down Wadi Arabah.

Like the mistral in the south of France, a strong wind often sweeps down the valley, in former times acting as giant natural bellows in the copper-smelting process in the mines at the head of the valley. The most important site excavated is *Tell el-Khalifa*, believed by archaeologists to be the ruined port of *Ezion-Geber* which the Bible records was beside Eloth (Eilat) in the land of Edom, on the shores of the Red Sea.

All that remains of medieval Aqaba is the fort in the palm-grove. Any evidence of Crusader occupation has long since been removed. Restoration to the fort was carried out in 1320 by the Mameluke ruler, Sultan Nasir, to whom there is an inscription, and in 1505 by the last Mameluke Sultan, Qansuh el-Ghuri. Above the double-edged portal is the twentieth-century addition by the Sharif of Mecca of the Hashemite Coat of Arms. In the evening, there are often one or two old Arabs there who remember Lawrence and the great Howeitat warrior, Sheikh Audeh Abu Taiyh, who were billeted in the fort after routing the Turks.

Colonel F. G. Peake, who was sent out to organise an Arab force in the Hejaz, has left a marvellous description of his meeting with Lawrence in Aqaba on 9 April 1918:

'The party was headed by a small man dressed in extremely good and expensive Bedouin clothes ... on his head a wonderful silk *kufaiyeh*[1] held in position by a gold *agal*.[2] His feet were bare and he had a gold *hegazi*[3] dagger in his belt, and in his hand he carried the usual almond-wood cane that every Bedouin [sic] camel rider uses ... As this regal looking person came in the tent door ... I imagined it must be Faisal himself ... I ceremoniously showed him to a chair, speaking the usual flowery Arabic words of welcome ... To my surprise he said in perfect English: "Well, Peake, so you have arrived at last! ..." It was Lawrence!'

Peake himself was an interesting character. He had a penchant for peacocks, keeping one hundred of them in his garden in Amman and whilst awaiting the arrival of Lawrence in Aqaba, he spent his time in collecting wild flowers.

As competent at riding a camel as the Bedouin, he is credited with the formation of Jordan's redoubtable Arab Legion. Founded in 1920 with 75 cavalry, by 1921 the legion had increased to 1,000 men and in 1926, when Ma'an was incorporated into the Emirate of Trans-Jordan, a further 300 men enlisted, 100 of whom were Camel Corps, to patrol the south-eastern border with Saudi Arabia.

---

[1] *Kufaiyeh* or, *Kiffeyeh*: a cotton head-robe usually white, but in Jordan frequently red and white check.

[2] *Agal*: the black cord used to secure the head-robe, said to originate from an old Bedouin habit of tying around his head, to avoid its loss, the piece of rope he would use to hobble a camel.

[3] *Hegazi* or *Khanjar*: a curved dagger, usually decorated and embossed on the handle.

Peake maintained strict discipline among his men. Writing his book *Arab Command*, Jarvis observes that the normal, workaday state of a police post rarely achieved the orderliness desired by a Commanding Officer, as a result of the Bedouin habit of dropping in for tea. Peake solved the problem by acquiring his pilot's licence, and was wont to arrive almost at the same time as a message was received to say that he was on his way. The legion, however, went one better, by devising a secret code, the cryptic *ghayamit*, meaning 'the cloud is coming', which they transmitted to warn their colleagues to spruce up. It is a credit to the efficiency of the legion that there has never been a case of misadventure concerning a traveller in Jordan.

Tourists who travel to the more remote areas in northeast and south-east Jordan will meet the desert police, whose star garrison is the eighty-strong Desert Camel Corps stationed at Wadi Rum, about an hour's drive east of Aqaba.

Lawrence adored Wadi Rum. Some of the most descriptive passages in his history of the desert campaigns, *Seven Pillars of Wisdom*, surround his admiration for the giant valley.

'Our little caravan fell quiet . . . ashamed to flaunt itself in the presence of such stupendous hills. . . .' he writes of his party arriving to muster assistance among the Rum Bedouin, for the assault on Aqaba.

A cavernous valley, over 130 kilometres in length, Rum is the result of an enormous upheaval that thrust granite and sandstone outcrops through the surface of the earth probably several million years ago.

Reaching heights of 1,754 metres (Jebel Rum), the cliffs stand like skyscrapers in the hot sand along either side of the wadi. As in Petra, one sees the same colourful phenomenon of ever-changing hues, depending on the hour of day. Purple at dawn, the cliffs turn mauve, then brown, at noon fading to the fawn of an old sepia-tinted photograph. After midday the colours flow the other way: from brown back to mauve, then orange, purple, a hot red at dusk to black, and finally silver under a full moon which many people consider is Rum at its most spectacular.

Vegetation is sparse, with coarse grass clumps, scattered shrubs and curling vines producing the gourd-like, bitter-tasting *handhal* or 'desert melon'. Growing in rocky areas, out of reach of goats, is the tall, lupin-like, white flowering *borsalan*.

Wild animals are now rare. The common fox, hyrax, desert hare, jerboa and gerbil still exist in remote parts of the valley but oryx and gazelle have been shot out. Birds sighted in Rum are Sinai rose-finches, blackcaps, fan-tail ravens, redstarts, desert larks and buzzards. The summer heat is so intense that birds are known to die on the wing.

The heat haze produces strange mirages on the drive through the neck of the wadi across the sunbaked *ghor*: illusions of shimmering lakes, dazzling white towns and camel riders all slowly melt into a stunted tamarisk.

On one crossing into Rum, we picked up an old Bedouin trudging along in the midday sun. Hearing the car he turned, half raising a hand; then on seeing me, he thought better of it, dropping it to his side. When we stopped, he shuffled up wearing camelskin thonged sandals and a ragged *thobe* (the long loose-fitting cotton robe worn by men) and I put him in my usual place, beside the driver, and passed him water.

'God is great, God is merciful, God be praised', he repeated, all the way to the police post.

Wadi Rum police post is a crenellated walled 'Beau Geste' type of fort located by a copse of *hena*, the local eucalyptus. All local Bedouin, the police take a great pride in their glamorous desert rig – a divided full-length khaki skirt, or *zaboun*, worn with a red and white check *kiffeyeh* tied at a rakish angle with a double knotted black *agal* pinned with the silver camel badge of the corps. Polished cartridge straps cross their chest and a small dagger is worn through another cartridge belt around their waist. A .32 Smith and Wesson on the left hip completes their attire.

The Desert Camel Patrol at the police post Wadi Rum near Aqaba

Much photographed by visitors, the police mount their caparisoned camels and parade around the fort like movie stars. One of them who speaks a little English is reminded to explain that some of them acted in *Lawrence of Arabia*, of which several sequences were filmed in Rum.

The Desert Camel Corps evolved from the Imperial Camel Corps whose task was to patrol the 1,000 kilometres-long border with Saudi Arabia, searching for gun-runners. Today their target is narcotics smugglers. Tall, lean and suntanned, like his officers, the sergeant said they patrol in pairs for a two- to three-day stretch, sometimes camping in the open, but more usually invited to stay as guests of local Bedouin. Another of their duties is to settle any disputes among the 250 Bedouin families in Rum.

Six different tribes live in the wadi, the main ones being the Beni Sakhr, the Sirhan and the Howeitat – the latter figured prominently in the Arab Revolt. Most are nomadic, but several families who pitch their tents near the police post earn money by taking tourists on camel rides.

An interesting trip either by camel, or landrover, can be made to a spring in the jebel where Lawrence bathed after returning from his historic meeting with Faisal, in Aqaba.

'. . . a climb of fifteen minutes . . . at the top the waterfall . . . falling with that clear sound into a shallow, frothing pool . . .'

Eager to see the spring, the obvious source of early settlement in Wadi Rum, I set out with the sergeant driving several kilometres east of the police post through drifts of ever deepening sand. Reaching a cleft in the rock where dark stains indicated a hidden water source, we looked up as a herd of black goats trotted nimbly along a conduit cut in the side of the cliff. The sergeant explained that it was the work of the Nabataeans, as was the graffiti carved in the low undercut of rock. Following his driver, I edged along the narrow ledge when, after several hazardous moments, we sidled round a bulge of rock and there, framed by ferns, was the spring. In the welcome shade, I unwrapped some *ka'ik* and eggs from my camera-bag, and sitting with our feet in the water, the three of us enjoyed a picnic.

Tourists who would like to spend a few days at random, making camel-rides in Wadi Rum, have the use of a small rest-house near the police post. While basic facilities are available, any other requirements including food, drink and personal requisites should be brought from Aqaba. A future project sponsored by an ex-army major, himself a Bedouin, is to accommodate tourists Bedouin-style, in tents. Extra time spent in Wadi Rum affords the increasingly rare opportunity of making contact with the

An Australian traveller enjoys traditional Bedouin hospitality, Wadi Rum

Bedouin who may be observed at close quarters. About 8 kilometres past the Rum turn-off, there is also an interesting desert reclamation scheme to extract some 60 million cubic metres of water a year from beneath the *ghor.*

In 1968, the Italian company responsible for the pilot project at Qa' Disi began sprinkler cultivation of the desert. With added nitrates and phosphates, the barren ground soon bore results with cereals, pulses, lucerne and vegetables yielding up to three harvests annually. Unable to believe the 'greening of Rum', the Bedouin travel from kilometres around to see for themselves. Now run by the Ministry of Agriculture, it is hoped that the farm will not only supply local needs, but also those of northern Saudi Arabia. Water in excess of requirements is pumped to Aqaba.

The road journey from Aqaba to Amman via the Desert Highway takes about four to five hours. Leaving the sea, the highway cuts across the neck of Wadi Arabah, then after the Rum turn-off it climbs the southern scarp of the central plateau.

The rest-house located on the 1,200-metre high headland of Ras al-Naqb affords a striking view, back across the outcrops of Wadi Rum and south, as far as one can see to the rocky region of al-Hasma, rolling towards Saudi Arabia. The longest part of the drive lies ahead, through the monotonous semi-desert landscape of the high plateau.

One hundred and nineteen kilometres north of Aqaba is Ma'an, chief town in the *muhafazat,* the district of southern Jordan. An oasis on the fringe of the desert, it is an attractive old settlement of *pisé* houses, high mud-brick walls and gardens sprouting date-palms, historically important as a staging-post on the pilgrimage from Syria and Turkey to Mecca. One hundred and twenty-one kilometres further south is Mudawwarah, on the frontier with Saudi Arabia.

Bedouin sheep market, Ma'an, last town on the edge of the eastern desert

Ma'an is an important market depôt for the Bedouin who travel great distances to buy essentials and to sell their animals. The town is particularly crowded prior to a feast day, such as Eid el-Fitr which follows Ramadan. Transactions take place at a slow pace, interspersed with bouts of coffee–drinking, a common habit throughout the Middle East. The market is at the end of the main street, before the railway station.

After a survey was made by a Turkish engineer, who simply followed the pilgrim route through Jordan, construction of the Hejaz Railway began in Damascus in 1900, reaching Ma'an in 1904, and Medina four years later. The first train left for Arabia in 1908.

To prevent the Turks from sending troops to crush the Arab Revolt, a total of 732 kilometres of track was blown up between Ma'an and Medina and the railway has since lain disused.

Plans now call for the reconstruction of the entire Hejaz Railway, a total of 1,300 kilometres, to widen the line from the original narrow gauge and to replace missing sections of the track. The 402 kilometres between Damascus and Amman will be modernised with Saudi Arabia underwriting the bill (King Saud pledged a gift of nearly $6 million). Restoration of the line will not only ameliorate conditions for people making the *haj*, or pilgrimage to Mecca, but will promote regional trade and industrial development, and encourage tourism.

From Ma'an, another road, finally petering out into a track, leads east-north-east for 65 kilometres to el-Jafr, and a further 183 kilometres to Bayir. It should not be attempted without a suitable vehicle and only in the cooler season. Bayir is a small oasis and a centre for the Howeitat Bedouin, who practise falconry in the area.

It is a soporific journey from Ma'an north to Qatranah the only village of any significance until Amman. The Desert Highway runs parallel to the railway, whose stations are situated at intervals of 30 kilometres. At al Hasa, a low, grey powder cloud marks Jordan's major mining centre for phosphates.

Driving on north through the desert, crossing and re-crossing the railway, one reaches Qatranah, an oil-stained village smelling of smoke and kebabs. Several cafés sell cold drinks. Dusty corners of the town occasionally display Bedouin jewellery and brass coffee-pots; however, the market is dependent on whatever the Bedouin have to sell. Qatranah will spring to life if a proposed shale-fuelled 300 megawatt plant is built in the area. A legacy of Ottoman domination is a ruined castle.

Three kilometres south of Qatranah a branch road leads from the Desert Highway to the King's Highway, a distance of about 30 kilometres where the countryside is unfarmed and in springtime is a mass of wild flowers. The rare black iris blooms along the roadside with *Glaucium arabicum*, a delicate red flower related to the wild red poppy and resembling an anemone. The spindly yellow *Hirschfeldia incana* (wild mustard) and blue anchusa flourish. The Bedouin call the latter 'hem-hem' after a larva living in its root, which they use for trapping birds. There are no facilities or settlements on this branch road between the highways.

North of Qatranah is Jiza, located near a large Roman reservoir on the left of the Desert Highway. Nearby are sites of archaeological significance at Zizia, Al Qastal and Dab'ah. None has any tourist facilities. Jiza has a small café and next door, potters shape crude, yet attractive earthenware on ancient kick-wheels. Most of the pottery is trucked to Saudi Arabia. Near Jiza, about 32 kilometres south of Amman, is the new Queen Alia International Airport.

It is common to see hitch-hikers waiting at the fork of the King's and Desert Highways, hoping for a ride to either Petra, or Aqaba. Travelling south, the best time to leave Amman is in the early morning. The afternoon is ideal for driving north from Aqaba, as the sun sets behind the car, over the Sinai Peninsula.

Chapter Six

The Heritage of Northern Jordan

Tourist attractions in northern Jordan range from Roman cities to Ummayad hunting lodges and Azraq Oasis. To explore the area requires two days, the ideal time being in spring when the hills are covered in marguerites, hollyhocks and mimosa. Although the eastern desert zone of Azraq is very hot in summer, the towns of Jerash, Umm Qeis and Ajlun, in the eastern escarpment, enjoy pleasant daytime temperatures with cool nights.

The most remarkable site is the Roman city of Jerash. Although the excavation has not yet been finished, it is considered by archaeologists to be the most complete of any Roman settlement in the world. Jerash looks its best either in the early morning, when photographers will find the lighting perfect until about 10am, or just before dusk. The city is an easy 48-kilometre drive north of Amman, via Suweilih.

Leaving Amman, the highway climbs through the rolling green Gilead Hills, then descends into al-Baq'a Valley, where the biggest Palestinian refugee camp in Jordan is located. Founded in 1968, its dwellings are still without running water, and, at an early hour, groups of women walk along the roadside carrying the day's supply in tins balanced on their heads, the weight giving them a peculiar swaying gait.

Forty kilometres north of Amman, the road crosses the

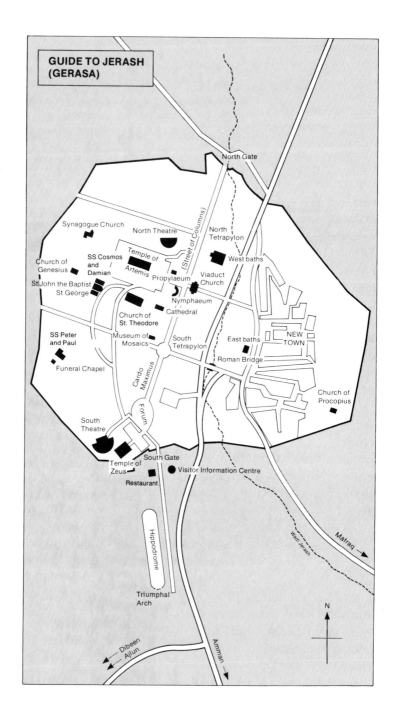

GUIDE TO JERASH
(GERASA)

North Gate

Synagogue Church

North Theatre

North
Tetrapylon

(Street of Columns)

West baths

Church of
Genesius

SS Cosmos
and
Damian

Temple of
Artemis

Propylaeum

Viaduct
Church

St John the Baptist
St George

Nymphaeum

Cathedral

Church of
St. Theodore

SS Peter
and Paul

Museum of
Mosaics

South
Tetrapylon

East baths

NEW
TOWN

Roman Bridge

Funeral Chapel

Cardo Maximus

Church of
Procopius

South
Theatre

Forum

Temple of
Zeus

South Gate

Visitor Information Centre

Restaurant

Hippodrome

Triumphal
Arch

N

Dibeen
Ajlun

Amman

West Jerash

Mafraq

98

River Zerqa, the biblical Jabbock which marked the northern limit of the Ammonite kingdom. For those in need of refreshment, about three kilometres past the bridge there is a small roadside café sheltered by shady *hena* trees. Otherwise one can take coffee in the rest-house at Jerash.

One's first sight of the city is the great Triumphal Arch built in honour of the visit to Jerash by the Emperor Hadrian in AD 129. Beyond this spot, invaded by lush vegetation, is the Hippodrome, where polo goal-posts are the only vestige of the Persian invasion in AD 614 which ended the illustrious Roman civilisation.

Like many towns in the Middle East, Jerash probably owes its settlement to a small stream, rather grandly named the Chrysoras, or 'Golden River'. The modern village stands on its east bank while ancient Jerash overlooks it from the windswept western plateau.

Historians believe the city was founded about 332 BC. The early name, 'Antioch on the Chrysoras', suggests its elevation to town status by one of the Seleucid heirs of Alexander the Great.

The importance of Jerash increased once it joined the Decapolis. The town is known to have traded extensively with the Nabataeans, whose influence is apparent in the characteristic 'crow step' pattern on some monuments, notably around the Fountain Court. From this wealth, and on proceeds from passing travellers, the Romans built grandiose baths, temples, forums and other edifices in Jerash.

As in Amman, Roman expertise in town-planning is evident from the lay-out of the city. In the centre is the Forum, from where the great 'Street of Columns', or *Cardo Maximus*, runs a distance of 600 metres to the North Gate.

The fortunes of Jerash further soared when the Emperor Trajan annexed the Nabataean Kingdom. Profiting from the increased trade, the Romans demolished many of the early buildings and built new, more elaborate ones: the Artemis Temple, the huge thermal baths and the Triumphal Arch date from this time. Archaeologists in fact believe the intention of the arch was to extend the city further south, but unless excavations reveal further settlement, the arch is isolated from the rest of Jerash.

Jerash reached the peak of its prosperity in the third century AD, when the boom began to level off. No more buildings were constructed and little maintenance was done to those already there. The rise of the Sassanian Empire in Iraq drew commerce farther east, away from the old caravan routes, and when Palmyra – the prosperous Roman city in present-day Syria – was destroyed in AD 273, Jerash also began a decline from which it never recovered. The erosion of Roman power also witnessed a resurfacing of the 'old predatory instincts of the Bedouin'.

By the middle of the fourth century AD a considerable Christian community was living in the city. The Byzantine Emperor Justinian ordered the construction of scores of churches, many of which were built of stones taken from temples and baths. Inscriptions reveal the construction of other civic buildings, and it is known that the licentious Maiumas Water Festival was held in Jerash as late as the sixth century AD.

So although their standard of living was less opulent than that of the Romans, it seems that the Byzantine citizens of Jerash indulged themselves to a degree of excess, while their contribution to the city, mainly in the form of churches, is considered inferior by comparison with the refined architecture of the Roman Empire.

The knell for Jerash sounded in AD 614 when it was sacked by the Persians. Some twenty-one years later the Arabs took it, and finally the great earthquake in AD 747 brought the remaining monuments tumbling down. Contributing further to the desecration of Jerash was the order of the Caliph Yazid II to destroy any remaining images, as a result of which statues and mosaics that survived the catastrophe were systematically smashed.

The tenth century AD found the ruined city still inhabited by a mixed Moslem and Christian population who directed no efforts towards its restoration. In AD 1120 the

Temple of Artemis was converted into a fortress which the Crusaders later razed to the ground. Visiting Jerash in the thirteenth century AD the Arab geographer Yaqut wrote only of lifeless ruins.

Over the subsequent centuries the city slowly succumbed to the elements, becoming buried deeper and deeper, until the Circassian settlers in the late nineteenth century AD considered it more suitable to start afresh, on the east bank of the Chrysoras.

Since no one at that time had an interest in excavating a Roman settlement, ancient Jerash remained thus – buried and almost forgotten – until its re-discovery in 1806 by a German traveller. Although excavations were begun in 1925, progress has been slow, largely through a lack of funds (although the World Bank has now promised $18 million).

Professor Haroutune Kalayan of the Department of Antiquities was responsible for some of the restoration of Jerash. Struggling with his labourers to replace the head, or capital, on a Roman column in the North Theatre, he told me that his greatest problem lies in the lack of records explaining from where stones were removed during archaeological excavations.

Entering the southern side of Jerash, near its Information Centre, brings one into the vast, oval-shaped Forum, or market place, embraced by a semi-circle of fifty-six columns topped by Ionian capitals. All stand in their original positions although many have been restored.

The Forum in Jerash is considered to be one of the most perfect in existence. Its once bustling market life has been resurrected in a spectacular 'Son et Lumière' when the audience can imagine it filled with stately, toga-clad figures, shopping and exchanging gossip with merchants and passers-by.

In summer, there is often a class of school-children seated in the Forum, or in the Theatre, learning about their country's history. The Theatre, built to seat 5,000, and the adjacent ruins of the Temple of Zeus (AD 163) provide a panorama of the Forum and the 'Street of Columns'.

It is the dream of many travellers to walk along the mighty *Cardo Maximus* in Jerash. No other Roman city that I know (Carthage, Leptis Magna, Busra or Baalbek) has such a majestic thoroughfare lined by soaring columns, some 260 on either side. An aqueduct once ran across their tops, carrying water to every corner of the city. The marks of chariot wheels are embedded in the paving slabs where the odd bold flower produces yellow bloom.

About 200 metres along the street one comes to a road junction. At this intersection and at a second cross-roads farther north, is found the lower part of a tetrapylon – a square edifice that once supported four columns, probably surmounted by a statue.

Beyond the second tetrapylon, on the western side of the *Cardo Maximus*, is the semi-circular Nymphaeum dating from the second century AD, which doubled as both a temple and a fountain. Jerash was renowned for fountains, but the Nymphaeum is considered the most elaborate: statues in niches once poured water from vessels, and lions' heads spouted into basins, one of which remains.

Beyond the Nymphaeum a flight of stairs leads to the Propylaeum, a solid structure beneath a second stairway leading up to the Temple of Artemis, the most imposing monument in Jerash.

Elevated to a height of 5 metres on a podium, or stage, the temple must have provided an awe-inspiring sight to travellers whilst still far-off from the city. The 15-metre-high surrounding columns topped with Corinthian capitals are the most photographed in Jerash. Although the marble has been stripped off and many of the temple's stones have been removed for other buildings, the shell remains fairly well preserved, standing about 160 metres long by 120 metres across. Behind the Temple of Artemis, two columns poke tantalisingly through the hillside – so much of Jerash remains hidden; Dr Kalayan estimated

Much of Jerash remains hidden, like these two Roman columns in the hillside behind the Artemis Temple

that only five to ten per cent had been excavated by 1981.

The ruins of thirteen churches so far discovered lie west of the temple: among them the churches of St John, St George and the larger church of St Theodore were built in AD 496. To the north is another church dedicated to the saints Cosmos and Damianus whose floor displays a vivid sixth-century AD mosaic. South of the Nymphaeum is the Cathedral dated AD 350, largely constructed of materials removed from the Temple of Dionysos. In front of the Propylaeum are the remains of the Viaduct Church which stood beside the road leading to the bridge across the river.

At the northern end of the *Cardo Maximus* are the West Baths, probably built in the second century AD, of which only four crumbling arches and a dome remain. Most visitors do not walk this far along the 'Street of Columns', which is usually devoid of crowds, even on a Friday. The North Gate was erected in AD 115 from where a road leads from Jerash to Busra, in southern Syria.

103

Standing on the modern highway below the old rest-house, one overlooks a Roman bridge spanning the stream which rushes merrily through Jerash. On the far side is the modern village whose setting amidst poplars and walnut trees adds to its charm. Attractive in springtime, it is equally picturesque in autumn (October – November).

After a morning spent exploring the city, one can eat lunch at the Jerash tourist centre restaurant, or at a Lebanese restaurant located south of the Triumphal Arch, by the road to Ajlun. Jordan's most pleasant rural restaurant, it serves Oriental specialities such as *mazza* – the Arabic hors d'oeuvres. In summer, the heady scent of gardenias drifts up from the garden; one may eat inside, or out on the terrace, and the restaurant is open for lunch and dinner.

There is a Sound and Light Programme in Jerash from May-November, at 7.30p.m. (English, French, German and Arabic.)

On each side of the road to Jerash and north to Irbid, are forests of a tree known locally as the *kharroub* (Ceratona siligra), whose leaves serve as fodder for cattle and whose fruit is crushed into a refreshing, wine-coloured though non-alcoholic beverage. During the past three years some three million Aleppo pines have been planted in the government afforestation programme for northern Jordan.

One hundred and forty kilometres north of Amman, Irbid is built on the site of Arbila which was a member of the Decapolis. A rapidly expanding industrial town, Irbid also houses the University of Yarmuk, which is expected by 1985 to be a learning centre for some 20,000 students. Sites of archaeological significance are at Tell al-Husn, dating from the Bronze Age, and Beit Ras Rehab.

It is a half-hour drive from here to Umm Qeis – the Greco-Roman city of Gadara – situated on the lip of the escarpment with views of Lake Tiberius, the Yarmuk River Valley and the strategic Golan Heights.

Thickets of tall bamboo hide the river from sight and an

almost tropical vegetation surrounds the hot springs village of el-Hammah which has the remains of Roman and
Byzantine baths. At present there is only simple accommodation and a café, but a new tourist hotel is planned for
the area which has been reputed for its hot springs since
ancient times. During the Roman Empire, many citizens
travelled there to seek a cure: archaeologists also believe
that this accounts for the presence of several theatres in
Umm Qeis, indicating its popularity, as a resort, with the
Romans.

Under Roman rule, Gadara joined the Decapolis along
with Jerash and nearby Pella, and like the other members,
it reached its golden age in AD 2 when the boundary of the
city extended as far as Lake Tiberias, about ten kilometres
away.

To date there has been little excavation work under-
taken in Umm Qeis, and without the knowledge of a guide
it is difficult to recognise many of its monuments.

Beneath the hillside covered with houses at the entrance of the town is the ancient Acropolis, dating from a
settlement on the site in 218 BC by the Seleucid king,
Antiochus III. Recognisable, but badly damaged, is the
North Theatre and in front, the remains of the Forum.
From here a colonnaded street, once bordered by shops,
runs westwards and as in the *Cardo Maximus*, discerning
tourists will spot chariot wheel marks in the stones.

Like Jerash, Gadara was enclosed by walls, and just
inside the West Gate is the ruined Nymphaeum and the
remains of a large Basilica. Basalt rubble lies where once
stood the West Theatre, on the bottom tier of which is
seated a headless white marble statue holding a cornu-
copia: a standing version of this goddess appears on
Gadarene coins.

The most famous biblical event associated with Gadara,
or Umm Qeis, is the miracle of the Gadarene swine.
Matthew 8:28–34 relates how Jesus exorcised two men
possessed of the devil and transferred their madness into a
herd of pigs, to the consternation of local farmers who

ordered Christ to leave the town.

I had visited Jordan several times before going to Ajlun, reached by driving south from Umm Qeis via Irbid, or an easy 87-kilometre journey direct from Amman.

Thrust against a mountain crowned by a splendid Arab castle, Ajlun is one of the most picturesque towns in Jordan. From its houses rises a solitary minaret, all that remains of an eighteenth-century mosque built over the remains of a former Byzantine church. This lonely minaret without a mosque and a giant *hena* tree on the main square, give Ajlun a distinctive character. Towering above it is the extraordinary Qalaat al-Rabaad, a castle-fortress built in 1184–85 by the Emir Izzeddin Usama. Saladin ordered the castle to be built – so as to contain the Crusader threat and to survey the caravan and pilgrim routes. Qalaat al-Rabaad was destroyed by invading Mongol forces in the thirteenth century AD, but was later restored by the Mamelukes who likewise restored the 'Crac de Monreal', at Shaubak.

Situated on the summit of the mountain at a height of 2,000 metres, the castle affords a bird's eye view of ancient Palestine and the jagged escarpment. Up here, on the roof of the Holy Land, one can see the River Jordan meandering through the valley to its rendez-vous with the Dead Sea. On a clear day, even Mount Hermon is visible to the north. Early morning is the best time to view the countryside from the castle, or Qala'at al-Rabaad. During winter, the road to Ajlun is sometimes closed by snowfalls. On a Friday, the road is crowded as Jordanian families drive to Dibeen National Park.

The Park lies 62 kilometres from Amman on a hillside overlooking the Zerqa River Valley. It is mainly planted with Aleppo pines, but there are also old Cypress pines, junipers, acacias, hawthorns and wild pistachios.

Wild animals that are still known to inhabit the hills of northern Jordan and particularly the Dibeen National Park are the Ethiopian hedgehog, the lesser mouse-tailed bat, horseshoe bats and Schreiber's bats, the Persian squirrel and the broad-toothed field-mouse. The brown bear, badger and fallow deer are extinct.

Another attractive settlement is Salt which can be visited en route to the Jordan Valley. During the Ottoman rule, Salt was the chief town in Trans-Jordan. Today it is the administrative centre of Balqa District with a population of 33,000.

Salt is like a smaller version of Amman, similarly built on several hills, on one of which stands a ruined citadel dating from 1220 and with the main street running downtown, through a steep wadi. Although Salt is known to

Travellers' choice: sign outside Azraq in north-east Jordan

date from the Iron Age, little is written of its history. There is a large Greek Orthodox Church behind the main square overlooked by an attractive clutter of old houses, reminiscent of Mediterranean towns.

The houses are the most picturesque feature of Salt whose name derives from the Latin *saltus*, meaning a wooded valley. One sees charming Ottoman-style buildings several storeys in height, built of ochre, or amber coloured stone with French-style shutters flung back on the streets. Many are built on top of older buildings whose porticos are visible at foundation level.

A second tour for visitors interested in nature as well as history is to Azraq Oasis, and Jordan's desert castles. This used to be a hectic day-trip from Amman, but Azraq today has a rest-house. A highway links it to the capital.

The best plan is to have an early lunch in Amman and leave by 2pm, for although this may be the hottest part of the day, the sun sets behind the car and one arrives in the late afternoon, ideal for sightseeing and photography.

There are several remote, solitary castles to be seen. They are a heritage of the Ummayad caliphs, the first rulers of Islam in the eighth century AD, who conquered all of Iraq, Palestine and Syria and who ruled from their capital in Damascus.

Originally a desert tribe, the Ummayads liked to exchange a crowded city life for an occasional reconciliation with their background. Passionately fond of hunting, they made reconnaissance trips by horse and camel, at first pitching tents and ultimately building castles in areas where game was found in abundance. Each castle, or *qasr* in Arabic, was a combination of fort and hunting-lodge; some were luxurious, such as Qasr Amra, others utilitarian, like the simple baths at Hammam es-Sarah.

In the wooded countryside of those days, their likely quarry was the Syrian bear, the Arabian oryx, deer, gazelle and boar, all of which are now extinct in the wild. Bringing huge entourages of retainers, poets, musicians and dancers, they often retired to the desert lodges for several weeks at a time.

Each building has its own character bearing the mark of its architect and craftsmen, the best example of which are the unique wall frescoes in Qasr Amra. Two of the castles, Qasr Azraq and Qasr Hallabat are of Roman origin with overlays from the Ummayad, Crusader and Mameluke periods. Qasr el-Mushatta, el-Kharranah and Qasr Amra are wholly Ummayad and although most are now beyond hope of repair, others such as Qasr Amra have been restored, and can give visitors a degree of insight into the past.

Lumps of basalt mark the way for wandering nomads in the rough *hammada* region near Azraq

Two of the castles can be missed unless one is extremely enthusiastic. Neither is on the castle circuit between Amman and Azraq, and Qasr el-Tuba in particular – 87 kilometres south of Azraq – is in poor condition and was only used as a staging-post. The other, Qasr el-Mushatta – near Queen Alia airport – was obviously destined to be built on a grandiose scale, but for some reason it was never completed. Traces of once elaborate friezes lie scattered about, the bulk having been stripped off and sent to Germany by the Ottoman sultan as a souvenir of the Kaiser's visit to the Holy Land in 1904. The remaining walls, sunk with circular towers, are slowly shedding their stones like a desert cactus dropping its fruit.

A new highway links Amman and Qasr el-Kharranah, which is a huge, solid block looking for all the world as if it has fallen off the back of a passing truck.

A massive structure sitting on the ancient east-west caravan routes, it appears to be the only castle to have been built solely for defence. A Cufic inscription dates it from AD 711, but almost obliterated Greek lettering on the jambs, or side posts of the door, suggest it may even pre-date Islam.

For centuries, Qasr el-Kharranah has been a solitary 'monarch' of the desert, but it does boast a curator who hurries out with the keys when he hears the sound of tyres crushing the flint-stone at the entrance. On a Friday, it is a popular spot for family picnics.

To reach Qasr al-Amra, you drive due north across pebble conglomerate towards the shallow depression known as Wadi Butum. The desolate landscape makes it hard to imagine that Qasr Amra once stood in thickets of *Pistacia atlantica*, a tree growing over four metres high and able to survive for more than 400 years. The pistacia suffered a similar fate to other woodland sacrificed by the Turks as sleepers for the Hejaz Railway. In the wadi, only one or two gnarled old trees remain, being almost sacred to the Bedouin who chew their salty brown seeds, which are also used for flavouring the local white cheese in Jordan.

A small, but obviously comfortable retreat built for the Caliph Walid I as a hunting-lodge, Qasr Amra is the most distinctive of the Ummayad castles. Beautifully preserved, it consists of three vaulted halls which are cross-vaulted to

Qasr al-Amra, Ummayad hunting-lodge lavishly embellished with frescoes

form different rooms for baths. Every wall is embellished with frescoes, once concealed under the soot of Bedouin campfires, but now restored by a team from the National Museum of Madrid.

The frescoes are remarkable, not only for the freshness of their colours, but being overtly frolicsome, they indicate that there was more to the after-hunting scene than just washing off the desert dust. The naked ladies cavorting in the *hammam*, or steam baths, bear a striking resemblance to a Botticelli fresco. Other scenes depict hunting dogs savaging a herd of gazelles. Art historians consider the frescoes are probably Syrian in origin, influenced by Greek rather than Byzantine art, and date between AD 705–715. Inside one needs a good torch to see the mosaic floors at the rear of the halls. The ceiling in the steam-room represents the night sky, with the various constellations.

Life was obviously lively after a hunt. One can imagine the smell of a boar, or a gazelle, roasting on the spit, musicians serenading the hunters, the trills of ladies splashing in the *hammam* and outside, in the darkness, a panting cheetah straining at its chain. Of all the castles, Qasr Amra is outstanding.

The drive from Qasr al-Amra to Azraq crosses the eastern steppe zone of the central plateau, a mix of sand and limestone and in the north, a black basalt plateau known as the *hammada*. The route is crossed and re-crossed by dozens of tracks like crab-trails etched in the sand. It is easy for the driver to miss the right direction, but even out here it would not be long before one was found by wandering Bedouin.

One of the Bedouin's major migration routes crosses the plateau from Syria to Azraq, then continues on to Wadi Sirhan where many spend the winter. Sometimes only their animals are seen: liquorice-coloured goats tearing at the sparse grass and herds of camels slowly plodding towards the scent of water in a distant well.

Azraq lies on a low basalt ridge. For several kilometres, the ridge is almost uniformly black and devoid of vegetation until the appearance of semi-woody perennials such as the unpalatable bush *Peganum harmala*. A richer flora takes over in the wetter *hammada* transitional zone and, as night falls, the first frog starts croaking in the marshes around Azraq, a welcome sound after the hot desert drive from Amman.

Unless one spends some considerable time in the desert, one cannot appreciate its miraculous oases, nor the fascination of the Bedouin for running water and their love of greenery, in any form.

'Ali screamed "Grass!" and flung himself off the saddle,' writes Lawrence in *Seven Pillars of Wisdom* when he and his Bedouin guide finally reached the oasis at Azraq. Westerners visiting the Middle East and staying in its luxury hotels may not find Azraq especially interesting, but to the Bedouin, out in this remote corner of north-east Jordan, it is something akin to paradise.

The crumbling basalt castle at the entrance of the town was security for Lawrence, after months of sleeping under the desert stars. Inscriptions over its entrance are in Greek, Latin and Arabic, but scholars generally put its date of construction at the time of the Roman Empire in about AD 300. Qasr Azraq is at the entrance to Azraq-Druze, the bigger of two villages making up the oasis settlement.

About 200 Druze families live in Azraq-Druze, distinguished from their Moslem neighbours only by religion, the basic tenet that it must be kept a secret from outsiders. This tends to make them appear somewhat taciturn towards strangers. At the top of their social scale are the *ajawid*, or elders, for whom the sight of a tourist taking photographs is likely to produce an angry reaction. A feeling of xenophobia pervades the village; pedestrians avert their eyes and despite the heat, many houses have their shutters closed. Seven kilometres south is the other small village of Azraq-Shishan, numbering about seventy families of Circassian stock.

Azraq's total settled population is about 2,000, with an estimated 40,000 Bedouin who are dependent on the oasis for water and grazing. The main tribes are the Bani-Sakhr, whose territory extends from el-Muwaqqar south-east of Amman to Wadi Sirhan, the Rwala who pass through north-west Jordan during migrations between Syria and Saudi Arabia and the Sirhan who gather around Mafraq and winter near el-Beidha.

The bulk of cultivated land is around Azraq-Druze, some of the main crops being tomatoes, melons, okra, beans, lucerne and sunflowers. But for both villages, the most important economic use of the land is the extraction of salt from Qa-el-Azraq, a flat area around the oasis, characterised by saline springs.

Special conditions apply to salt extraction, the main one being that rights are only granted to locals. Of some 200 families, both Druze and Shishani, 120 are wholly or partly engaged in this activity. A co-operative markets the salt on their behalf with current production about 200,000 sacks, each weighing 140 kilogrammes. The system works by each member of the Azraq Co-operative Society being allowed an annual quota of 70 sacks for himself and each member of his family. The head of the family is entitled to an additional 120 sacks of the same weight.

Salt extraction normally occurs from May through to July after winter rain has compacted the soil, forming a crust on the bottom of the pans which prevents earth from mixing with the crystals and spoiling the quality. Rain also moistens the *qa* and prevents contamination of the salt by wind-carried dust. Something the villagers fear is the *Rih el-Sharqiyah*, a sand-laden wind blowing off the eastern desert. Obliged to work in mid-summer, they begin at six o'clock and stop by ten when many are already weak from actual salt depletion as they sweat heavily while wielding their shovels. Equal status between the sexes being one aspect of Druze society, women are seen shovelling and stacking the salt beside the men.

In former times, wildlife was attracted to these natural salt-licks on the *qa*, but today mammals are very rare. Sadly, the word 'rare' appears all too frequently on a list of Jordan's wildlife: the European wildcat, the caracal or

Hassan Mosque in Amman, Winter 1980

Wadi Rum: desert patrol

Landscape in Wadi Arabah, western Jordan

Fresco in the steam-bath in Qasr Amra, a hunting-lodge built by the Ummayad caliphs

Zarqa Ma'in: hot springs

Crumbling vestige of Crusader occupation, the Crac de Monreal near Shaubak

Sharing the summer harvest near Tafila, King's Highway

Crystallised salt forms hot-weather 'icebergs':
Dead Sea shoreline near Zara

The Dead Sea seen from Mt. Nebo in the eastern escarpment

'Street of Columns' in Jerash, the Roman city in northern Jordan

Playful anemone fish, Gulf of Aqaba

Well camouflaged in the shallows off Aqaba, the lionfish can inflict a painful sting

The beautiful Black Iris of Jordan

Spring sees the West Bank ablaze with wild flowers

Aqaba offers year-round sunshine

The ancient city of Salt

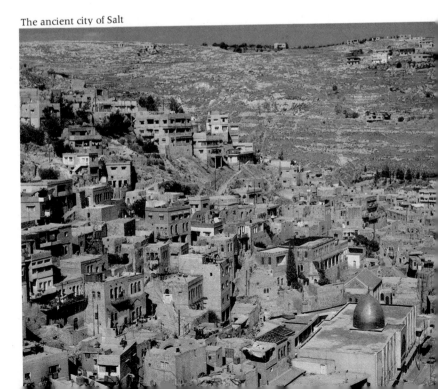

Druze families hold hereditary rights to salt collecting on the *Qa* near Azraq

Bedouin camp beside the royal tombs in Petra

Dress smock from Gaza

Intricacies of Bedouin hand-weaving

Tasty fish and pine-nuts served on a bed of rice.
Creamy dish is hommous dip

Ka'ik, left, a popular bread eaten in Jordan

Aromas of East Jerusalem

Samples in the souq, Amman

Petra tomb displays the unique 'crow-step' concept of Nabataean architecture

An 'Aladdin's Cave' of artifacts in East Jerusalem souq

One of Islam's most sacred shrines, the Dome of the Rock in East Jerusalem

The welcoming smile of Jordan: son of the sheikh of the Bani Sakhr

sandcat, the fox and the wolf (*Vulpes arabica*) are all believed extinct. Like the wolf, the habitat of the striped hyena was the remote basalt ridge, where it raised its litters in impenetrable caves in the lava. However, the hyena's penchant for nocturnal attacks on local livestock has seen its virtual demise by poison baits, and the small Asiatic jackal which bred in the marshes and fed only on frogs, fish and carrion, has suffered a similar fate. Catfish are still abundant in the deeper pools.

Of the order of *insectivores*, Azraq has the Ethiopian hedgehog, an animal of desert and steppe country, the white-toothed shrew inhabiting wooded land and commonly found in the oasis with Savi's pygmy gerbil, a tiny creature whose body length, including the tail, does not exceed 40–50 millimetres. A dozen different types of rodents have also been recorded, but like the rare five-toed jerboa, they frequently fall prey to hungry dogs. Once abundant in the tall reed swamps, the wild boar has disappeared and the Syrian wild ass, whose stronghold was the basalt range south of Jebel Druze, is now extinct.

Provided there is no interference in its water-table, Azraq will probably remain one of the world's most important sanctuaries for migratory birds, since its marshes lie on the major migration route between Europe and Africa.

Some birds spend weeks feeding there; others only rest their wings a few hours before continuing their long flight to Africa. For ornithologists, spring is the best period to visit Azraq when, prior to breeding in Europe, many birds return from the southern hemisphere already in nuptial feathers. Over sixty species have been observed to breed at Azraq and the Mountfort expedition counted over 200 species at the oasis.

The best time to observe the birds is dawn, another valid reason for spending a night at the Azraq rest-house. Fortified by a small cup of strong Arab coffee, one can then sneak into a hide made of tamarisk branches to observe the pageant of song and flight on the marshes. One morning there might only be red-throated pips, blackcaps and blue-cheeked bee-eaters, the next, thousands of Kentish plovers could be sprinting across the flats, with hawks and eagles spiralling in the warm air currents. No two mornings are similar, except of course for herons, storks and egrets constantly stabbing at frogs in the slimy feeder canals, and the sand-martins dipping for insects on the surface of the marsh.

When the pools are full and the *qa* is a quagmire after winter rain, thousands of waterfowl wing in: teal, widgeon, mallard, moorhen and other water-birds. Hunting is now prohibited, but the effect of shooting other species concerns members of Jordan's Royal Society for the Conservation of Wildlife. The continued migration of birds to Azraq will also depend on the outcome of a scheme to pump water to Amman, since excessive demand may lower the water-table, thus interfering with the region's ecological system.

The oasis is the focal point of a self-contained hydrological system. The water comes from two sources: shallow, hand-dug wells and deep springs of which 'Azraq I' exceeds 1,000 metres in depth. Pumping water from here to Irbid has already lowered the water-level and any additional demand could cause a marked reduction in the water-table with subsequent encroachment of alkaline water from the *qa*. This would not only render the water unfit for human consumption, but drastically affect the flora and fauna of the surrounding marshes.

The Shaumari wildlife reserve, located eight kilometres west of Azraq, covers an area of mainly semi-desert, about 22 kilometres long, within which animals associated with arid conditions are protected – though being mainly nocturnal, such as the gerbil, jerboa and hedgehog, they are rarely seen.

Shaumari is also a breeding centre for endangered species such as the oryx, ibex, gazelle and ostrich. It is fenced to prevent Bedouin grazing, similar to the Masai encroachment of Kenya's great game reserves.

The most interesting breeding programme surrounds the Arabian oryx – *Oryx leucoryx* – the beautiful cream and chocolate-coloured antelope which was originally widespread in Palestine, Jordan and the Arabian peninsula. Perfectly camouflaged for its environment, the oryx occasionally fell victim to Bedouin who hunted it for food; but when it was discovered in Saudi Arabia and Kuwait, parties of Arabs systematically hunted the oryx resulting in widespread slaughter.

Such tragedies in the developing Arab states have prompted an international effort among naturalists to save the oryx from extinction. 'Operation Oryx' managed to capture three animals in the Sultanate of Oman which, with captive oryx donated by zoos in England and Qatar, now forms the nucleus of a 'world herd' living in Phoenix, Arizona. It seems oryx do not mind captivity and happily thriving on a diet of lucerne, corn and processed pellets, herds in both Qatar and Arizona have more than tripled since being established. Prompted by Jordan's interest in establishing a breeding centre, the San Diego Zoo sent four male oryx to Shaumari in 1979, the first oryx bred in captivity to return to their homeland.

My own visit to Shaumari coincided with a decision to introduce the four brothers to four females, also born in San Diego. The rangers erected extra barriers to prevent any animal escaping, then standing back, they opened the entrances between the separate cages. One of the oryx, a shy character known as Halim, scampered into his hut while the other two manifested nervousness by brisk backward and forward pacing, showing no interest in passing through to the females.

The attitude of Fareh, the fourth oryx, was different. It was not an interest in his potential paramour, but in me. Walking over to where I stood taking pictures, he poked his nose through the mesh and licked my hand. Not wanting to interfere with the experiment, I crouched down behind the barrier, but this made him angry, and backing up, Fareh charged, striking the wire with his horns and pushing with his forehead like a fighting bull.

Frightened that he might break a horn, I straightened up and called his name. At once his mood changed and he walked quietly across, pushing his nose out to lick me again.

The probable explanation for such a display of emotion in a fully mature oryx is simple. In San Diego, Fareh's mother had abandoned him as a baby and unlike his brothers, who ran with the herd, first-born Fareh had been bottle-fed. The sight of a tall woman in a blue denim skirt must have conjured up memories of an old American girlfriend!

Poignant though it was, Fareh's 'human connection' soon vanished when he mated with one of the females. Naturalists say that once the 'world herd' has reached 1,000 animals, the oryx can be said to have been saved from extinction, and thanks to the consciousness of wildlife conservation, Shaumari has been able to release Fareh's off-spring into the wild.

On Friday, Azraq is crowded with residents from Amman who drive up in a day to picnic by the palm-fringed ponds. Tourists, therefore, should choose to visit Azraq on another day. As for the outward trip, water for the return journey to Amman should be taken along: Azraq local mineral water is as pure as any in Europe.

A short detour off the highway, about half-way to Amman, leads to Qasr el-Hallabat, the last castle to be seen on the journey to Azraq. The building is thought to have been built by the Romans as protection against marauding desert tribes. Modifications were made to it by the Greeks and the remains of a mosque indicate the site was inhabited by the Ummayads. The general state of Qasr el-Hallabat is poor, but the nearby bath-house, Hammam es-Sarah, has been restored and is worth a visit.

The highway now leads to Mafraq, a town of little significance; but 11 kilometres east is the unique basalt city of Umm el-Jimal, in Arabic 'mother of the camel', indicating probable use as a caravanserai.

Seen from a distance, the town has the appearance of a settlement razed by napalm; but closer, some of the black buildings are seen to have endured the test of time – even the severe earthquake that wreaked havoc in Petra, Jerash and Jerusalem.

Covering about 80 hectares, Umm el-Jimal has extensive Roman, Byzantine and Ummayad ruins, but historians believe the original inhabitants were Nabataean. The builders of 'the black city' manifested great skills in

The eerie basalt ruins of Umm el-Jimal which was destroyed by an earthquake after the Ummayad period

shaping the basalt into buildings, carving beams as though they were of wood and constructing ceilings by laying the massive structures on cantilevered supports jutting out from the walls. Doors were carved from whole lumps of basalt, and judging from the remains of the houses, they seem to have followed the traditional Eastern design of rooms opening on to a central courtyard. Further evidence of the talents of the early inhabitants of Umm el-Jimal are the cisterns for storing the limited amount of rain falling in this dry area of northern Jordan. Subsequently channelled along aqueducts, the water was used for irrigating fields in the nearby wadi.

The city is surrounded by a wall entered through six gates. An inscription on the main West Gate of Commodius dates it from the reign of Marcus Aurelius. Historians consider the Romans must have taken Umm el-Jimal from the Nabataeans. There are no known records of the history of the town during the early Christian era, but numerous churches indicate that it was an important religious centre. In the north-west corner, the church of St Julianus, built in AD 345, is the earliest documented Christian church in Jordan. Crosses are to be seen cut in the basalt, and a well-defined 'Jerusalem Cross' is engraved on one of four arches supporting the church, dating from about AD 577.

Several thousand people are believed to have once lived in Umm el-Jimal. A strange place by day, it is quite eerie at night when desert winds sigh through the broken arches of its crumbling churches.

Chapter Seven

The Black Tents of Jordan

Jordan has an estimated population of 40,000 Bedouin nomads, still following the historic migrations of their ancestors. Tribal membership varies from a few thousand, as with the Sirhan, to large tribes such as the Bani Sakhr thought to number 30,000, plus some 23,000 Rwala who pass through Jordan annually from Arabia to Syria and Iraq.

Other major tribes are notably the Howeitat, the most traditional of Jordan's Bedouin tribes who claim descendency from the Prophet through his daughter Fatima, the Bani Attiya and al-Hajaya from the district of Kerak, and the Bani Khalid and al-Isa who originally migrated from Iraq. In 1948, several tribes from the Negev, including the Tarabin, the Azazimah and the Jibarat moved into Jordan.

Bedouin tribes can be likened to Scottish clans, with all the members (in theory) related to a common ancestor, sharing the same family name. Each tribe is further divided into sub-groups which comprise the closest relatives whose first loyalty is to each other. Known as the *hamoula*, the group is responsible for avenging the murder of a member; and alternately, any crime committed by one of the group places everyone at risk of retaliation.

Traditional to Bedouin everywhere, murder used to be avenged according to the old desert maxim of taking 'an eye for an eye'. Debts were settled in blood money and, today, the paying of money to the relatives of a victim in a car accident has its roots in this Bedouin custom.

The Bedouin are the only peoples who actually live and survive in the desert; but since an individual stands no chance in such a hostile environment, the infrastructure of Bedouin life is welded to tribal society, its philosophy comprising complex social and economic rules to ensure survival. In former times, and still today, loyalty, bravery and hospitality are the qualities most esteemed by the Bedouin: resourcefulness, self-reliance and vigilance are other qualities that enable them to live together in the desert.

Each tribe has a leader, the paramount sheikh, elected by a tribal council, or *majlis.* In effect, tribal administration is quite democratic, since anyone is free to express his opinion at a sitting.

Under the leadership of the sheikh, the *majlis* judges minor crimes, but for serious offences, the tribes follow government law, which affects all citizens in Jordan. In any event, the premise of tribal law was not to inflict harsh punishment on an offender so much as to examine the extent of compensation to be paid to a victim.

Although there is no class structure in a tribe, the sheikh has to be more affluent in comparison with the others, in order to be able to assume the responsibility of offering hospitality to travellers, whether they be friends or strangers. Should he be unable to entertain in a manner befitting a sheikh, word soon passes around to other tribes and the reputation of his own tribe is ruined.

The strength of a tribe historically depends on the character of the sheikh whose task remains that of arbitrator – not by autocratic means, but through his wisdom and natural qualities of leadership. In former times, an important consideration in the choice of a sheikh was his record as a leader during tribal warfare when bravery was quickly established.

Jordan's most famous Bedouin warrior was the Howeitat leader, Sheikh Audeh Abu Tayeh, whom Lawrence considered to be 'the greatest fighting man in northern

Arabia'. Sheikh Audeh is reported to have slain over seventy-five men and, as befitting a sheikh, he was also humble, keeping for himself only 5 out of 400 camels that his tribe had taken in a raid.

Warfare grew more serious when the Bedouin obtained rifles, and battles for tribal supremacy in the early twentieth century saw tremendous depletion among their ranks. Had the government not intervened, certain tribes could have faced annihilation; the Howeitat, for instance, recognised as the best Bedouin fighters, had their numbers reduced from 1,200 to less than 500 in just over a decade. In her book *The Bedouin*, Shirley Kay notes that four-fifths of the Rwala also died in battle.

Strange as it seems, beautiful Bedouin girls often rode into battle ahead of the army, beating their breasts and encouraging the men to fight. If accidently captured, it was a matter of honour that the enemy should return them, unharmed, to their own tribe.

As with all aspects of Bedouin society, warfare and raiding followed a strict code of ethics of which a fundamental rule was a formal declaration of the intention to attack. Thus the element of surprise became the most thrilling part of a raid, but it was also a question of honour never to attack a sleeping tribe. Most raids took place at dawn, giving the enemy the chance to track down animals which had taken fright and escaped.

Tribal relations were regulated by these conventions in the same manner as the unwritten rules set for travellers. A member of a tribe wishing to cross enemy territory would request the goodwill of the sheikh, who could not refuse, since this would have been considered shameful. Granted protection, the traveller then passed in safety, since all members of that tribe were obliged to agree to a temporary truce.

Raiding, where the aim was to loot, rather than to kill, was the highlight of a mundane existence. Raids were plotted for months in advance, the Bedouin believing it was their 'divine right' to attack another tribe who had found good grazing when their own herds were depleted. Historians see raiding as an alternative to trading and, more often, it was the only means of survival. A raiding party included all able-bodied men over the age of twelve and numbered anything from twenty to several hundred. Camels were used to travel to the scene of a raid, but horses were deployed in the actual attack.

One can imagine a raiding party lying low, some six kilometres from a group of tents pitched around a desert well. A moment before dawn, the raiders rise, rinse their mouths and pray. Tying their camel's mouths, they then break camp, leading their horses up the dunes. On the other side of the sands, some fifty members of a *hamoula* are beginning to rise. A cock is crowing and the first woman is preparing coffee on a sluggish fire. As the yawning men shake the creases from their *thobes*, a long cry echoes from the highest dune and the raiders fan out down the sands. Two riders head for a group of mares, slash their ropes and urge them away. Others grab water-bags, bags of flour and strips of gazelle meat drying on the roof of a tent. The woman resists and her coffee-bag is torn, scattering the contents on the ground; but according to tribal law, she and the other women and children are not harmed, and with no real resistance the raiders escape. Back at the camp-site, the marauders reload their camels, taking count of their gains: two horses, a bag of flour, a rifle and sufficient meat to last a week. They have not been pursued, but until they reach the next well, some 30 kilometres distant, they will pause neither to eat, nor to drink. The rest of their tribe is camped another 80 kilometres south, but safety is only relative since, having carried out a raid, they can only anticipate retaliation. The traditional eating position of the Bedouin – squatting, without the knees touching the ground and with the right shoulder inclined towards the food – is symbolic of past feuds, permitting the eater to jump up quickly if attacked.

The very nature of the Bedouin's itinerant life precludes the acquisition of superfluous objects: true Bedouin possess only simple articles for personal and social requirements. Their most important possession is the tent.

Even those Bedouin who have moved into the government re-settlement homes still like to erect their tents nearby. One woman whom I spoke to in the village of Kariah, not far from Ma'an, told me she only used the new house for cooking and washing, as the family preferred to sleep and to entertain in the tent. The reason is also deeply psychological, as for thousands of years the tent has been the Bedouin's only protection against the environment. Tourists visiting Jordan may find the black tents pitched by the roadside to be barely habitable, but for the Bedouin living outside urban society they represent the security of home.

A tent varies in size according to the owner's wealth and the number of his family. It is normally supported on two or three poles, and measures from 9 metres long by 3.5 metres wide. The largest tent I ever saw in Jordan was a four-poled structure pitched at the steps of a mansion built on the edge of the desert, near el-Muwaqqar and belonging to the paramount sheikh of the Bani-Sakhr.

The dark brown, or black colour, of the low-slung tent enables it to be seen from a great distance against the neutral background of the desert. Called *al-bayt*, it is woven from a mixture of sheep and goat hair, the cloth being sewn together in strips so that it can easily be replaced when worn. Several strips of white cotton cloth are inserted into the back to give added strength. Ideally suited to the environment, the tent can be quickly erected and just as easily dismantled and loaded on to a camel for transportation to new grazing. Its cloth is waterproof for the rare occasions when it rains, and during chilly nights the tight weave acts as a reasonably effective wind-break, whilst on hot days its sides can be rolled up for ventilation.

A central curtain divides the tent into male and female quarters, its patterned side facing the male domain.

The focal point of the male domain is a fireplace sunk in

the sand, surrounded by utensils for preparing tea or coffee: a pestle and mortar, an enamel kettle, brass coffee-pots, a tray with small coffee-cups and glasses, spoons, tongs for raking the embers, a ladle for roasting the beans and a decorated coffee-bean bag hanging from the tent-pole. Carpets or mattresses are laid on the ground, with cushions and camel saddles for the guests to lean on. Guests are always entertained in the male section of the tent: if food is to be served, it is cooked and carried in from the women's quarters, where the bulk of family possessions are stored.

The women's domain, or *al-mahram*, is mostly occupied by bedding-rugs, quilts and mattresses which are rolled up during the daytime and stacked against the back of the tent. Many families also own a large tin trunk, or suitcase, that is kept permanently packed, creating the impression that the family is about to move but in effect serving both for storage and for easy transportation.

The women's cooking area is less tidy than the men's quarters, with blackened pots and pans scattered about the fireplace. Sacks of flour and rice, bags of ghee (clarified butter) and pungent-smelling cheese are lined along the side of the tent: in springtime, there are also bags of *laban* (yoghurt). Two battered kerosene cans standing near the entrance contain water filled from black goat-skin water-bags. There may also be a child's cradle and a loom.

Fundamental to all Moslem societies, jobs are precisely allocated in a Bedouin household. A man may help his wife to erect their tent but it would never occur to him to assist with anything that was traditionally designated as women's work.

It is a man's job to move his family to new grazing areas, to look after the camels and, if an opportunity arises, to shoot something for the pot. It is frequently the man who does the shopping when the family needs provisions.

Bedouin women work exceptionally hard. Tired and prematurely aged, they shuffle slowly about performing their tasks in a lacklustre fashion that may also arise from a vitamin deficiency stemming from their meagre diet.

A woman's job is to cook, raise the children, supervise the grazing of the sheep and goats, to weave the tent, the dividing curtain and the bedding rugs, to fetch water and collect firewood. The number of Bedouin women seeking relief at the mineral springs at Zarqa Ma'in is evidence of their back-breaking work.

What I find puzzling is the apparently strange choice of camp-sites, possibly motivated by the direction of the wind, particularly around Kerak, where men pitch their tents in seemingly impossible places in the crags with the result that women have a good hour's climb down to fetch water from the wadi. On one occasion near Azraq, I saw a tent pitched against the Irbid water-pipeline. And as if this were not tantalising enough, the women had to walk three kilometres to the closest spring. I met two Rwala women returning one morning. Whilst stepping over the pipeline, the younger one tripped, and spilled her precious load of water. I asked why they did not camp nearer the local facilities and was told that they did not like the townspeople. . . .

Hauling and carrying water is not their only hard job. According to Shelagh Weir's study of the Bedouin (a Museum of Mankind Publication), weaving on the simple Bedouin loom also requires great strength and dexterity. After shearing, the goat hair and sheep's wool is teased, ready for the spinning process. The fibres are spun from a crude wooden spindle with the 'rove', or loose ball of teased fibre either wrapped around the wrist, or allowed to float behind the shoulder. Using the 'drop and spin' method with the spindle suspended, the women wander about chatting to others and herding the goats.

In former times, the women used to dye the wool themselves, but today synthetically coloured yarn can be purchased in any village. Shelagh Weir says the Howeitat at one time spun cotton cloth from raw fibre, but this, too, can now be bought.

I have watched Howeitat women weaving inside their

tents, but as the ground loom takes up a lot of space, a small shelter is often rigged up outside where they sit under the shade of rugs with the warp pegged out in front. The loom has no mechanical aids. The cloth is woven in and out with a wooden 'sword beater' and as it lengthens, the women sit on the fabric to help maintain tension. The 'beating hook', or implement for beating in the weft, is usually made of steel, although some women still use the old-fashioned gazelle horn inherited from their mothers. The maximum width of the cloth is that which two women can accomplish while working together – approximately a metre across.

Women of the sheep and goat-breeding tribes weave more regularly than the camel-herders, who do not have sufficient wool, and who are, of necessity, more frequently on the move. As a result of the demand for their cloth in some villages bordering the desert, a subsidiary weaving industry has evolved to supply tent strips, rugs and other articles.

The most important product of the loom is the tent cloth, but the most striking item is the curtain, *sahah*, which gives scope for the development of colourful patterns, red, orange, cream and brown being especially popular.

Since the Quran forbids the representation of human life, the forms are always geometric patterns based on squares, stripes, diamonds and triangles. The sharp outlines are no doubt influenced by images in their environment, the jagged outline of a *jebel*, or a dune whipped into a knife-like edge by the wind. Even the shape of the black tent, and the angle it is pitched against the sky, is echoed in a purely abstract design.

Decorative weaving is also expressed in rugs, cushion covers, saddle-bags, camel-halters, girdles, belts, marriage bags and woven and plaited straps which a bride wears around her neck. Small cowrie shells are often sewn on to the cloth as an added decoration. The Naif Museum in Aqaba has a collection of traditional Bedouin articles, in particular large, tasselled camel-bags used singly to store items in the tent, and in pairs for transporting goods during a move.

Today Bedouin women are becoming less productive in these crafts. Most of the curtains, rugs and decorated bean bags are family heirlooms, but there is a parallel in western society where women no longer embroider the beautiful tablecloths and doilies that were once an essential part of a Victorian trousseau.

There is a growing trend among the more affluent Bedouin families for the women to own a treadle sewing-machine. A Howeitat woman told me she found it much quicker to run up cushion covers and other pro-ducts using the fancy, mechanical stitches. Tourist demand for traditional Bedouin handiwork may result in a revival of the craft: in Wadi Rum, some women embroider dresses and shirts which have a ready market among tourists.

Until 1940–45, Bedouin women in Jordan wore a black cotton dress of voluminous proportions, which served as a combination of over-garment, under-garment and night-dress and was over three metres in length. Whilst work-ing, they hitched it around their waists, and at night it would untuck to be wrapped around their feet as a protec-tion against the cold. A modified version of this costume is still worn by the present generation of Bedouin women who have settled into houses, but as their children are educated, they will inevitably adopt alternative fashions, a trend occurring throughout the Middle East.

Bedouin women dress discreetly, as required by Islam. Their dress is usually black nylon, or some other synthetic material, full length with wide sleeves, embroidered across the bosom and the hem.

Married townswomen wear a cloth over their heads known as *al-waqah* which they often cover with another garment of red, or black silk. They usually wear an outer veil over the *waqah* which is called the *miqna'a*, around which is a band interlaced with silver threads known as *al-a'sbah*. The women of Salt are dressed especially colourfully, setting off their attire with a long over-mantle, *al-jubbah*, reaching to their knees. In Madaba and Kerak it is shorter and called *ad-damer*. Exposed to western fashions in Amman, many young girls are replacing *al-waqah* with a western-type, patterned, or plain headscarf.

Although the variety of colours available for machine embroidery sees the custom petering out, in certain parts of Jordan a woman's clothing still denotes her marital status, the colour of the embroidery being especially significant. Unmarried girls, for example, may only wear blue embroidered dresses and red is restricted to married women. Unaware of this at the time, I was disappointed when a pretty young Bedouin girl refused to let me photograph her in a red-patterned Bedouin robe that I had bought in Aqaba.

Until the middle of the twentieth century, Bedouin men wore the long *kiber* and an outer short coat, the *damer*, with a flowing cloak, or *abayah* and the typical head-dress, or *kuffeyeh*, secured with the black *agal* cord. Sheikhs and wealthy traders wore a more elaborate *abayah* of silk, or woven camel hair embroidered round the sleeves and hem in gold thread. Their *agal* was also of twisted gold.

Today Bedouin men wear a long, generally plain coloured *kiber* or *thobe* with a red and white check, or plain white, *kuffeyeh*. When it is cold, many also wear the incongruous mix of *kuffeyeh* and western sports jacket: in Amman, I have also seen men wearing a western suit and tie with an Arab *kuffeyeh*.

Whilst Bedouin women in Jordan have never worn an excessive amount of jewellery (as do certain Negev tribes who literally cover their faces behind a mask of coins and other trinkets), each woman has a collection of jewellery given to her on the occasion of her marriage. She does not choose it herself; having received the bride-price, her father visits a jeweller, or buys from itinerant traders –

usually a local gypsy race known as the Sulubbas, or Nawars.

As the Bedouin are poorer than the townspeople, the silversmiths used to provide them with a cheaper, lower grade of silver, the source of which was the former Austrian currency, the Maria Theresa dollar. Mixed with the other metals, usually copper, the Maria Theresa dollar provided the ideal substance for metalling Arab jewellery.

Much of the old Bedouin jewellery is cumbersome and rather crudely worked; however, the art of filigree and particularly of granulation (soldering small drops on to a silver base, frequently seen in the form of a Quran case), has more appeal to the western shopper. Also popular are pendants, rings and necklaces set with small pieces of amber, coral and turquoise.

Circassian and Armenian craftsmen who migrated to Jordan early this century introduced black enamel, or nielloware. Whilst not especially appealing, it is worth noting that the silver must be of a good quality to withstand the insertion of the metal.

A Bedouin woman's jewellery is her 'bank', which she removes only to sell. Because of the current inflated prices of the few things she may require – such as coffee, *kohl* (eye-liner used by Arab women), cloth, some foods, and, at most, a sewing-machine – there is a growing tendency, and a need, for more and more women to sell their jewellery. The first objects to go are usually the anklets, which are no longer fashionable; but as prices continue to escalate, the Bedouin women are experiencing a gradual erosion of their only assets.

The soaring price of gold has seen this precious metal replace silver jewellery as the traditional dowry for a Bedouin bride. Goldsmiths abound in Amman, but to my knowledge there are no longer any silversmiths to be found. One goldsmith said that a visitor from one of the Gulf States spent £20,000 on gold jewellery for his daughter's wedding.

The Bedouin in Jordan do not have this wealth; but,

whatever the case, a bride still acquires her jewellery: amulets, pendants inscribed with the name of Allah or a verse from the Quran, bangles, earrings, rings, necklaces and *kohl* cases.

Like the women, Bedouin men own few possessions, in order to maintain their freedom and mobility. Most own a rifle, the butt of which is often decorated with slivers of bone and silver. There is also a growing fashion for transistor radios.

All Bedouin are passionately fond of music which, with story-telling and poetry, has always played a significant role in their lives. Poetry is the perfect medium for self-expression. Love and war remain the favourite themes, with extensive use made of the simile: comparisons are made with familiar things in the desert, such as the thousand virtues of the camel, or the stars. . . .

Present-day poems and stories have been passed down over the centuries by word of mouth. The arrival of a poet, or a renowned story teller, is a signal for everyone to gather round the camp-fire. Shirley Kay makes the interesting observation that the metres used in the odes are thought to correspond to the walking pace of the camel, or the horse, indicating that many of the poems must have been composed on long, monotonous desert treks.

The ode (*qasida* in Arabic) is composed of 20–100 couplets with the rhyme maintained through the poem. Since Arabic has only three vowels and many words have standard feminine endings, it is not as difficult as it may sound to find some 200 rhyming words. Some form of music usually accompanies the poems.

Although much less sophisticated than the instruments of classic Arabic music heard in the city, Bedouin instruments are adequate for simple entertainment. The traditional instrument, still widely used, is the one-string *rababa*, a type of 'desert violin' made of goatskin stretched over a wooden frame. The bow produces a weird 'keening' sound which, heard in a Bedouin tent, epitomises centuries of nomadism. I recall, whilst climbing alone in Petra, that I caught the bitter-sweet sound of a *rababa* being played by a shepherd boy, seated on a rock like some raffish violinist.

If one member of the *hamoula* owns a *rababa*, another will have a drum and percussion instruments such as the *rig*, or *daff* – a circular tambourine which, when shaken vigorously, is an invitation to dance.

Normally there is not a great deal of dancing in cloistered Bedouin society but one popular dance is the *sahja*, symbolising a woman's need to defend her vulnerability. A young girl, brandishing a sword or a camel-stick, dances, followed by men shuffling in pursuit; but there is no development of any type, the same steps being repeated over and over again.

The time of greatest rejoicing is at a wedding when celebrations follow fixed formalities, before, during and after the event.

First a preliminary delegation requests the bride's hand and agrees on the dowry. In the old days, this would be a previously agreed number of horses, camels, sheep or goats, but today it is in the form of money – except among the very poorest families.

A symbolic form of procession known as a *qitar* precedes the wedding: a group of friends and relatives jovially go to 'fetch' the bride, the men firing their rifles and the women ululating shrilly. The true procession, or *fardeh*, is an all-female affair when only the bride's relatives and closest friends go to her tent, where they spend hours painting henna patterns on her hands and feet. Finally she is dressed and taken to a section of the tent that is curtained off, where she remains until led to her future husband.

A great deal of singing and dancing accompanies the wedding, which may continue for seven days. Singing plays a major part in the celebrations with the singer, always an older, self-confident woman, moving around the circle, arousing clapping and enthusiasm amongst the onlookers. She too wields a stick, or a dagger, held symbolically to ward off any attempt to touch her which would be considered shameful for her and her children.

During all the merrymaking, the newly-weds remain inside their tent which is pitched slightly apart from the others. A tradition, still practised, is the symbolic caning and stoning of the bridegroom by his relatives, to prove his toughness. At the entrance to the bridal tent or *al-bazeh*, he ritually cuts the throat of a sheep, or a goat, which will be cooked as part of a huge *mansaf* (see Chapter 7).

The birth of a child, particularly if it is a boy, is another time of rejoicing in the desert. Circumcision is also occasioned by the slaughter of an animal.

Once, near Shaubak, I saw a large Bedouin tent pitched under the trees; approaching cautiously, I was courteously invited to sit inside on the carpet, with about thirty of the male relatives. In the centre was a huge tray of mutton and rice, pyramids of apples were stacked in the corners and crates of orange-cola reached the roof. Unable to converse, I could not discover where the womenfolk were, so I could only assume they must have been busy preparing the bride. Obviously these Bedouin were well-off, for it is difficult to imagine a poor desert family preparing such a sumptuous feast.

When game was plentiful, hunting was a popular pastime among the Bedouin whose austere life-styles afforded little leisure. Hunting doubled both as a sport and a means of providing food. In the heat of the desert, the Bedouin never killed to excess – just what they could eat, or share, or salt down for future meals. Their quarry was the oryx, the gazelle, the desert hare and the *hubara*, or McQueen's bustard. In the old days, they tracked game from camel, or on horseback, using the desert dog, saluqi, to flush prey from the dunes.

The origins of the desert hunting-dog are vague, but it seems possible that it was the first animal domesticated by man, 4–5,000 years ago in Arabia. Although many cities in the Middle East claim to be the dog's ancestral home, historians say the saluqi is first recorded in the Arabian city of Saluq, long ago buried under the desert sands. The saluqi's expertise as a hunter is depicted on Mesopotamian pottery and in Egyptian bas-reliefs; and the beautiful murals seen in Qasr Amra, in north-east Jordan, depict the dogs attacking a herd of gazelles.

Many Bedouin still own a saluqi. It resembles a small Afghan hound, having the same tapered head and fine muzzle, downward hanging ears and upward curling tail, but standing only 70 centimetres at the shoulder. Its legs are straight and sturdy to withstand the punishment of racing across the hard terrain: saluqis have been recorded at speeds of 60–65 kilometres an hour, and running in long, loping strides, they can seize a hare, or a jerboa at full stride.

Although a hunter, the saluqi makes a gentle, sensitive pet and the Bedouin allow it to share the tent as one of the family, despite their natural aversion to dogs.

The falcon is also allowed into the tent. The legendary sport of desert nomads, falconry reached its zenith under the Ummayads who hunted with falcons, saluqis, and also with trained cheetahs.

The method of capturing and training a falcon is the same as in years past, but the cost of feeding it fresh meat, the scarcity of falcons and the ban on hunting bustard has resulted in a big drop in the number of falconers in Jordan. Bedouin are still known to hunt in the desert around al-Bayir, but the great hunting parties of the past are today the exclusive privilege of wealthy Arab sheikhs.

When a woman herding goats, or a child fetching wood, sees a falcon in the area, the man at once sets about digging a pit which he conceals with tamarisk boughs and other debris. To attract the falcon's attention, he ties a string to the leg of a dove, or other small bird, and conceals himself in the hide, allowing it to flutter above him.

Spotting the victim, the falcon plummets down, killing it and tearing at its flesh. And since the falcon always feeds upwind, the man is able to pull the corpse slowly towards the hide, extend an arm, and throw a net over the falcon.

Taking it back to the tent, he stitches the bird's eyelids and attaches 'jesses' to its legs to prevent it flying away. During the training period, lasting from thirty to fifty days, the falcon is never apart from the man who carries it about on his wrist, talking to it and stroking its feathers. Training is by subtle force: food is withheld until the bird realises its dependence on its captor. When it is calmer, its lids are unstitched and the falcon is allowed to sit on a small stool, watching family life in the tent.

The final training is to teach the bird to attack a lure, usually the wing of a bustard that is swung in the air by an assistant. Long strings attached to the jesses prevent the falcon from escaping as it is repeatedly provoked to attack the lure, rewarded each time with a piece of fresh meat (an obvious difficulty in the desert).

Ultimately the falcon is taken on a hunt, and now that hunting bustard is banned, its likely quarry is the hare. In ancient times, a good falcon could bring down five bustard on the wing in the aerial combats the Bedouin consider are the most spectacular part of the hunt. History records that a flock of falcons trained by the Ummayads brought down a herd of terrified gazelles by swooping down and clawing at their eyes.

The Arab thoroughbred horse has been associated with the Bedouin since time immemorial. Long before the advent of Islam, Bedouin horse-breeders were considered masters in the art of selective mating to develop a horse of great speed, stamina and purity of line. Most Bedouin believe that every noble strain goes back to Kuhayla, a mare in ancient times from whom the five major breeds are descended. More important than sires in breeding, mares were also preferred for desert raids because of their greater stamina. If the camel is the most useful animal to the Bedouin, the Arab horse was his pride and protection; but sadly, because of today's high costs, it is rare to see one in a Bedouin encampment. A story relates how an old sheikh, when asked why he had a bicycle leaning against his tent-pole, replied: ... 'bicycles do not eat. ...'

The horse is becoming rare in Bedouin society. These guides are employed at Petra

Whilst it is no longer correct to link the Bedouin and the Arab horse, there is excellent bloodstock in the royal stables of His Majesty King Hussein. His Majesty's Arab horses, whose lineage dates from the stables of the Sharif Hussein, were rescued from the royal stables at Shuna on the invasion of the West Bank, and swum to safety across the River Jordan.

The camel, however, remains an integral part of Bedouin life, although their numbers are decreasing, as seen by a recent FAO study which puts the estimated total at some 18,000, compared with a million at the turn of the century.

The decline in Jordan's camel population points to the decreasing dependence on the animal by those Bedouin now living a sedentary life. But while tribes along the perimeter of the desert can lead a relatively comfortable existence breeding sheep and cultivating crops, the Bedouin is still unable to exist without his camel, nor indeed the camel without him.

Probably arising from an admiration of the hardships they endure, the camel-breeders are regarded as the élite by other Bedouin. The Bedouin in fact categorise themselves into three groups: the *hadari*, or settled tribes; the *arab* or sheep-breeders; leaving the term *badawi*, or *bedouin*, strictly only applicable to the noble camel-breeders. It is therefore incorrect to call all nomads *bedouin*, but the term is normally used by writers as it is the word most familiar to Westerners.

Passing through Wadi Arabah once, I was fortunate in witnessing a tribal migration, or at least part of a *hamoula* moving north for the summer. First came the husband, then his wife riding in an old-fashioned camel litter, and their three sons, urging on their pack camels with that peculiar *hut-hut-hut* language used by the Bedouin to their beasts.

The earliest known representation of a camel is found on Egyptian earthenware dating from 3–5,000 BC. By the end of the second millennium they were probably being used as beasts of burden, a harbinger of the great caravans that crossed Jordan during the Middle Ages.

A camel in prime condition is a splendid animal, its finer points admired by the Bedouin as much as those of an Arab horse. The Austrian scholar, von Hammer Pungstall, claims to have discovered 5,744 different names and epithets for describing the camel in Arabic. The Arabic name, *jamal*, has the same root as *jamil*, the word for beautiful.

As with the saluqi and the falcon, where beige, or albino is preferred, the Bedouin place great emphasis on the colour of their camels. In Jordan pure white animals are a mark of prestige, their hair also making the finest woven *abayahs*. During a raid, white camels were always the first to be captured and during a retaliation, the first to be retrieved. Adeb, my driver, could not fathom my enthusiasm when, crossing the desert south of Azraq, we spotted six cream-coloured camels loping across the horizon. But whilst researching a book on the Gulf states, I had become accustomed to the dark brown camels which are preferred in Arabia.

Physically and metabolically, the camel is ideally adapted to withstand the harsh desert environment. It has thickly fringed eyelashes acting as a shield against wind-blown sand, a second transparent lid that can be lowered during a driving sandstorm, and muscular nostrils it can partly close, for the same reason.

The camel's broad, flat feet spread out on the sand like snowshoes and its distinctive hump (the Asian Bactrian camel has two humps), in effect a lump of fat weighing between 40–50 kilos, acts as a useful source of energy on long treks. The hump mirrors a camel's condition. In weak and impoverished animals I have seen in the drought-stricken areas of the African *sahel*, it had shrunk to a mere flap of skin.

The camel's ability to survive for long periods without water is its greatest advantage to the Bedouin, who live in regions where wells are few and distances between them great. In summer a camel can survive for two or three days without a drink compared to a man, who will die in extreme temperatures within twelve hours.

Its whole metabolism is geared to resisting heat and dehydration. A camel does not sweat, yet its body temperature can vary by as much as six degrees centigrade without causing it distress. Its stomach, consisting of four fleshy pockets, regulates the slow digestion of food. A camel's recovery rate is also astonishing: a thirsty beast can drink 114 litres in one burst and regain its normal composure within half an hour.

Endurance is one of the camel's greatest attributes and in Jordan, as elsewhere in the Middle East, female camels are preferred as mounts. The Bedouin claim they are more courageous than bulls, but after a long, forced march, it has been known for a camel to drop dead.

A small problem is the camel's surly disposition. Its bad temper is evident particularly when it is roused, and the eerie groaning of a camel herd is audible for several kilometres across the desert. Bull camels become quite violent during the rutting season when the Bedouin hobble their front legs so they cannot fight. In this way they can only move in restricted hops, gnashing their teeth and groaning with annoyance.

As the majority of bull camels are slaughtered at birth, the arrival of a bull at a campsite causes great activity as everyone brings his she-camels to be served. A legend among the Bedouin in Oman says that camels dislike to copulate in front of human beings, but in the flat expanse of eastern Jordan, there is little privacy.

The main difference between the sheep-herders and the camel-breeders is the distances they must travel in search of food. Life for the *badawi* is an almost permanent quest for pasture since every ten days or so the tent is dismantled and its contents loaded as the family, or *hamoula* – or indeed the entire tribe – migrates elsewhere, sometimes travelling up to 1,500 kilometres in one year.

During autumn the migratory trails follow the rain-clouds hanging like a grey blanket over northern Jordan. A member of the tribe always watches to see if distant thunder brings rain: the sight of rain falling on the horizon is the signal for a race to see who can be first to reach the grass that springs up miraculously in the hitherto barren ground.

Camels are bred carefully to ensure they drop their young only when pasture is available. Apart from its superior qualities as a mount, another advantage of the she-camel is her milk. On good grazing, she can suckle her young, yet still yield up to 5 litres for family use either as milk, or made into *ghee* and yoghurt. Camel milk is the basic diet of many Bedouin and some families often have nothing to sustain themselves but milk, and its by-products, during an entire day.

Taking photographs early one morning, I came across a Sirhan encampment while a camel was being milked. Straightening up, with the usual words of welcome, the owner handed me a warm, frothy mug, fresh from her udder. Gaunt yet austere, he also insisted that I sit with his family, and share their sandy dates. This, he non-chalantly informed my driver, was the only food they had eaten for a week, but that in three days, on the occasion of a tribal wedding, they would slaughter a goat. A Westerner can have no idea of the extent of Bedouin hospitality when even the poorest family, such as these Sirhan, will share their last morsel, even with a complete stranger such as myself.

Generosity ranks high among the criteria by which a person is judged in Bedouin society. There are also other reasons, one being the fundamental Moslem belief that if one is generous to one's fellows on earth, then Allah will reward one in Paradise. And whilst there is no denying the generosity of the Bedouin, visitors also provide them with the company they crave in their monotonous desert lives.

A further example of Bedouin hospitality is the story of two surveyors who ran short of water while working near the border with Iraq. Needing only a drink before returning to Amman, they called with this request at a black tent. Invited in, however, they were offered coffee, then the man's wife prepared dinner and they were asked to spend the night. Rather than cause offence, they were obliged to accept the invitation; the following day a goat was slain for a *mansaf* and they did not get back to the city until the next night.

In an interview with the *Jordan Times*, a Bedouin policeman, an authority on Bedouin customs, explained that the origin of many contemporary habits in Arab urban society stems from Bedouin traditions. He said that scores of gestures, imperceptible to a Westerner, even to an Arab born and raised in the town, surround even the most simple act of hospitality. The whole coffee ritual, for example, can be likened to silent language in a complex pact that is binding to both guest and host.

The repeated smiling greeting: *'Ahlan wasahlan'* – 'Welcome, twice welcome' – invites a guest to take a place around the fire in the men's section of the tent. The host then digs into the coffee-bag and puts some beans in a ladle to roast on the embers. When they have cooled, he pounds them with the pestle and mortar, or *mihbash* (which may be of traditional carved wood, or of modern brass).

A skilful coffee grinder can pound out an appreciable rhythm audible at some distance, which announces to neighbours the presence of guests. The beans are tossed into boiling water and after boiling several times, the contents are poured into another pot over freshly ground cardamom seeds. This is allowed to simmer for about fifteen minutes, its pleasantly bitter aroma pervading the tent.

The coffee-pot is one of several brass pots of different sizes made in Syria, with the craftsman's name engraved on the side, or on the base. A bunch of twigs stuck in its spout acts as a filter and the bearer, or whoever has made the coffee, pours a few drops into a tiny cup, about the size of an egg-cup without a handle, and hands it to the host.

The following gestures, though now largely symbolic, remain essential protocol in the Bedouin coffee ceremony.

The first cup offered to the host is deemed the 'unworthy cup', assuring the guest that the coffee is safe to drink and satisfying the host that it is hot, since it is a terrible insult to serve cold coffee. Like the other cups, the second cup is poured with the left hand, the bearer holding a stack of cups in his right. This cup is offered to the guest whose acceptance signifies that he is pleased with the hospitality.

The third cup, even more significantly, has its roots in the days of tribal feuding. It silently concludes the protec-

Bedouin coffee-ceremony follows timeless rituals. Note the tamarisk twigs which act as a strainer in the spout

tion agreement, meaning that the guest is safe from any attack while under the auspices of his host. Apparently this cup, known as the 'sword cup', is binding, even against attack by one or the other's brother. Sometimes a fourth cup is offered confirming the silent defence pact.

It is not usual to drink more than this, but if a guest

wants more (only a few drops are poured into each cup), he simply holds out his cup to be refilled by the attentive bearer. Alternatively, to signify he has had enough, he flicks the cup a couple of times with his wrist, a final silent gesture concluding the coffee ritual.

As is frequently so in western society, the serving of coffee, or tea, is the first gesture of hospitality, with an invitation to eat the ultimate form of generosity, also following similarly specific protocol.

Essentially there are two types of meals: either the ordinary meal that is offered upon the arrival in the tent of an unexpected guest, or the special feast, to honour an esteemed guest, at tribal marriages and on festive occasions such as *eid el-fitr*.

A simple meal means precisely this in Bedouin society – a little rice and yoghurt, or *ghee*, eaten with thin, unleavened bread and dates. At the other end of the scale is the *mansaf*, a meal of gargantuan proportions. (For recipe and explanation see Chapter 8). One such *mansaf* held in southern Jordan in honour of King Faisal consisted of an entire baby camel which was stuffed with sheep, in turn stuffed with turkeys, inside which were chickens, the whole spread on a bed of rice that would have covered a small room.

Fundamental to Moslem custom, a *mansaf*, or any other meal, is only ever eaten with the right hand. The custom is to take three mouthfuls of rice before eating the meat – a gesture corresponding to the three symbolic cups of coffee and signifying that a guest is under his host's protection. Eating less meat is also considered to be a sign of humility.

Another point of etiquette surrounding a Bedouin *mansaf* is not to allow one's fingers to enter one's mouth. This is avoided by picking up the rice with three fingers, rolling it in the palm of the hand and popping it in from a distance of a few centimetres, an art requiring a certain dexterity. It is also polite only to eat from that portion of the plate directly in front of one and to accept graciously the choice pieces offered by the host.

Tourists will probably not have the opportunity of eating with the Bedouin, but a *mansaf* which I ate at Amman's Oasis Restaurant approaches the real experience. Set outdoors under a Bedouin tent, the *mansaf* was eaten seated on cushions, using one's fingers, or cutlery, as desired. Coffee was served in the traditional manner with the beans ground by a Bedouin using a traditional wooden *mihbash*. The restaurant was evidently popular not only with Western visitors, but with Amman residents seeking to sample a part of their ethnic background.

Chapter Eight

The Jordanian Cuisine

A bonus of a visit to Jordan is the thousand and one delights of Arab cooking.

As with many Middle Eastern dishes, Jordanian food stems from traditional Bedouin cooking, but while interpretations of this have evolved in countries such as Syria, Turkey and Lebanon, in many instances Jordanian cooking remains faithful to the original recipe. A good example is *mansaf* which has come down through the ages undiluted by modern adaptations. Also typically Jordanian is the fondness for cooking in yoghurt.

The most common varieties of main course dishes are: *yakhaneh* a combination of meat, small onions, tomatoes, cabbage and other vegetables, cooked as a casserole; *mahshi*, vine leaves and vegetables – usually eggplant, courgette or cabbage stuffed with rice and minced meat, or rice with onions, and *rosto* which is meat, or chicken, usually charcoal-grilled in the form of kebabs or *shawarma* (spitted lamb).

The main course is usually started with several varieties of the *mazza*, or hors d'oeuvres. Salads are an important side dish and a meal is often finished on a sweet note, with dessert, or fresh fruit.

Bread is traditionally eaten with every meal – either dry, or as a dip. There are more varieties to the flat, round bread, or *khoubz*, in Jordan than anywhere else in the Middle East.

The following are some of the different kinds of *khoubz*, of which there are over a dozen: *khoubz sh'rak*, the large, thin, round, unleavened break baked in a *tanour*, or oven, popular for *shawarma* sandwiches (some villages may still only have a communal *tanour* where people carry their bread and dishes to be cooked); *ka'ik tawil*, which is a long, hard loaf; bread-rings sprinkled with sesame seeds, known as *ka'ik bilsimsim; khoubz* and *margoug*, the typical flat, unleavened bread, sometimes 40 centimetres in diameter and considered the best bread to have with *mansaf*. Then there is *taboun*, a bread cooked by less affluent people, being thick, leavened and baked on hot rocks, which is why the base is uneven. Many shops in England sell a variation of this flat bread, known as *pitta*.

Probably the most famous feature of Middle Eastern food is the Lebanese *mazza*, or hors d'oeuvres, which is served in restaurants throughout Jordan.

A *mazza* consists of many small appetisers, both simple and elaborate foods, eaten either hot or cold. A *mazza* may be eaten as an accompaniment to drink (when it is normally arak), as an hors d'oeuvres, or as a meal in itself. Recipes for some of the most popular appetisers appear at the end of this chapter. Other delicacies are cold stuffed vine leaves, fried calves' liver, white cheese, black olives, radishes, artichoke hearts, stuffed spleen, brains drenched in a lemon and olive oil dressing and fried bean rissoles, or *falafel*.

Some restaurants offer a house speciality with the *mazza*. I particularly enjoyed *qusa*, a purée of grilled courgettes, lemon juice and yoghurt at the Abu Ahmed Restaurant in Amman. *Kishki*, laban mixed with chopped walnuts and olive oil and sprinkled with *sumak*, was another interesting dish at the *Semi Ramis* in Aqaba. Crisply grilled chicken wings with lemon juice sauce was also a novelty at the Oasis Restaurant in Amman.

Taken with bread, soup is often a meal in itself; but broadly speaking soups are not popular. A reason is probably the rich sauces that frequently accompany a main course such as *mahshi*, or *mansaf*. Soups made from lentils, meat and vegetables and *frieka*, made from cracked, smoked green wheat, are most common, especially in the towns of the east bank escarpment.

Fish is a rarity, although no doubt when Jordan had a Mediterranean access it was a popular dish. The very good Lebanese House in Jerash serves freshwater bream from Lake Tiberias. In Aqaba, the Basman Garden serves fresh fish and chips, *faridi*, a type of local bream, being recommended. The Aquamarina restaurant also serves Aqaba fish. A recipe appears at the end of this chapter for fish cooked in a typically Middle Eastern manner.

Experts say there are more than 500 different ways of cooking chicken in the Middle East, of which *shishtaouk* and *musakhan* are especially popular in Jordan. The chef at the Amman Holiday Inn supplied his recipe for *shishtaouk*. *Musakhan* is chicken, steamed in a sauce of olive oil, onions and *sumak* (see list of spices and herbs later in chapter), then baked on bread layered with more onions and *sumak*. Several Amman restaurants specialise in cooking this very rich dish.

In deference to Jordanians of Circassian descent, there is a recipe for Circassian Chicken. Traditional Circassian cooking has been very little changed, but recipes are closely guarded. Cooks are vague about quantities and cooking times – largely speaking, a common trait throughout the Middle East.

Historically the food of the rich, meat is still considered a luxury by the Bedouin in Jordan. Even today they eat only mutton, or occasionally a young camel. Lamb is the most common dish in urban society although beef is becoming popular. As the majority of Jordanians are Moslems, pork is not seen (although international hotels serve bacon for breakfast).

Meat is usually grilled, or cooked in a casserole. Like poultry, it is usually marinated, both to tenderise and to absorb other flavours. A local habit is to add coriander fried with garlic to almost every meat and vegetable recipe. A small wooden pestle and mortar used solely for grinding this mixture, known as a *taklia*, is kept in every kitchen.

Shawarma – slices of lamb layered on a vertical spit and rotated on a grill – is a great favourite. It is eaten plain, in bread, or with chopped parsley, onion and tomato. Restaurants sometimes have a *shawarma* positioned by their door,

Meshwi, grilled meats, are also popular with the best known probably shishkebab or meat on skewers. Cafés in Qatranah and Ma'an sell them, a tasty snack during the long drive to Aqaba.

The Jordanians have a passion for minced meat dishes of an endless variety and cooks can develop a reputation for their skill in preparing the delicate shells of *kubbeh*, minced meat and *burghul*, or cracked wheat. Mincing machines and electric blenders make easy work of mincing today, but kneading and repeated mincing is the key to success. Amman hotels invariably include a *kubbeh* in their Friday lunchtime buffet. *Kubbeh* served with yoghurt is a Jordanian speciality, especially in Kerak.

Mahshi is the mainstay of the Jordanian cuisine. The most common vegetables used are eggplants, courgettes and marrows stuffed with a filling of minced meat, rice, onions and spices. A *mahshi* is an economical dish to make, if rather elaborate to prepare, but the advantage is that it can be chilled, then re-heated in the rich sauce just prior to serving.

At the other end of the scale are the lavish dinners, more like feasts, on occasions such as weddings, circumcisions and religious holidays. Such elaborate dishes usually mean extravagant recipes: one given to me called for a whole roast lamb to be rubbed with a pound of salt and a pound of butter. The stuffing required a pound of pine-nuts!

Jordan's national dish is the Bedouin *mansaf*, meaning 'the large tray', or dish, on which this traditional desert repast is served. A vast communal dinner, the *mansaf* consists of chunks of stewed lamb, rice, bread and *jameed* (a dried yoghurt made of sheep's milk crushed, then melted and poured over the food).

Preparing a *mansaf* whilst squatting in a tent is one thing, but it can be accomplished in the kitchen if one uses one's imagination. *Jameed* is one of the few ingredients that is not obtainable in England or America, since it is made from sheep's milk yoghurt that has been rolled in a ball and dried for one, even two years. Although it is much richer than normal yoghurt, a reasonable substitute is obtained by stabilising plain yoghurt (as described in the recipe for *Kubbeh bil-laban*). The best *mansafs* in Jordan are said to come from Salt and Kerak.

Following *mansaf, fatir* is a popular people's food, consisting of unleavened bread soaked in yoghurt and topped with *samn'a balqawiah*, a fat made from unclarified butter normally made from sheep's milk. Typical of Balqa Province, though perhaps not for Western taste, *fatir* is a warm, sustaining dish on a cold winter's night.

'Vegetables in the Middle East do not play second fiddle as "two veg" to meat in England', writes Claudia Roden, in *A Book of Middle Eastern Food*. 'They hold a dignified ... position in the hierarchy of food ... in turn, *mazza*, pickles and salads. They can be stuffed and ranked as a main course....'

The most common vegetables are: tomatoes, okra, cabbage, cauliflower, potatoes, string beans, onions, peppers, cucumbers, lettuce, eggplants and marrows.

Rice is also a basic side dish, the long-grained variety being most popular, while for *mansaf*, Italian or Egyptian rice with its high starch content is preferred.

Perhaps the most exotic foods are the Arab pastries and desserts. Jordan does not have a typical sweet since pastries such as the honey and nut *baklava* are eaten all over the Middle East, particularly in Lebanon and Syria. Also popular is *eish assaraya*, a special sweet filled with bread, cream and pistachios. Another, *kataif*, much in demand during Ramadan, is like a pancake, made of the thin Greek philo pastry, stuffed with cheese or nuts and triple cream. There is also the famous creamy *knaffeh* which comes from Nablus. *Ghrabieh* are pine-nut biscuits cooked at festive periods such as Easter and Christmas.

The rich desserts *ma'mounia* and *muhallabia* are basically Syrian specialities, although they appear in Jordanian cooking. The basis of many desserts is ground rice, or semolina. Chopped, ground and whole nuts, usually almonds, walnuts and pistachios, are common ingredients. Flavourings are orange and rose water. *Muhallabia* is found on dessert trolleys of all good Jordanian restaurants and the recipe is given here. A smooth blend of subtle flavours, it is easy to make and palatable at any time of the year.

On occasions during my travels, I have been delighted by different dishes, only to be disappointed when I could not find the recipe. This is why I have listed some of Jordan's best-loved dishes – all of which I have tested in my own home. With the exception of *sumak*, all the ingredients are obtainable. The following is also a handy alphabetical list of spices and herbs, to enable people to buy them fresh locally:

Bagdonis	parsley	*Rihan*	basil
Simsim	sesame seed	*Shomar*	stems of the root
Fil-fil	pepper		fennel
Girfe	cinnamon	*Sumak*	red coloured,
Hasal ban	rosemary		lemon-tasting,
Zaatar	thyme		almost crystalline
Jawz al-tib	nutmeg		spice which comes
Kamoun	cumin		from seed husks
Krunful	cloves	*Tarkhoun*	tarragon
Miramieh	sage	*Thoom*	garlic
Nanaa	mint	*Yansoun*	anis
		Usfur	Indian saffron

Hors d'Oeuvres *(Mazza)*

Six of the most popular dishes served in a *mazza* are:

tabbouleh (mint, burghul, parsley and tomato salad)
hommous (chick pea and sesame seed dip)
babagannouj (eggplant and *tahini*, or sesame seed paste)
salata fil-fil (green pepper salad)
salata bi-laban (cucumber and yoghurt salad)
kubbeh nayeh (minced raw meat fingers and soaked burghul).

In the following recipes the cup is equivalent to ¼ pint (142 ml), and the conversions for the weights and measures are approximate.

Hommous

500 g (1 lb 2 oz) whole chick peas
1 tsp. (5 ml) bicarbonate of soda
Crushed garlic clove
½ cup (70 ml) tahini (sesame seed paste)
3 tbsp. (45 ml) fresh lemon juice
1 tbsp. (15 ml) olive oil
Salt, paprika, parsley

Soak the chick peas overnight. Drain, add bicarbonate of soda and cover with water in a pressure-cooker. Steam for about 20 minutes (1–1½ hours in a saucepan). Drain and shell, putting aside 6 peas to use as a garnish. Using the juice, reduce the rest to a purée in a blender. Add the crushed, salted garlic and finally the tahini, blending constantly. Lastly add the lemon juice, by which time the *hommous* should have a rich, creamy consistency. Tip into a shallow concave dish (about the size of a side plate), pour a pool of olive oil into the centre and garnish with the extra chick peas. Sprinkle a little paprika and chopped parsley as a decoration around the rim of the dish. *Hommous* should be served at room temperature as a dip, with warmed Arab bread. It is also a tasty accompaniment to kebabs.

Serves about six.

Tabbouleh

1 cup of fine *burghul*
½ cup diced cucumber
3 tbsp. finely chopped onion (spring onion is best)
1 cup diced fresh tomato
1½ cups finely chopped parsley
½ cup fresh mint
3 tbsp. (45 ml) olive oil
3 tbsp. (45 ml) lemon juice
Salt and pepper to taste

Soak the *burghul* in cold water for about an hour prior to preparing the salad. Drain, squeeze out the moisture and spread on a cloth. Now mix the *burghul* with the chopped onions, ensuring the onion juices penetrate the grains. Add the parsley, mint, tomatoes, cucumber, lemon juice and olive oil. Add salt and pepper to taste. The salad should have a distinctive lemon flavour. Serve on a dish the size of a side plate (glass is attractive). Decorate the centre with a slice of tomato and several black olives. The salad is eaten scooped up with a fork, or in fresh lettuce leaves, served in a separate dish beside it.

Serves six.

Babagannouj

1 large, or two medium-sized eggplants
½ cup (70 ml) *tahini* (sesame seed paste)
½ cup (70 ml) lemon juice
2 tbsp. chopped parsley
2 garlic cloves chopped
Salt

It is most important to slit the skins of the eggplants to enable steam to escape. Cook slowly under the grill until their skins are crisp and beginning to crack. Remove and allow to cool, then peel, squeezing out as much of the bitter juice as possible. Crush the garlic with salt. Place the eggplant pulp in a blender, blend for one minute, then add *tahini*, lemon juice, garlic and salt, and continue blending. Cold water when added to the *tahini* will give it a whiter colour, as desired. More lemon juice and salt can be added, according to taste. Serve the creamy dip in a shallow, concave plate. Make a pool of olive oil in the centre and garnish with a black olive. It is eaten with bread as a dip.

Serves six.

Salata Fil-Fil

4 medium sized green peppers
⅓ cup (45 ml) fresh lemon juice
Dash of vinegar
½ cup (70 ml) olive oil
Salt to taste
1 clove crushed garlic

Remove seeds from the peppers, quarter lengthways and cook under the grill until the edges are brown and crisp. Make up the sauce with the remaining ingredients and when the peppers are cool, drench them with it on a medium sized plate. Garnish with one or two black olives.

Serves about four.

Salata Khiar Bil-Laban

454 g (1 lb) carton yoghurt
3 cucumbers
1 tsp. salt
2 cloves garlic
1 tsp. dried mint leaves

Stir yoghurt until smooth. Crush and blend in the garlic. Wash and slice cucumbers (leaving the skin on for colour), and add to mixture. Salt, and serve in a salad bowl sprinkled with the dried mint.

Serves about six.

Kubbeh Nayeh

454 g (1 lb) minced lamb (prime quality)
1 large onion
Cup fine *burghul*
Salt and black pepper

Adding salt and pepper, mince the meat several more times at home. Pound the onion and mix well into the meat, adding 1–2 tbsp. (15–30 ml) cold water to achieve a smooth texture. Meanwhile, rinse the *burghul* in a sieve and squeeze out the moisture. Add this to the minced meat and knead vigorously. The secret of *kubbeh nayeh* is to obtain the finest mixture possible, so it is necessary to put it through the mincer several more times.

Now take small portions of the meat and roll into small fingers between the palms. Place them all, side by side, on a glass plate and splash evenly with a little olive oil and lemon. *Kubbeh nayeh* is usually served with a bowl of young lettuce; it can also sit on a bed of lettuce leaves.

An advantage is that it can be prepared and refrigerated prior to serving.

Serves about six.

Shourabat Al-Kebab Bil Riz (Feastday Soup)

454 g (1 lb) minced lamb
¼ cup of rice (or vermicelli)
1 medium onion
1 tbsp. chopped parsley
1 tbsp. (15 ml) fresh lemon juice
Cinnamon, salt and pepper

Season the mince well and either knead, or put through a mincer. Chop onion very finely and knead into the mixture. Wetting the hands, roll the meat into marble-sized balls. Boil the rice in about 8 cups (1¼ litres) of water, reduce heat and add the meat-balls, plus lemon juice, cooking for about 15 minutes. Remove from heat and leave to stand about 30 minutes. Re-heat prior to serving, dot with butter and sprinkle with parsley. For variation, tomato purée can be added.

These quantities are sufficient for about four bowls, but more water may be added during cooking if more soup is required.

Shourabat Addas (Lentil Soup)

2 tbsp. butter
1 large finely chopped onion
1 large cup red lentils
1½ litres (2¾ pints) meat stock
1 tbsp. (15 ml) lemon juice
2 tbsp. (30 ml) olive oil
1 tsp. ground cumin
Salt and pepper

Fry onion in a large saucepan until transparent. Add the lentils and stir until glossy, then pour in the stock, add the cumin and simmer until almost disintegrated (1 hour or more, depending on the age of the lentils and whether they have been soaked). When the lentils are cooked, add the salt and pepper and allow to cool. Now put the soup through an electric blender, return to the stove and bring to boiling point. Add olive oil and finally add the lemon juice. Decorate with croutons of bread fried in butter and crushed garlic. Sprinkle with a little fresh parsley.

Serves four.

Vegetable Soup

454 g (1 lb) cubed stewing beef
1 large onion, finely sliced
1 large potato, sliced
1 red pepper, seeded and sliced
2 carrots, sliced
1 cup white cabbage, shredded
1 tbsp. (15 ml) tomato purée
2 tbsp. (30 ml) olive oil
1 tsp. dill
¼ cup (35 ml) tarragon vinegar
Salt and pepper
2 litres (3½ pints) bouillon (or meat extract)

Heat the oil in a large saucepan and fry the onion until lightly browned. Add the meat, shaking frequently to prevent sticking. Now add the vegetables and cook for about five minutes. Finally add the stock, tomato purée and seasoning. Simmer gently over a low heat for about 2 hours. Allow to cool and scrape off any fat. Heat again. During the last few minutes add the vinegar and the dill and sprinkle with parsley.

Serves six.

Shishtaouk (Chicken in lemon juice)

Although not strictly a Jordanian dish, this item features on the menu of most hotels.

1 chicken weighing about 1½ kilos (3 lb) or two smaller chickens – boned and cut in cubes
2 medium sized onions, sliced
½ cup (70 ml) lemon juice
1 tsp. salt
½ tsp. pepper
3 cloves garlic, crushed
Pinch paprika

Marinate chicken with all the other ingredients for 12 hours. Melt some butter in a saucepan and sauté the chicken adding ½ cup (70 ml) water, or a little more lemon juice, as necessary. Press down and cover the chicken, allowing to simmer about 30 minutes, or until the flesh is tender. Serve garnished with parsley. (If the sauce is too thin, mix a little cornflour paste and add to the saucepan with a dash more paprika.)

Serves four.

Circassian Chicken

1 chicken weighing about 1½ kilos (3 lb)
1 cup milk
1 clove garlic
2 stalks celery
125 g (5 oz) walnuts
2 tbsp. (30 ml) oil
1 tsp. paprika
454 g (1 lb) *burghul* (crushed wheat)
2 tbsp. butter
1 tbsp. plain flour

Place the bird in a saucepan, add garlic, celery, salt and pepper, cover with water and bring to the boil, simmering about one hour, or until the chicken is tender. Remove and drain, allowing the stock to cool and scooping off the fat as it settles. Cut the chicken into reasonably sized serving portions.

For the sauce, pound the nuts and place in a clean pan. Now sieve 250 ml (about ½ pint) of stock into the pan and bring it to the boil, stirring constantly, adding flour and milk to thicken. Season with salt as necessary. Mix the paprika with the oil until it is bright red.

To serve, arrange the warm chicken pieces in a ring of boiled *burghul*, pour the nut sauce over both, and garnish with a trickle of the red oil.

Serves four.

Samak Bi-Tahini (Fish baked in sesame seed paste)

Ideally a whole rock fish to bake weighing 1 kilo (just over 2 lb), or fillets according to the number of guests
1 tbsp. (15 ml) olive oil
⅓ cup (45 ml) lemon juice
½ cup (70 ml) water
½ cup (70 ml) *tahini*
1 cup chopped onions
Salt and pepper
Parsley for garnish

Rub the fish with salt, pepper and olive oil, then place in greased foil in a baking dish. Cook about 15 minutes in a moderate oven until the flesh is flaky. Add the water and lemon juice to the *tahini*, mixing it into a paste. Gently fry the onion in the remaining oil, then sprinkle it over the fish. Pour the *tahini* over the fish and bake a further 10–15 minutes in opened foil. Garnish with parsley and serve with boiled rice and a salad.

Serves four.

Bamiyeh (Okra Stew)

3 tbsp. (45 ml) cooking oil, or vegetable fat
1 kilo (just over 2 lb) lamb, cubed
3 small garlic cloves, sliced
¾ kilo (1 lb 6 oz) young okra
250 g (9 oz) ripe tomatoes, sliced (or use a 454 g (1 lb) tin, including the juice)
2 cups (284 ml) of stock
1 tsp. ground coriander
2 tbsp. (30 ml) lemon juice
Salt and pepper

Wipe okra and carefully remove stems. Fry the garlic and coriander, until transparent. Add the meat, browning well. Now add the okra and fry gently. Next add the tomatoes, allow to simmer for 5 minutes, then cover with the stock. Season with salt and pepper, stir slowly bringing the stew to boiling point, then simmer on a low flame for 1–2 hours. By this time the meat should be tender and the sauce rich (dilute with water, if it is too thick). Finally add the lemon juice and serve hot, with rice.

Serves six.

Moujaddara

This is a common dish, cheap to buy and easy to prepare. It is very filling.

1 cup of lentils
½ cup rice
2 cups chopped onions
½ tsp. salt
½ cup (70 mls) olive oil

Steam lentils for five minutes in a pressure-cooker. Mix with the rice and steam a further five minutes. Meanwhile, brown one cup of onions in the oil and add to the rice and lentils. Brown the remaining onions (margarine can be used instead of oil) and garnish with this and fresh parsley. Moujaddara can be eaten hot, or lukewarm with a green salad, or laban.

Serves about four.

Kubbeh Bi-Laban (Meat balls in yoghurt sauce)

Prepare *kubbeh* according to the recipe for *kubbeh nayeh*, except that the meat balls should be rolled the size of large walnuts and stuffed with a mixture of fried onions and pine nuts.

Yoghurt Sauce:

1 litre (1¾ pints) yoghurt
1 tbsp. cornflour
3 cloves garlic, crushed
2 tbsp. dried crushed mint
3 tbsp. butter
Salt

Fry the *kubbeh* balls in oil so that the outside is very crisp and brown, but the inside tender.

To stabilise the yoghurt as a sauce, pour into a large saucepan and beat until it becomes liquid. Mix the cornflour in a light paste and add to the yoghurt with a pinch of salt. Bring to just below boiling point, stirring continuously with a wooden spoon in the same direction. Stir for ten minutes on the lowest heat, until the sauce is a rich consistency. Do not cover the pan, or overheat the contents. The yoghurt can now be mixed and cooked with other ingredients without danger of curdling.

Now fry the crushed garlic in butter, add mint and mix well into the yoghurt. Finally return the meat balls to the mixture and heat; serve with plain boiled rice. *Kubbeh bi-laban* may also be eaten cold.

Serves about four.

Kufta Bis-Sayniyyeh

Translated this means 'hamburger in the pan'.

680 g (about 1½ lb) minced lamb
4 medium sized potatoes
2 medium sized diced onions
454 g (1 lb) fresh tomatoes (remove skins)
2 tbsp. tomato paste
2 tbsp. fresh parsley
1 tbsp. fresh mint
Salt and pepper to taste
Butter

Ideally the meat should be put through a mincer. Parboil the potatoes so they are firm, but half-cooked, setting one aside as a final garnish. Mix the meat, onions, parsley and seasoning to taste. Spread down firmly in a buttered baking dish 23 cm × 30 cm (9 in × 12 in). Place the potatoes and onions over the flattened meat, then layers of tomatoes, and diluted tomato purée over the pan. Add salt and pepper as desired. Sprinkle the top with mint and dot with butter. Bake for 30 minutes in a medium-hot oven. Garnish with the extra sliced potato and cook a further 15 minutes until it is brown and crisp.

Serves four.

Kufta bis-Sayniyyeh can be served as a main course accompanied by cold cooked green beans, with a lemon, olive oil and garlic dressing. Other suggestions for salads are shredded cabbage using the same dressing, or lettuce, cucumber, radish and green peppers with lemon and olive oil.

Sheikh El-Mahshi (Eggplant stuffed with meat)

8 small cylindrical eggplants
250 g (9 oz) finely minced lamb, or beef
⅓ cup pine nuts
½ tsp. salt
1 tsp. allspice
3 tbsp. tomato paste
3 medium size chopped onions
2 tbsp. butter

Wash the eggplants, trimming the stems, but leaving the fruits whole. Peel in alternate strips, leaving some skin on them since this acts as a binder during the cooking. Fry them whole in hot fat, and drain. Gently fry the meat, pine-nuts, chopped onions and season. While this is cooking, make a lengthwise slit in each eggplant. When the mince mixture is cool, press some filling into each one, and arrange the eggplants in an oven-proof dish. Blend the tomato paste with water to just cover the eggplants. Bake in a medium oven for 30 minutes, when the sauce should be thick. *Sheikh al-mahshi* may be served with rice.

Serves six.

Kebabs (Lamb or beef grilled on skewers)

Allow about 250 g (½ lb) meat per person which should make up two skewers.

Choose a good cut of meat – cheap stewing steak will not do. Cut into cubes, about an inch square, and rub with salt, pepper, lemon juice, olive oil and marjoram. Impale on skewers and cook under the grill.

Most countries use lamb in preference to beef, since it is cheaper. In either case, chunks of green pepper, onion and thick wedges of tomato can be interspersed with the meat.

Similarly, halved kidneys previously marinated in a mixture of two parts olive oil to one part lemon juice, seasoned with salt and pepper, make a delicious *kebab*.

Hommous can be used as a side dip. The *kebabs* may be eaten with salad, or plain boiled rice, according to taste.

Serve whilst still on the skewers, on a bed of watercress and with wedges of lemon.

Kharouf Bi Lamoun (Roast lamb in lemon juice)

Again, although this is not strictly a Jordanian dish, it is a great favourite.

1 medium sized leg of lamb (a shoulder will do for fewer guests), well seasoned
1 large cup of yoghurt
½ cup (70 ml) fresh lemon juice, plus rind
3 garlic cloves, sliced
Olive oil

Stick garlic slivers in the joint and sear in oil in a hot oven. Cool slightly, then pour over the lemon juice and rind, plus half the yoghurt. Bake in a moderately hot oven at first, then reduce the heat to low after about 15 minutes. Keep adding the remaining yoghurt bit by bit. Add half a cup of water if the lemon juice dries up. Turn meat once only, then allow the yoghurt to form a crust. Cooking time, depending on the size of the joint, about 1½–2 hours.

Serve with plain boiled potatoes, a tomato and lettuce salad, or a green bean salad.

A leg serves six.

Lahmi Bis-Saniyyeh (Braised chops and vegetables)

8–10 fleshy chump chops
1 large onion, sliced
2–3 cloves garlic, chopped
6 ripe tomatoes
Salt and pepper
Sliced marrow, courgette, beans or whatever vegetables desired
1 tbsp. chopped parsley

Trim chops of excess fat, and brown in hot butter on both sides. Remove and place in greased baking dish. Sweat the onion and the garlic (adding a pinch of coriander to taste). Then add the tomatoes, salt and pepper and half the parsley. Simmer for 10 minutes, then add ½ cup (70 ml) of water. Mix this well into the sauce. Place the sliced vegetables on top of the chops, then drench with the sauce mixture. Add more seasoning as desired. Cook until the chops are tender, the vegetables are ready and the sauce is aromatic. Garnish with the rest of the parsley. Serve with a green salad.

Serves about four.

Malfouf (Stuffed cabbage leaves)

1 cabbage head which should be boiled to separate leaves
³/₄ kilo (about 1¹/₂ lb) minced shoulder of lamb
Several lamb bones, or a shank
3 cups rice
3 garlic cloves
Butter or margarine
¹/₂ cup (70 ml) lemon juice
Salt and pepper, allspice, cloves

Mix the semi-cooked rice with the butter and mince, and season with the spices. Cut the core out of the cabbage and separate the leaves. Place each leaf on a wooden board, arrange about a tablespoon of mixture in it, then roll firmly into a cigar shape. Repeat this procedure using all the leaves, or until there is no filling left. In the base of a large pot arrange the stuffed leaves, placing garlic between the rows and leaving one or two loose cloves. Place a dish on top of the rolls to keep them flattened down and add water, or stock, to cover. Finally add more salt to taste and cook 30–50 minutes in a medium oven. *Malfouf* can be served with a side dish of yoghurt.

Serves four to six.

Bedouin Mansaf

1 whole lamb
2 kilos (4 lb 6 oz) rice
20 pieces Arab bread (variety *khubz mashrouh*)
1 kilo (2lb 3 oz) *jameed* (or subsitute yoghurt)
¹/₄ kilo (¹/₂ lb) clarified butter, or margarine
¹/₄ kilo (¹/₂ lb) pine-nuts
Salt, pepper, allspice, cardamom

Cook the lamb in pieces in a small amount of water together with spices, until the meat is half done. Add the cooked yoghurt and simmer until tender. Add the browned butter, reserving a small quantity to brown the pine-nuts. Meanwhile in another large saucepan, cook the rice. Keeping some bread aside as a dip, break open the rest over a large tray, leaving an edging around the rim. Spread more of the yoghurt sauce over this and pile with rice. Arrange the pieces of lamb on top of the rice. The Bedouin decorate the *mansaf* with the cooked head of the lamb whose brain, tongue and eyeball muscles are considered delicacies to be offered to honoured guests. Sprinkle the entire bed of rice and lamb with the cooked pine-nuts. Western taste might prefer to leave out the head and garnish with chopped parsley. The remaining yoghurt is passed around as a dip with the bread. It is also drunk in side glasses.

Serves eight to ten.

Muhallabia (Ground rice pudding)

1 tbsp. cornflour
3 tbsp. ground rice
1.13 litres (2 pints) milk
6 tbsp. of sugar
1 tbsp. (15 ml) rose-water (or orange-water)
1 cup ground almonds
Chopped almonds, or pistachios and freshly grated nutmeg to garnish

Using a little of the milk, mix the cornflour and the ground rice to a smooth paste. Add the sugar to the rest of the milk and slowly bring to the boil adding the paste and stirring constantly with a wooden spoon. Simmer the mixture, taking care it does not stick on the bottom of the saucepan – a burnt taste will spoil the delicate flavour of the *muhallabia*. After 10–15 minutes, the mixture should have thickened, signifying it is cooked.

Now add the rose-water or orange-water, plus the ground almonds, blending well on a low heat. Allow to simmer a few minutes, then remove from the stove and allow to cool slightly. Pour the mixture into a large glass bowl, or in individual glass dishes. Decorate with slivers of almonds or pistachios and a hint of nutmeg, then chill well. *Muhallabia* requires 3–4 hours to chill properly.

Serves six.

Ma'Mounia (a rich dessert made from semolina)

3½ cups (½ l.) water
1 tsp. (5 ml) lemon juice
1 cup of semolina
3 cups of sugar
112 g (¼ lb) unsalted butter
1 tsp. ground cinnamon
3–4 tbsp. double cream

Boil together the water, sugar and lemon juice, allowing to simmer for 10–15 minutes until the mixture has thickened. Gently fry the semolina in the butter for 5–10 minutes then add the syrup, stirring well with a wooden spoon. Let the pan sit on a low flame for several minutes then remove it and leave to rest for 15 minutes. Sprinkle the warm dessert with the cinnamon, then cover with the cream. Serve in this fashion, slightly cool on top and warm underneath.

Serves four.

Chapter Nine

East Jerusalem and the West Bank

Although East Jerusalem and the West Bank of the River
Jordan are under Israeli occupation, many tourists take
the opportunity to visit the Holy Land.

People who are not travelling with a group can take a
private or a shared taxi from Amman to Jordanian control, about five kilometres from the King Hussein Bridge.

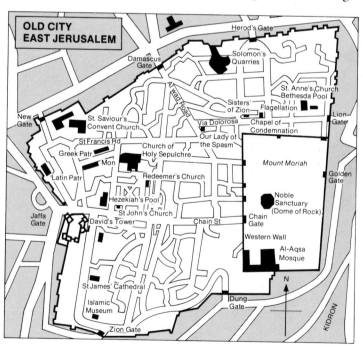

OLD CITY EAST JERUSALEM

Herod's Gate
Solomon's Quarries
Damascus Gate
St. Anne's Church
Bethesda Pool
Al Wad Road
Sisters' of Zion
Flagellation
New Gate
St. Saviour's Convent Church
Via Dolorosa
Chapel of Condemnation
Lion Gate
St Francis Rd
Our Lady of the Spasm
Greek Patr
Church of Holy Sepulchre
Mon
Mount Moriah
Latin Patr
Redeemer's Church
Golden Gate
Hezekiah's Pool
Noble Sanctuary (Dome of Rock)
St John's Church
Jaffa Gate
David's Tower
Chain St
Chain Gate
Western Wall
Al-Aqsa Mosque
St James' Cathedral
N
Islamic Museum
Dung Gate
Zion Gate
KIDRON

Following exit formalities, one then catches a bus a further 2 kilometres to a final control post on the river bank. Amman is only 40 minutes' drive from the bridge, but as Israeli entry procedures are slow, people are advised to leave the Jordanian capital by 7 o'clock in order to arrive in the West Bank by noon.

Having crossed the bridge, it is a good idea to have lunch in the attractive al-Rawda Park Garden restaurant in nearby Jericho. Following a tour of Jericho, one can visit the Qumran Caves, then travel on to Jerusalem, arriving at dusk.

Jericho sits like an emerald in a bowl of barren hills, the semi-tropical vegetation thriving on water from historic sources such as 'Elijah's Spring' which Elijah is said to have sweetened by casting in a handful of salt (2 Kings 2:21).

Huge flame trees, or *Poinciana regia*, shade the streets where traders sit outside their stores on stools, chatting and drinking coffee. Only the fruiterers seem to do a brisk

The River Jordan, setting of many Biblical events, flows slowly into the Dead Sea

business. When a coach halts, they spring into action, polishing melons and pressing glasses of orange-juice which tourists stand drinking in the road. Dates are a good buy; the date industry in Jericho is older than the Bible.

Archaeologists consider Jericho to be one of the oldest continuously inhabited sites in the world, settled from 8–7,000 BC. One excavation at Tell es-Sultan has exposed a Neolithic watch-tower. Joshua's attack on Jericho when the priests blew their trumpets and the 'walls came tumbling down' is well chronicled in the Bible (Josh. 6). Verse 21 records that having gained an entry to the city, the Jews then '... utterly destroyed all there was ... both man and woman, young and old, and ox, and sheep, and ass, with the edge of the sword'. The summit of the *tell* overlooks the forlorn refugee-camps of Jericho, vacated when the Palestinians fled in 1967 – many for a second time – to the east bank of the River Jordan.

Five kilometres north of Jericho are the ruins of an Ummayad Palace, built as a rural residence for the Caliph Ibn Abdul Malik (AD 724–742).

The excavations give a clear idea of the lay-out of the palace which was destroyed by an earthquake before completion. The complex is entered by ante-rooms with seats cut in the walls where visitors waited to be summoned. There are ruins of a colonnaded court and an audience hall, two small mosques and baths. Overlooking the baths is a chamber where the Caliph used to retire. Its floor is covered by one of the world's most beautiful mosaics. Known as the 'Tree of Life', it is an allegorical representation of a tree heavy with fruit and a lion savaging a gazelle. Close examination of some of the rose-coloured columns reveals the presence of Byzantine crosses indicating that they were filched as building material from former churches. The Hisham Palace is open daily, from 8.00–17.00 hours, and a charge is made for admission.

West of here is the stark aspect of the Mount of Temptation where Jesus resisted the devil for 40 days and 40 nights (Matt. 4:8–9). There is a Greek monastery half-way up and on the summit the ruins of a fort dating from 160 BC. Flat-topped and wind-swept, the mountain overlooks the deceptively beautiful waters of the Dead Sea.

The 30-kilometre road-trip south of Jericho to the Qumran Caves runs parallel to the Dead Sea, then swings into the escarpment.

The story of the Bedouin shepherd who found the Dead Sea Scrolls in 1947 is well known. Wandering with his goats, he abstractedly tossed a stone into one of the caves. Hearing pottery shatter he investigated, and discovered the scrolls rolled inside earthenware jars, which had been hidden by a community of Essene monks fleeing from the Roman legions. It is not surprising that the scrolls were not found for nearly 2,000 years, since the area, in the Judaean Hills, is dry, deeply eroded, unsuited to grazing and uninhabited, even by the Bedouin.

East Jerusalem was captured from Jordan in 1967. Its population of about 80,000 is mainly Moslem with a Christian minority.

Situated at an altitude of 755 metres, the city's climate is affected by the eastern desert and prevailing Mediterranean breezes. The eastern slopes of the Judaean Hills (the western upthrust of the rift valley depression) lie in a rain shadow, with most rain falling during the winter months. Snowfalls are not uncommon. Summer temperatures reach 37 °C in the shade although, as in Amman, there is an appreciable drop at night.

Driving up from Jericho as the sun sets behind the Old City ramparts is a sight to behold. Whilst still far off, one can see the Tower of Ascension on the Mount of Olives. Sea-level is passed about half-way from Jericho, and as one drives through the Kidron Valley, the evening prayer-call echoes from the great al-Aqsa Mosque.

East Jerusalem sleeps early since most tourists are tired from sightseeing. There are several good hotels within walking distance of the Old City. The National Palace is a clean, well-run establishment with a good restaurant.

An alternative place to stay is on the Mount of Olives. While I consider it is more convenient to have lodgings near the Old City, few experiences compare to awakening in the Inter-Continental Hotel overlooking Jerusalem. Early rising tourists are also greeted by a shrewd old 'camel man' who plods up from the Kidron Valley to be photographed against the stunning backdrop of the Holy City. A stroll from the hotel is the Garden of Gethsemane, where an order of Franciscan monks tend the flower-beds divided by hedges of pungent rosemary.

In the gardens, facing the Golden Gate across the Kidron Valley, is the Church of the Agony, built over the spot where Jesus is believed to have spent His last night, praying and waiting for His arrest.

Also known as the 'Church of All Nations', it displays twelve cupolas and is noted for a superb mosaic above the altar depicting Jesus kneeling on 'the rock of agony'. A shrine was first built on the site by the Byzantines in AD 380. In the churchyard are eight olive trees. Twisted and gnarled with time, they are held to be cuttings of trees growing in the Garden of Gethsemane during the life of Christ. Towering above is the beautiful Russian Church of Mary Magdalene, its seven golden onion domes gleaming in the sun. Built in 1888 by Czar Alexander III, the church enshrines members of the Russian royal family.

Nearby is the white chapel called Dominus Flevit where Jesus is supposed to have wept for Jerusalem whilst riding in to the city on a donkey on Palm Sunday (Luke 19:41). Other important shrines in the area are the Dome of the Ascension and the Pater Noster Church.

The Crusaders enshrined what was believed to be the site of Christ's ascension with a small, open, polygonal chapel. The Moslems covered it with the traditional Islamic cupola and it has been since known as the Dome of the Ascension.

The Pater Noster Church occupies the place where Jesus is said to have forewarned His disciples of the forthcoming destruction of Jerusalem and the beginning of the New

Kingdom (Matt. 24). In one of the cloisters, the Lord's Prayer is set in tiles in fifty different languages. In 1868, the Princesse de la Tour d'Auvergne commissioned a church and a Carmelite Convent for the holy site.

Easily accessible for people staying on the Mount of Olives, its most noticeable landmark is the soaring Gothic spire over the Russian convent. It is widely held that this tower, the Tower of Ascension, marks the true place where Christ ascended into Heaven. The convent is known for stirring masses, exquisite examples of mediaeval ecclesiastical music. From the top of the tower – a climb of 214 steps – is a sweeping view back towards the River Jordan.

Excellent views of the Old City are obtained from the surrounding wall, 4 kilometres in length, in part built by Suleiman the Magnificent. The wall encloses the Christian, Moslem, Armenian and Jewish quarters of the Old City and is entered via seven gates: Jaffa Gate, in Arabic *Bab al-Khalil* (Gate of the Friend), the main thoroughfare for traffic into the Old City; Zion Gate, in Arabic *Bab en-Nabi Daoud* (Gate of the Prophet David), giving access to David's tomb; Dung Gate, adjacent to the Western Wall, the exit through which the city's rubbish has been carted since the second century AD; Lion Gate, named for its lion relief, and called *Bab Sittna Miriam* by the Arabs (St. Mary's Gate), leading to the Virgin's tomb; Herod's Gate, named for pilgrims who sought in this vicinity the house of Herod Antipas, from where Jesus was sent to Pilate, facing the commercial centre of East Jerusalem; Damascus Gate, in Arabic *Bab el Amoud* (Gate of the Pillar), named on account of a column depicted in the mosaic map of Jerusalem in Madaba, at the start of the road leading to Damascus; and New Gate, built in 1889 to facilitate Christians access between the Christian Quarter of the Old City and their properties outside the walls. An eighth gate, an elaborate Byzantine structure known as the Golden Gate, has been sealed for the last four centuries.

In order to visit the shrines of the Old City, the most

convenient approach is through the Lion Gate, seeing first the Moslem sanctuaries on Mount Moriah, and then following the Stations of the Cross, along the Via Dolorosa, to the Church of the Holy Sepulchre.

The *Haram esh-Sharif*, or Noble Sanctuary, encloses the two great Moslem shrines – the Dome of the Rock and al-Aqsa Mosque. Christians will find the area no less inspiring since the mosque was pre-dated by Herod's Temple, in the time of Christ. One can picture Jesus as a young boy talking to the priests and elders and later, as a man, driving the money-changers from the temple (Matt. 21:12–13).

Standing in the centre of the terrace is the Dome of the Rock, a great octagonal shrine built over the 'rock', which to different religions signifies different events – Moslems believe that it was from this rock that Mohammed ascended into Heaven.

The shrine was commissioned by Abdul Malak Ibn Marwan, a founder of the Ummayad dynasty in AD 691. Byzantine architects based the design on a fourth-century shrine marking the ascension of Jesus, on the Mount of Olives. During an early renovation of the shrine, the Caliph Mamun erased Malik's name from the foundation plaque, inscribing his own, but neglecting to change the date ...

The huge golden cupola of the Dome of the Rock is actually aluminium bronze alloy, made in Italy. The Quranic inscription on the drum refers to the misdeeds of the Israelites, the Prophet's visit to the mountain and his spiritual ascension into Heaven (Quran, Sura 17:1–7).

Inside the dome is a blaze of red, black and gold stucco while the gold frieze around the base is inscribed with further verses from the Quran. Many of the stained-glass windows set in the drum date from the reign of Suleiman the Magnificent. The floor is strewn with rich Oriental carpets, while crosses seen on some of the marble columns supporting the dome indicate former association with Christian worship.

A severe earthquake in the eleventh century caused the great dome to collapse. The architect responsible for rebuilding it has left a description of a marble balustrade encircling the sacred rock, of silk carpets covering the floor and a ponderous silver candelabrum swinging from the ceiling – this later crashed, but the chain is still to be seen.

In place of the marble balustrade, a high carved wooden balustrade now encircles the sacred rock in the centre of the shrine. A footprint type of indentation in the surface is believed to have been left when Mohammed leapt to Heaven. Tradition says that the rock tried to follow the Prophet, but was restrained by the angel Gabriel, and a second imprint is said to be the palm of the angel who held it back. During the reign of Abdul Malak, fifty-two cleaners were employed to wash the rock with a solution of saffron, musk, rose-water and ambergris. Five thousand lamps were kept burning with tamarisk and jasmine to perfume the mosque. Near the imprint of the foot of the Prophet is a tall shrine decorated with a grill in which, it is said, are relics of the Prophet.

Below the rock is a cave above which is an inscription in Arabic, which translated reads: 'O God, Pardon the sinner who cometh here, and relieve Ye the sick'.

The places of prayer of Elijah, Abraham, David and Solomon are shown within the hollow known to Moslems as the 'Well of Souls', where the dead are supposed to meet twice a year. The cave is small, so it is as well to visit it before too many tourists are about. When I was there, a *khamsin* was buffeting Mount Moriah, the wind sounding like the whisperings of souls awaiting passage to Paradise.

In return for a donation to the shrine, one is sometimes permitted to climb up to the roof. At this height there is a wonderful view of the *Haram esh-Sharif* and other structures of interest; the adjacent silver-domed *al-Aqsa* Mosque, the beautiful *Sabil Qait Bey* Fountain donated by one of the Mameluke sultans, the pagoda-shaped Dome of the Chain, once used by the Arabs as a treasury, and the graceful *minbar*, or pulpit, erected in 1456. In the southern corner of the compound is the entrance to vaulted, sub-terranean passages known as 'Solomon's Stables', which were used as such by both Herod and the Crusaders. The Dome of Ascension, dating from 1200, is a replica of the structure on the Mount of Olives. Elegant arcades stand at the head of the eight stairways leading up to the terrace on which the Dome of the Rock is built. Next to the Islamic Museum, the Mograbi Gate gives access to the Western Wall, thought to be part of the retaining wall of Herod's temple. The Mograbi Gate is the nearest access to *Haram esh-Sharif* from the south, where the beautiful al-Aqsa Mosque is situated.

Although Moslem places of worship vary in the lavish-ness of their embellishments, the atmosphere is always quiet and a sense of humility pervades as people prostrate themselves in prayers.

The ritual begins with the traditional ablutions in a courtyard fountain; then on removing their shoes or san-dals, Moslems enter the mosque for a spiritual cleansing with Allah. What is not generally known is that Moslems allowed Christians freedom of worship, unlike the Crusaders who massacred thousands of Jews, Moslems and even local Christians in Jerusalem.

Al-Aqsa, which means 'the distant place' in relation to Mecca, is, after Mecca and Medina in Saudi Arabia, one of the holiest shrines in Islam. The first mosque on Mount Moriah was built by the Caliph Walid (AD 705–715) but it and subsequent mosques were destroyed by earthquakes: the present building dates from the eleventh century. The distinctive portal with the seven arched doorways dates from the thirteenth century.

Al-Aqsa remained a mosque until Jerusalem was cap-tured by the Crusaders when the Knights Templars made it their headquarters. A century later, following the city's surrender to Saladin, its golden cross was again replaced by the crescent of Islam.

Like the Dome of the Rock, the mosque suffered great damage from earthquakes, but on each occasion it was rebuilt: the Carrera marble columns were a gift from Mussolini, after an earthquake in 1938, and the cost of the lavishly decorated ceiling was born by King Farouk of Egypt. The dome is embellished with silver and mosaic reliefs, while the floor is covered with some of the most beautiful carpets in the Middle East. Measuring 90 metres long by 60 metres wide, the mosque holds 5,000 worshippers for Friday prayers.

The most tragic event associated with al-Aqsa was the assassination, in 1951, of King Abdullah of Trans-Jordan as he was entering the mosque to pray, accompanied by young Prince Hussein. Then in 1969, a deranged Australian set fire to an exquisite pulpit of carved and inlaid cedar of Lebanon, brought by Saladin from Aleppo in 1187.

Non-Moslems are welcome to visit both al-Aqsa and the Dome of the Rock, from 9.00–17.00 hours, except on Friday. A charge is made for admission.

The *Bab al-Silsilal*, or the Chain Gate, is one of ten gates leading off the *Haram esh-Sharif* into the Old City. Others are the Cotton Merchants' Gate, the Iron Gate, the Prison Gate and the Ghawanmeh Gate on the western side of the compound – and on the north, the Gate of Gloom, the Hutta Gate and the Gate of the Tribes. Leaving by the Ghawanmeh Gate, one follows Christendom's most sacred road, the Via Dolorosa, or the 'Street of Sorrow', where Jesus carried the cross to the crucifixion on the hill of Calvary.

Tracing the 'Way of the Cross' sharpens one's image of Jerusalem at the time of Christ as the cobbled street runs beneath arches and winds round churches and chapels through the bazaar district in East Jerusalem. Every Friday, at 15.00 hours, the Franciscan fathers trace Christ's journey accompanied by pilgrims of all denominations, with volunteers taking turns to carry a replica of the cross.

Those who prefer to visit the Stations of the Cross alone will find the Bible is the best guide, but whilst the 'Way of the Cross' is well chronicled in John 19 and Luke 23, the

Tracing the 'Way of the Cross' sharpen's one's image of Jerusalem

Stations where Jesus halted are not specified. Over the centuries, Christians have reached agreement on ten places where Jesus halted along the Via Dolorosa, with a final three being located within the magnificent Church of the Holy Sepulchre, the present basilica dating from the Crusader period, in 1149.

Adjacent to the Ghawanmeh Gate and minaret are the remains of the Antonia Fortress, built by Herod in honour of his friend, Mark Anthony, and destroyed by Titus in AD 70. Within this compound Jesus was tried, mocked and given the cross carved from an olive-tree probably cut in nearby Kidron Valley.

Station I is fixed as the place where el-Omariya School stands in the ruins of the fortress (the starting point for the re-enactment of the 'Way of the Cross'). Christian tradition holds that here Pilate interrogated Jesus, handing Him over to the crowd with the words, *'Ecco Homo'* – behold the Man. John 19 relates how Pilate subsequently washed his hands of Jesus, who was jeered at and crowned with thorns.

Station II, where He received the cross, is marked by the Roman numerals 'II' at the entrance to the Condemnation Chapel, within the Franciscan compound, opposite el-Omariya School. This marks where Jesus was sentenced by Pilate and some of the flagstones inside the chapel are held to be the original pavement. The Chapel of Flagellation stands where it is believed that Jesus was scourged. Beautiful stained-glass windows depict the act of Pilate washing his hands and the triumph of Barabbas:

'. . . will ye therefore that I release unto you the King of the Jews? Then cried they all again, saying, Not this man, but Barabbas. Now Barabbas was a robber.' (John 18:39–40.)

Station III where Jesus fell the first time is marked by a small Polish chapel with a relief of Jesus stumbling, above the entrance portal. At this point, the Via Dolorosa veers left, into el-Wad Street.

Station IV is where Jesus saw His mother among the crowd lining the route. Mosaic footprints within 'Our Lady of Spasm' Armenian church are reputed to mark the actual spot. Here, the Via Dolorosa turns a sharp right.

Station V is where Roman soldiers forced Simon of Cyrene, who was visiting Jerusalem from Libya for the

Passover, to help Jesus carry the cross. It is marked by a nineteenth-century Franciscan oratory.

Beginning the incline to Calvary is Station VI. It was at this point that a woman stepped forward to wipe the sweat and blood off Jesus' face which left an imprint on her cloth. Her name, Saint Veronica, probably stems from the Latin 'true image' – *vera icone*. The famous *veronica* pass made with the magenta coloured cape in the bull-ring comes from this incident. There is a Greek convent on the site.

Station VII is where Jesus fell a second time under the burden of the cross. The site is noted above a doorway in *Souq Khan ez-Zeit* opposite a junction with the Via Dolorosa.

At Station VIII, Jesus addressed a group of wailing women with the words: 'Daughters of Jerusalem, weep not for me, but for yourselves, and your children' (Luke 23:27). A Latin cross cut in the wall of a Greek Orthodox convent marks this site, where Jesus also prophesied the destruction of Jerusalem.

A column built into the doorway of a Coptic Church marks Station IX where Jesus fell a third time.

The final Stations are found within the Church of the Holy Sepulchre (see map): Station X, where Jesus was stripped of His garments (John 19:23), Station XI where He was nailed to the cross (Luke 23:33) and Station XII where He died on the cross (John 19:30). A thirteenth site is where Christ was removed from the cross (Luke 24–53). It is useful to employ a guide to indicate these sites, which are among fifty of Christendom's most sacred shrines within the church.

Many visitors express a disappointment on discovering that the basilica is propped up with steel supports. The church is in need of repair, but although there is no shortage of funds, the different sects relegated to rights have been unable to reach agreement on a procedure for repair. As a result, one is unable to obtain an attractive photograph of the exterior, but flash-lights are permitted, even within the sacrosanct Holy Sepulchre – a small, claustrophobic enclosure containing the marble 'tomb of Christ'.

Throughout the day a colourful pageant of people circulates around the church: prelates of the various religious orders – Latin Catholic, Greek, Copt, Syrian, Armenian and Abyssinian – performing their various rites, and

Throughout the day, prelates of various religious orders perform their rites in the Church of the Holy Sepulchre

179

groups of tourists, listening attentively to the explanations of their guides in half-a-dozen different languages.

Early evening, when the crowds have dispersed, is the best time to visit the Church of the Holy Sepulchre. As bells ring out a deafening peel, one can wander through the opulent old basilica, hoary with centuries of incense and smoke from candles, glowing with brass crosses and dangling oil-lamps, rich drapes, gold and jewels – votive offerings made by pilgrims to an antique olive-wood bust of the Virgin Mary. Then, at the site of the fifth Station, is the great mosaic depicting Abraham sacrificing Isaac – an allegorical reference to the sacrifice of Christ. In the Greek sacristy leading off the Chapel of Adam is a splinter of wood claimed to be a remnant of the cross.

Whilst visiting the holy sites in East Jerusalem, one crosses and re-crosses the *souq*, descending by flights of stairs into the depths of the city from the Jaffa and Damascus Gates.

From research and travel, I have discovered that *souqs*, or bazaars, are more than merely colourful attractions. Functional markets, they are still an important part of a city's economic life and the best place to gauge local foods, fashions, customs and crafts.

Historically *souqs* have always delighted foreign visitors. In 1664, for example, a young French traveller named de Thevenot witnessed a parade of craftsmen from the *souq* in Aleppo and subsequently wrote a fascinating account of the sight.

It included, he wrote, shoe-makers wearing cone-shaped hats and carrying muskets and swords; eight men carrying a float on which two little boys were making sandals; and a company of confectioners carrying castles of sugar on their heads.

Next, de Thevenot said, came the 'gold spinners', two apprentices on a float actually spinning gold as they were carried through the streets. There were also bakers, tailors and dyers – with an apprentice dyeing cloth red before the eyes of the crowd – and, in order, a procession followed by coffee-sellers, butchers, silk-weavers, saddlers, carpenters, gardeners, smiths and barbers.

The parades, in those days common in many Middle Eastern cities, were not simply for entertainment. They were held to demonstrate the importance of commerce and crafts of the great cities of those regions: Damascus and Aleppo, Isfahan and Shiraz, Baghdad and Jerusalem, for example.

It was probably during the early spread of Islam that *souqs* assumed a definite pattern, with the traders and artisans of a particular craft grouped together: goldsmiths and silversmiths, shoemakers, carpenters, tailors, candlestick-makers and so on. It makes sense, since artisans of a particular craft all use the same raw materials and, in another way, it permits a buyer to compare price and quality with very little trouble. It was and still is socially appropriate too, since men plying the same trade, or craft, naturally have much in common. The location of the *souq* is always in the centre of the city – or in the case of Jerusalem, in what used to be the city centre, enabling people to reach it easily.

The *souq* in the Old City of East Jerusalem compels one to stop and look, time and time again. One should devote an entire morning for desultory strolling, or shopping, in the labyrinthine alleys. I have visited the bazaar at all hours of the day, but consider the best time to be in the early morning when the light is good for photography and the shop-keepers are fresh (late afternoon finds them somewhat jaded). By nine o'clock, most have arrived, unclicking a padlock and rolling up their shutter with a loud bang, signalling that they are open for business.

More than anything, the *souq* in East Jerusalem is a *souq* of sounds: the sharp noise made by the coffee-seller dropping beans on brass scales, the rattle as the nut-seller plunges his spoon into a sack of pistachios, the jingle of wind-chimes, ceaseless conversations, someone noisily blowing his nose, the clip-clop of shoes on the stone alleys, the soft, hurried patter of a passing donkey and the heavier tread of a mule, its owner whistling a warning to pedestrians, a cobbler tapping brass studs in leather belts, children wailing, radios blaring, the rubbish collector yelling as he pushes his cart towards the Dung Gate, the harsh squawk of chickens and the dull *thwop* of a butcher chopping meat, the irregular whirr of ancient air-conditioners, and a similar sound from equally ancient sewing machines, the water-seller, walking with that flat-footed step, common to all water-sellers in the Middle East, ringing his bell; then drowning other sounds, the bells peeling in the Church of the Holy Sepulchre.

The market people are as interesting as the shops. In East Jerusalem, for instance, I especially remember a fragile, blind old Palestinian lady, groping her way along the 'Street of the Sweet-Sellers'. No doubt she knew her way and was probably a familiar figure – small, wrinkled and wearing the red embroidered costume of Ramallah. Stopping at the entrance of one shop, she felt around, then held up a bar of *halwa* (an Oriental sweet made with honey and nuts, usually pistachios, resembling nougat), handing her purse trustingly to the owner for him to extract payment. While waiting, she popped a handful of sultanas in her mouth; then, smiling like a guilty child, she continued her shopping. I watched her buying bundles of mint and some coriander, before losing sight of her in the jostling crowds.

If the *souq* is a functioning day-to-day market for locals, it is also the best place to buy souvenirs.

Expensive, but veritable museum pieces, are the hand-worked Palestinian dresses which I saw for sale at No. 13, el-Khawajat Street. Costing from £50 upwards, they are guaranteed to make any woman the star of a party. The majority are black, most cotton, some silk, embroidered around the sleeves or hem, but mainly across the bosom, with traditional motifs from Bethlehem, Hebron, Ramallah and other Palestinian towns.

Wherever one travels in Jordan, but particularly in the occupied West Bank, one sees women in local costume. It is said that a young man seeking a bride still studies the embroidery on a woman's clothes, since it indicates a woman's skill. Embroidery takes many forms, but it is mainly geometric: the two basic styles are cross-stitch, using different coloured threads (red and blue are popular) and running stitch, in gold and silver thread. Sometimes old coins, fringes and beads are sewn on to the dress as added decoration.

Another item of clothing which finds popularity with tourists is what is known as the 'Crusader jacket', of corded silk, or velvet, usually black or burgundy and embroidered with gold thread. Loose-fitting kaftans abound, selling for around £5. Adults' and children's embroidered 'peasant blouses' are also attractive. Cosy sheepskin jackets are good buys for winter; several shops specialise in coats and mittens.

Pottery, Hebron glassware, olive-wood carvings, old mosaics reproduced in ceramic tiles, dolls in West Bank costume and charming Christmas cards from the Holy City, featuring nativity scenes made from pressed wild-flowers, are some of the myriad souvenirs to be purchased in Jerusalem's *souq*.

Antique Bedouin silver jewellery, modern coral and turquoise jewellery and decorative *mihbash*, or coffee-grinders are other attractive items, but probably the most popular are mother-of-pearl crosses and candles. Christian Street, near the Church of the Holy Sepulchre, is the 'Street of the Candlestick-makers'. Candles, bells, rosaries and other religious reliquaries may be blessed in the Church of the Holy Sepulchre.

Christendom's other sacred town, Bethlehem, is only a short distance from Jerusalem, seen as a pilgrimage rather than a tour, although as in the Church of the Holy Sepulchre it is useful to employ a guide. In this instance one can make an organised tour and return later independently: taxis charge about £2 for the 11-kilometre journey from East Jerusalem to Bethlehem and buses depart regularly from near the Damascus Gate.

Two kilometres outside the city walls, the village of Bethany is a popular stop for Christian pilgrims as it sets the scene for many biblical events such as Jesus' association with Lazarus, his sisters Martha and Mary, and Simon the Leper. In Simon's house, Mary anointed Jesus' feet with oil and dried them with her hair; and it was from Bethany, on Palm Sunday, that Jesus rode into Jerusalem on a donkey.

In 1953, a Franciscan church was built and dedicated to Lazarus whom Jesus miraculously resurrected. The church incorporates Crusader and Byzantine relics, former shrines once decorated with mosaics depicting the events in Bethany. In order to visit the tomb of Lazarus, one should obtain the key from the custodian who runs a small souvenir stand opposite: elderly visitors should watch their footing on the slippery steps leading down to the cave.

The cave, or grotto, beneath the Church of the Nativity in Bethlehem, has a special aura. A silver star, with an inscription dated 1717, is sunk in the site of the manger where Jesus was born. Crowds tend to spoil the atmosphere, but if one returns quietly in the evening, one can light a taper, and pray.

The first Church of the Nativity was built above the grotto in AD 326. After being destroyed two centuries later it was rebuilt by Justinian, in the sixth century. During the assault on Jerusalem, soldiers of the First Crusade, led by Godfrey de Bouillon, planted the Christian banner on the spire before advancing to capture the Holy City.

The interior of the church is modest. There are no pews, but four rows of Corinthian-type, amber-coloured limestone columns line its length. The English oak ceiling was donated to the church by King Edward IV. Some of the floorboards are raised, exposing fragments of the original beautiful mosaic. The church was reputedly spared during the Persian invasion that destroyed the Church of the Holy Sepulchre in AD 614 because the mosaic depicts the Magi wearing Persian robes.

Marble stairs on either side of the main altar descend into the 'Grotto of the Nativity'. During the cleaning of this small rectangular room, a medieval mosaic of a nativity scene was found beneath the centuries of smoky grime. Adjacent to the grotto is the Chapel of the Manger, and to the north of the basilica is the Church of Saint Catherine from where, on Christmas Eve, the Franciscan patriach removes an effigy of the Christchild and places it on the Altar of the Manger where it remains until Epiphany.

Rights in the church are shared by three Christian denominations: Latin Catholic, (Franciscan), Armenian and Greek Orthodox. Following much bickering, better relations between the three evolved during the British mandate of Palestine. Each religion has its own chapels and observes strict schedules: the Greek Orthodox prelates must have completed the censing of the 'Altar of the Nativity' by 4.30 a.m., when the Franciscans celebrate their first Mass. Following the Armenian service held at 8 a.m. the grotto is open to the public.

Four hundred metres from the church is the 'Milk Grotto' where, according to legend, Mary was suckling Jesus when drops of milk fell on the rock, turning it white. In 1872, the Franciscans erected a chapel on the site.

Before the road from Jerusalem reaches Manger Square and the Church of the Nativity, a road branches east to Beit Sahour and the 'Shepherds' Field'. The field, which is not dissimilar to others in the vicinity, is reputedly the one where '. . . the angel of the Lord came upon them . . . and said fear not . . . unto you is born . . . a Saviour, which is Christ the Lord . . .' (Luke 2:8–11). On Christmas Eve, services are held in the field and from above, at midnight, bells in the Church of the Nativity announce the dawn of Christmas to the world.

When I stood in the field under the brightness of the evening star, a Bedouin woman dressed in scarlet was urging her flock homewards before the gathering night. She aimed a stone at a straggler, sending sheep scattering and the woman, now yelling and holding up her skirts, ran in pursuit. Shortly afterwards came the gentle sight of a boy, presumably her son, descending the limestone crags, cradling a new-born lamb.

Bethlehem is a town of narrow streets lined with solidly built, cubical, flat-roofed stone houses, whose population of 35,000 is mainly Christian. Always crowded, on market days the town is especially animated when farmers in rural costume throng the *souq*.

On the outskirts of Bethlehem I stopped at the Jamer Restaurant, a clean, quiet place for lunch or dinner. Its verandah overlooks a small domed building in an olive-grove, marking the site of Rachel's tomb (Gen. 35:16). The restaurant menu features 'Cremisan' wine, made in a Franciscan monastery near the village of Beit Jalla, west of Bethlehem.

The Italianate monastery was founded in 1185 by a Father Belloni. From donations, he also bought 50 hectares of land and built a school for orphaned boys, where he taught them viniculture using imported Italian vines. Revenue from the sale of wine supported the school, as is the case with the present monastery of eighteen monks. The Father in charge of the wine-shop says their August harvest usually yields 300,000 litres. The detour to the monastery is a rewarding hour; the setting is pure Mediterranean and one may sample the wines – a bottle of Cremisan white wine cost me only 60 pence.

The sight of Bedouin grazing their herds along the road to Hebron quickly reminds travellers that they are in the Middle East. Four kilometres beyond Bethlehem is a Turkish fortress dating from the seventeenth century, called *Qala'at el-Burak* (the Castle of the Pools), built in order to protect three vast reservoirs, set in a cypress grove, and still supplying some water to Jerusalem.

South-east of Bethlehem are two interesting sites – one a huge circular bastion known as the Herodium, or Herod's Fortress, and the other the Monastery of Mar Saba.

The fortress, one of a chain of defences ordered by

Herod in Jordan, is reached by climbing up a rough path to the summit which commands a panorama of the Judaean wilderness to the Dead Sea. It is open from 8.00–17.00 hours daily.

Founded by Saint Saba of Cappodocia in AD 486, the five-storey monastery clings to the steep escarpment like a wasp's nest. The interior is said to have a 110 rooms, but as women – and it is said even female animals – are forbidden by the monks to enter, I am unable to describe it.

Forty kilometres south of East Jerusalem lies Hebron, a town of 50,000 inhabitants, believed to have been continuously inhabited for over 5,000 years. There are many references to the town in Genesis: chapter 13, verse 18 relates how Abram, a frequent visitor to the town, '... removed *his* tent, and came and dwelt in the plain of Mamre, which *is* in Hebron, and built there an altar unto the Lord'.

'Abram' was later changed to Abraham, in Arabic *Ibrahim*, the first Moslem saint. The great *al-haram al Ibrahim al-Khalil* (translated as the Sanctuary to Abraham, God's Friend) is found in Hebron.

As well as Abraham's tomb one may also see the tombs of Sarah, his wife, and of Isaac, Rebecca, Jacob and Leah. Above the entrance to the mosque are beautiful twelfth-century stained-glass windows. Note too the *mihrab* or pulpit, made of marble and mosaics, and the *minbar* or prayer niche, a masterly carving in walnut. One may visit the Sanctuary from Saturday to Thursday from 7.30–11.30 hours and 13.30–17.00 hours but it is closed on Friday.

A conservative town, for obvious reasons holy to both Moslems and Jews, Hebron inspires much religious fervour. Tourists should dress discreetly and not attempt to photograph the local people.

Hebron has been known for the art of glass-blowing since the Middle Ages. It costs nothing to watch this craft in shops or small factories along the road.

In one shop I met a man of seventy, his cheeks flabby from fifty-eight years of glass-blowing. He could neither read nor write, but excelled at shaping beautiful glass objects ranging from biblical-type pitchers to modern ash-trays. Glassware tends to be cheaper in Hebron than in Jerusalem, but many craftsmen are reluctant to bargain as they consider it is an insult to their work.

The round-trip to Hebron, including detours, should not exceed 100 kilometres.

A second sightseeing tour of the occupied West Bank visits the towns of Ramallah, Nablus and the site of Samaria, modern day Sebastiya. The journey takes only half a day. A suggestion is to pack a picnic lunch, buy local 'Latrun' wine on the way and *knaffeh*, the famous Arabic sweetmeat, in Nablus.

Beginning at the Damascus Gate, the Nablus Road runs for 16 kilometres to Ramallah, a predominantly Christian town with a population of 35,000.

The town was settled in 1492 by a small Christian community who fled from Shaubak in order to avoid an arranged marriage between a young girl and a local Moslem sheikh. Situated on hills clad in pine-trees, Ramallah is a clean town with attractive villas, gardens and a civic park. It is a popular summer resort with residents of East Jerusalem: the Mediterranean Sea is visible on a clear day.

Linked to Ramallah by a round-about is the Moslem town of el-Bireh, where on the left of the Bir Sharia-Nablus road I visited a good antique shop.

A road from Ramallah leads a distance of 17 kilometres to Latrun, situated on the western boundary of the 1948–49 ceasefire line. The Trappist monks in Latrun produce a popular, rather sweet wine that is widely sold in Jordan.

Three kilometres north of Ramallah is the village of Beitin, the biblical Bethel, mentioned many times in Genesis, where Abraham built an altar to God (hence the Arabic name, *Beit-Allah,* meaning 'the house of God'). Beitin is further associated with the popular parable of Jacob's dream of a ladder ascending to heaven (Gen. 28:12–19).

Farther north, the road crosses Wadi el-Haramiyah (in English, The Valley of the Robbers), an intensely culti-vated valley. Sixty-three kilometres north of Jerusalem one reaches the well dug by Jacob, reputedly where the Samaritan woman offered Jesus a drink when He revealed Himself to be the Christian Messiah (John 4:5–26).

The site, with Crusader and Byzantine relics, is the responsibility of the Greek Orthodox Church. An atten-dant monk will drop a pitcher into the well and haul up some fresh drinking water. The tomb of Joseph, identified by a white dome, is found near the well. To the north-east, the present-day village of Askar used to be the New Tes-tament Sychar, where the Samaritan woman lived.

With a population of 80,000, Nablus is the largest town in the occupied West Bank. Founded by Titus, who called it *Flavia Neapolis* (hence the Arabic Nablus), the town is supplied with abundant water and is important in the cultivation of olives.

The market sells a rich harvest of fruit and vegetables from the West Bank. There are also baskets of the 'St Peter fish' netted in the Sea of Galilee. A 'mouth-carrier', the fish holds its eggs in its mouth prior to hatching or alterna-tively, a small pebble (Matt. 17:24–27). Of the carp family, St Peter fish makes delicious eating.

Also sold in the market are trays of the mouth-watering *knaffeh*; and since one needs to be an expert to make the sweetmeat at home, it is worth watching how it is accom-plished.

The pastry-cook fills a utensil shaped like a large, inverted salt-shaker, and with great panache for the benefit of onlookers, pours fine streams of liquid dough on to a sizzling hot-plate. Instantly the strings crisp into fine vermicelli which he scrapes off like bunches of hair. Plac-ing them on a large, round, buttered tray, a layer of soft white cheese is added, then a further layer of vermicelli. The tray is popped into the oven and when the upper side is cooked, it is buttered and reversed for a further 15 minutes' baking. Removed and cooled slightly, it is drenched with syrup and served on cardboard plates to hungry customers. I have bought *knaffeh* in London, but it is a far cry from that of the narrow backstreets of Nablus.

Although the inhabitants are predominantly Moslem, there are also about 300 members of the Samaritan sect, descendants of the surviving Israelites, who inter-married with the alien population who came there after the fall of Samaria in 722 BC.

The Samaritans have never effectively had a common cause with Judah and have been regarded historically by the Jews as a heretical sect. They worship God and take their authority from the Five Books of Moses (Genesis to Deuteronomy). Samaritans further differ in claiming that Abraham sacrificed Isaac on Mount Garizim, near Nablus, rather than on Mount Moriah, in East Jerusalem. Annually on Mount Garizim, they celebrate their Feast of the Passover on the evening before the full April moon.

The road forks north of Nablus, the right bifurcation leading to Sebastiya, a village near the ruins of ancient Samaria.

Archaeologists believe the site was occupied in the Bronze Age, but an actual settlement was not made until 880 BC by Omri, sixth king of Israel. Denounced by Jewish prophets for wickedness and corruption, Samaria was destroyed after a long Assyrian siege. After being fought over by the Babylonians and the Persians, it was then conquered by Alexander the Great, from which time it assumes the Hellenistic name of Sebaste (Sebastiya). Pompey annexed the town in 63 BC, bestowing responsibility on Herod the Great who erected many ornate buildings. Under Septimus Severus the city became a Roman colony, but after the fourth century AD it began to decline.

In spring, red poppies and wild mustard bring colour into the drab ruins. A Roman wall, 3,700 metres long, once surrounded the city. Stumps are all that remains of the Hippodrome, while to the south is the Forum and on a small hill lie the fallen stones of an Acropolis.

South of here are the ruins of the Crusader-built church

Palestinian view of the West Bank

of John the Baptist, reputedly built on top of an earlier basilica above the tomb of the saint.

History differs at this point; according to one legend, Salome danced for the head of John the Baptist in Sebaste. Other stories quote Jericho, or Macherus, near Madaba. There is also a tomb to John the Baptist in the Ummayad Mosque in Damascus; but wherever he may be buried, the town of Sebastiya in the occupied West Bank attracts many pilgrims, among them many Baptists. . . .

Information for Visitors to Jordan

Although specific details, especially costs, addresses, times, etc., given in this chapter were correct at the time of writing, there can be no guarantee that they have not subsequently altered, and should therefore be checked if some time elapses before use.

Travelling to Jordan by air

FLIGHT ROUTINGS

FLIGHT NO.	ROUTING
101	Amman – Rome
102	Rome – Amman
103	Amman – Paris – London
104	London – Paris – Amman
105	Amman – Geneva – Madrid
106	Madrid – Geneva – Amman
107	Amman – Belgrade – London
108	London – Belgrade – Amman
111	Amman – London
112	London – Amman
121	Amman – Frankfurt – Copenhagen
122	Copenhagen – Frankfurt – Amman
125	Amman – Frankfurt – Brussels
126	Brussels – Frankfurt – Amman
131	Amman – Athens
132	Athens – Amman
133	Amman – Larnaca
134	Larnaca – Amman
135	Amman – Damascus – Larnaca
136	Larnaca – Damascus – Amman
145	Amman – Tripoli
146	Tripoli – Amman
171	Amman – Istanbul – Belgrade
172	Belgrade – Istanbul – Amman
173	Amman – Istanbul
174	Istanbul – Amman
175	Amman – Bucharest – Berlin
176	Berlin – Bucharest – Amman
170	Amman – Bangkok

FLIGHT NO.	ROUTING
181	Bangkok – Amman
182	Amman – Singapore
183	Singapore – Amman
190	Amman – Dubai – Karachi
191	Karachi – Dubai – Amman
241	Amman – Damascus
242	Damascus – Amman
261	Amman – Amsterdam – New York
262	New York – Amsterdam – Amman
263	Amman – Vienna – New York
264	New York – Vienna – Amman
265	Amman – Vienna – Chicago – Los Angeles
266	Los Angeles – Chicago – Vienna – Amman
300	Amman – Aqaba
301	Aqaba – Amman
302	Amman – Aqaba
303	Aqaba – Amman
343	Amman – Tunis – Casablanca
344	Casablanca – Tunis – Amman
401	Amman – Beirut
402	Beirut – Amman
501	Amman – Cairo
502	Cairo – Amman
503	Amman – Cairo
504	Cairo – Amman
505	Amman – Cairo
506	Cairo – Amman

FLIGHT NO.	ROUTING	FLIGHT NO.	ROUTING
507	Amman – Cairo	701	Jeddah – Amman
508	Cairo – Amman	702	Amman – Riyadh
600	Amman – Bahrain – Muscat	703	Riyadh – Amman
601	Muscat – Bahrain – Amman	704	Amman – Dhahran
602	Amman – Abu Dhabi – Dubai	705	Dhahran – Amman
603	Dubai – Abu Dhabi – Amman	800	Amman – Kuwait
604	Amman – Abu Dhabi	801	Kuwait – Amman
605	Abu Dhabi – Amman	802	Amman – Kuwait – Dubai
606	Amman – Dubai	803	Dubai – Kuwait – Amman
607	Dubai – Amman	804	Amman – Kuwait – Abu Dhabi
608	Amman – Bahrain – Doha	805	Abu Dhabi – Kuwait – Amman
609	Doha – Bahrain – Amman	806	Amman – Kuwait
610	Amman – Doha	807	Kuwait – Amman
611	Doha – Amman	812	Amman – Baghdad
700	Amman – Jeddah	813	Baghdad – Amman

Flying times to Amman from European and Middle East Cities

Europe	Flying Time	The Middle East and Arab World	Flying Time	The Middle East and Arab World	Flying Time
Amsterdam	6.30	Abu Dhabi	2.45	Doha	2.30
Athens	2.15	Aden	3.50	Dubai	3.00
Belgrade	5.10	Algiers	5.25	Jeddah	2.00
Brussels	5.50	Ankara	2.15	Kuwait	2.00
Cologne	5.10	Aqaba	0.40	Medina	1.30
Copenhagen	6.50	Baghdad	1.15	Oman	4.20
Frankfurt	4.30	Bahrain	2.20	Rabat	7.05
Geneva	5.45	Beirut	0.50	Riyadh	2.05
London	5.30	Cairo	2.15	Tehran	3.05
Lisbon	6.50	Dhahran	2.15	Tripoli	6.50
Madrid	5.45			Tunis	6.10
Milan	4.50				
Paris	5.00				
Rome	3.45				
Zurich	5.10				

Travelling to Jordan by road

A fascinating overland trip from Europe through Turkey and Syria reaches Jordan at Ramtha, about two hours' drive from Amman. Jordan has some 12,000 kilometres of roads with excellent main highways running north and south of the country. An ordinary sedan car can manage most of the roads. Diesel engine vehicles are not permitted to enter Jordan except in transit. Four wheel drive is essential on desert tracks.

A car-ferry service operates daily between Suez – Aqaba – Jeddah: Telstar Maritime Agency: P.O. Box 9360, Amman (Telephone 36162).

Packing your case The quantity of clothing one packs naturally depends on the length of a visit to Jordan: a golden rule for travellers is – if in doubt, leave out. Travel as lightly as possible. Tourists crossing the King Hussein Bridge to the occupied West Bank will be rigorously searched by the Israeli authorities.

Accustomed to tourists, Jordanians are discreetly polite about their occasionally strange attire. Women should endeavour not to wear dresses that reveal too much neck, or leg. Slacks may be worn anywhere. Shorts are acceptable in Petra and Aqaba, but not elsewhere. Bikinis are in order for hotel pools in Amman and Aqaba.

Winter clothes are essential between December and March. A quilted jacket suffices in lieu of a top-coat. Amman is very windy at this time of year, but the Dead Sea can be warm by day, so pack accordingly. Remember, too, that even mid-summer temperatures in Jordan can drop dramatically at night. A long skirt is suitable for evenings in Amman and Aqaba. Although locals dress up, it is not expected of tourists.

Businessmen are expected to wear a suit and tie.

In addition to the main suitcase, a small hold-all, or airline bag, is useful for essential requirements on day trips outside Amman. Moisturised tissues are suggested for long drives. Comfortable shoes or plimsolls are invaluable, as are a hat and sunglasses. Binoculars are especially useful for bird-watching at Azraq. Most films are available in Amman, but they are very expensive.

Laundry is dealt with promptly and efficiently in Amman hotels.

Hairdressers are excellent.

When to go Generally speaking, spring and autumn are the best times to visit Jordan. Mid-summer is hot although the hill resorts of Madaba, Jerash and Ajlun enjoy cooler temperatures. Aqaba remains warm during the winter months. Both tourists and businessmen should avoid the month of fasting during Ramadan when many businesses close early and most Moslems abstain from eating and drinking between dawn and sunset.

The Weather

Month	Amman	Aqaba
January	8.1° (46.5°)	15.6° (60.0°)
February	9.0° (48.2°)	17.0° (62.6°)
March	11.8° (53.2°)	20.1° (68.2°)
April	16.0° (60.8°)	24.3° (75.7°)
May	20.7° (69.3°)	28.4° (83.1°)
June	23.7° (74.6°)	31.8° (89.2°)
July	25.1° (77.2°)	32.5° (90.0°)
August	25.6° (78.0°)	33.0° (91.4°)
September	23.5° (74.3°)	30.4° (86.7°)

Information for Visitors to Jordan

Month	Amman	Aqaba
October	20.6° (69.0°)	27.1° (80.7°)
November	15.3° (59.5°)	22.1° (71.7°)
December	10.0° (50.0°)	17.2° (62.9°)

Centigrade (Fahrenheit)

Entry Regulations An entry visa is required, which may be obtained at the Jordan Embassy, 6 Upper Phillimore Gardens, London W8. The visa may also be obtained from immigration authorities at the airport.

Health Regulations During the Haj (for a period of 40 days after the end of Ramadan) an anti-cholera vaccination is required for all visitors. For the moment, Jordan does not require other vaccinations unless travellers are coming from an infected area. As regulations alter suddenly according to the world health situation, visitors are advised to check again prior to their departure.

Customs Regulations 200 cigarettes, 25 cigars and 1 litre bottle of spirits, per person, but these details should be checked on departure.

Currency The unit of currency is the dinar which is divided into 1,000 fils. 10 fils are sometimes referred to as a piastre. Denomination of notes: 500 fils, 1, 5 10 and 20 dinars. Exchange facilities are available at the airport, and local currency may be changed when leaving Jordan.

Time GMT + 2 hours, and during summer, BST + 1 hour. For U.S. travellers this would be Eastern Standard Time + 7 hours.

Weights and Measures Metric

Electric Current 220 A.C. volts, 50 cycles. Round, two-prong wall plugs are used.

Telephone Jordan has direct dialling communications with Europe, North America, the Middle East and the Gulf States.

Mail The central post office in Amman is located in Prince Mohammed Street, and is open seven days a week. Branches are conveniently located throughout the town; there is one in the Inter-Continental shopping complex which is open from 8–18.00 hours. Airmail letters to England take about five days and to the USA and Australia seven to ten days.

Shopping Hours 8.30–13.00 hours and 15.30–18.00 hours.

Banking Hours 8.00–12.30 hours.

Government Offices 8.00–14.00 hours.

Private Offices In summer they are normally open from 8.00–13.00 hours and from 15.30–19.30 hours, and in winter from 8.30–13.30 hours and from 15.00–18.30 hours. Moslem enterprises are closed on Fridays, and Christian enterprises on Sundays. Earlier closing takes place during Ramadan.

National Holidays Arab League Day – 22 March; Labour Day – 1 May; Independence Day – 25 May; Arab Revolt and Army Day – 10 June; His Majesty King Hussein's Accession to the Throne – 11 August; His Majesty King Hussein's Birthday – 14 November.

Moslem Holidays The Moslem, or *Hegra* calendar is a lunar one, the first year corresponding with the Prophet Mohammed's flight from Mecca to Medina in AD 622. 1980 is the Moslem year 1400.

The *Hegra* is eleven days shorter than the Gregorian calendar, so that holidays vary from year to year and it is difficult to predict on which day in the Gregorian calendar a Moslem feast will occur.

The major Moslem holidays are: *Eid el-Fitr*, a three-day feast, falling after the end of the fast of Ramadan; *Eid al-Adha* which celebrates the end of the *Haj*, or pilgrimage to Mecca, and lasts four days; *Muharram* is New Year's Day; *Moulid el-Nabi* falls on the twelfth day of *Rabi 1*, the birthday of the Prophet; *Rajab 27* or the feast of *al-Miraj*, commemorating the journey of the Prophet Mohammed to Heaven; and *Sha'ban 9*, Arab Renaissance Day, commemorating the Arab revolt.

Christian Holidays Easter celebrations fall according to the Eastern Church date which may be three to four weeks behind the Western celebrations. Easter is considered more important to Christians in the East. Christmas is observed on 25 December. New Year is also observed.

Jordan Accommodation List

Given below is a list of recognised hotels, graded from 5–3 stars:

Amman

Jordan Intercontinental, PO Box 35014, Jabel Amman 3rd Circle (tel. 41361)
Holiday Inn/Amman, PO Box 6399, Al-Hussein Ben Ali Str. (tel. 663100)
Regency Palace, PO Box 927000, Amman – Sportcity (tel. 660000)
Amman Marriott, PO Box 926333, Shmeisani (tel. 660100)
Middle East, PO Box 19224, Shmeisani (tel. 667160)
Jerusalem International, Melia, PO Box 926265, Shmeisani (tel. 665121)
Grand Palace, PO Box 6916, Near Al Hussein Sportcity (tel. 661127)
Commodore Hotel, PO Box 3330, Shmeisani (tel. 665186)
Ambassador, PO Box 19014, Shmeisani (tel. 665161)
San Rock, PO Box 9032, Om Othaina (tel. 813800)
Tyche, PO Box 3190, Shmeisani (tel. 661115)
Amman Crown Hotel, PO Box 1318, Radio & Television Road (tel. 71256)
Amra Hotel, PO Box 292, Jabel Amman 6th Circle (tel. 815071)
Ammon, PO Box 950271, Jabel Amman 4th Circle (tel. 67113)
Gandol Hotel, PO Box 2082, Jabel Amman 5th Circle (tel. 24631)
Um Othaina Hotel, PO Box 3444, Jabel Amman 7th Circle (tel. 816146)
Hala Inn, PO Box 182423, Near Alkaldi Hospital (tel. 44542)
Philadelphia, PO Box 10, Al-Hashimi Street (tel. 25191)
Amman International, PO Box 2500, Jordan University Str. (tel. 841712)
Hisham, PO Box 5398, Jabel Amman 4th Circle (tel. 42720)
Al-Manar, PO Box 21730, Shmeisani (tel. 662186)
Omar-Al-Khayyam, PO Box 3075, Shmeisani
Merryland, PO Box 9122, King Hussein Str. (tel. 30217)
Royal, PO Box 19112, Opp Jordan University (tel. 843334)
Shepherd, PO Box 20200, Al-Khattab Str. (tel. 39197)
City, PO Box 2734, Prince Moh'd Str. (tel. 42251)
Granada, PO Box 2321, Jabel Amman 1st Circle (tel. 22617)

Al-Ghusein, PO Box 8234, Jabel Al-Hussein (tel. 665178)
Cameo, PO Box 5058, Jabel Amman 4th Circle (tel. 44579)
Firas Wing, PO Box 9119, Jabel Weibdeh (tel. 22103)
Holyland, PO Box 922294, Jordan University Str. (tel. 841309)
Ramallah, PO Box 182157, Prince Moh'd Str. (tel. 36122)
Select, PO Box 853, Jabel Weibdeh (tel. 37101)
Al-Cazar, PO Box 1210, Al-Hashimi Str. (tel. 36305)
National, PO Box 19287, Near Sport City (tel. 668459)
Sultan, PO Box 151325, Al-Amaneh Str. (tel. 39710)
Saladin, PO Box 6820, Al-Amaneh Str. (tel. 24508)
Amman Grand Hotel, PO Box 2006, Jabel Amman Ibn Sina Str. (tel. 44528)
Rum, PO Box 109, Basman Str. (tel. 23162)
New Park, PO Box 1790, King Hussein Str.
Caravan, PO Box 9062, Police College Str.
Canary, PO Box 9062, Jabel Weibdeh (tel. 38353)
Al-Jebel, PO Box 926167, Jordan University Str. (tel. 662327)

Aqaba

Holiday Inn/Aqaba, PO Box 6399, Aqaba (tel. 2426)
Aqaba Tourist House, PO Box 1060 (tel. 5165)
Al-Cazar, PO Box 392, Aqaba (tel. 4131)
Al-Miramar, PO Box 60, Aqaba (tel. 4341)
Aquamarina, PO Box 96, Aqaba (tel. 4333)
Coral Beach, PO Box 71, Aqaba (tel. 3521)
Aqaba, PO Box 43, Aqaba (tel. 2056)

Al Azraq

Al-Azraq, Al-Azraq (tel. 140)
Assayad, PO Box 70 (tel. 94)

Petra

Petra Forum, PO Box 30, Petra (tel. 61246/7)

Irbid

Al-Razi, PO Box 2132, Irbid (tel. 75515)
Al-Nassim, PO Box 1268, Irbid (tel. 74310)

Sweileh

Balga Palace, PO Box 9665, Sweileh (tel. 843291)

Zarqa

Tirawi, PO Box 1869, King Faisal Str./Zarqa (tel. 82947)

Ajlun

Grand Ajlun Hotel, P.O. Box 483, Irbid (tel. 3997)
There are rest-houses in Azraq, Petra, Dibeen and Kerak.
Single room rates are from JD2 in a 1-star hotel to JD16 in a 5-star hotel.

Tipping Most hotels and restaurants add 10–12 per cent service charge to the
bill. Porters require 100 fils per item of luggage.

Health Precautions The water is safe to drink in Amman. Outside the capital,
the excellent local mineral water is recommended. Caution should be exercised

in eating uncooked food at roadside cafés and in small towns. Fruit should be peeled. Medicine for stomach upsets is readily available in Amman and Aqaba; elsewhere it is prudent to carry a supply.

Dining out in Amman

Town Centre

Jordan Restaurant, Prince Mohammed Street (tel. 38333)
Popular restaurant serving Oriental food and pastries; also take-away
Jabri Restaurant, King Hussein Street (tel. 24108)
Popular restaurant serving Oriental dishes, notably chicken and onion, and Oriental pastries
Dar Assorour Restaurant, King Hussein Street, opposite the Arab Bank
Chicken and chips, shawarma sandwiches. Seating and take-away
Indian Chicken-Tikka Inn, Prince Mohammed Street, Wadi Seir Road, opposite Citibank (tel. 42437)
Speciality chicken *tikka*

First Circle: Jebel Amman

Diplomat Restaurant, Sidewalk Cafe, on the circle opposite ALIA (tel. 25592)
Snacks and sandwiches
Queens, First Circle (tel. 36776)

Second Circle: Jebel Amman

Estanbouli Restaurant, side street between 1st and 2nd Circles (tel. 38212)
Turkish and Jordanian cuisine in informal atmosphere. Good food and moderate prices
Babalu Restaurant, near 1st Circle (tel. 41116)
Local and Western food

Third Circle: Jebel Amman

Maatouk Restaurant, facing the circle, a short walk from the Inter-Continental Hotel. Tasty Oriental dishes are served, such as *shawarma* and *musakhan* – also pastries. Simple decor, fast service, also take-away. Moderate prices.
Nouroz Snack, on the Circle. Excellent pizzas and kebabs are served, the price for two people, with wine, being about JD4.
Abu Ahmad (New Orient Restaurant), near the Inter-Continental Hotel (tel. 41879). Popular garden restaurant serving Oriental dishes. If you want *mazza*, order when booking. Try *qusa* – grilled courgettes with yoghurt and lemon.
Omar Khayyam Restaurant, near the Inter-Continental Hotel, entrance opposite Citibank, top floor of shops and office complex (tel. 42910). Excellent though expensive Oriental cuisine; view of Jebel Weibdeh.
Royal Crown Rotisserie, rooftop Inter-Continental Hotel (tel. 41361). Expensive French cuisine.
Okaz Coffee-Shop, Inter-Continental Hotel (tel. 41361). Daily Arab buffet; good service.
Holiday Inn Restaurants: al-Hussein Ben Ali Street (tel. 63100). *Churchill's*: English food; *al-Liwan*: Oriental cuisine; *Relais*: French cuisine; *Ambassador's*: dinner dancing.
Taiwan Restaurant (tel. 41093). Chinese cuisine, moderately priced.

Shmeisani
Gardens, Lebanese food (tel. 664155)

Al Jabal. Near Sport City (tel. 662327)

La Terrasse Restaurant (tel. 62831). Situated in a second floor apartment block in a residential area, this restaurant offers a French cuisine.

Leonardo da Vinci Restaurant: Italian food. (tel. 662441)

Al Mansaf and Alwaloemeh Restaurants: M. Eastern and European food.

Marriott Hotel (tel. 660100)

Al Diwan Middle East Hotel (tel. 667159)

Ambassador Hotel Restaurant (tel. 665161)

Tyche Hotel Restaurant (tel. 661114)

Jebel Weibdeh
Le César Restaurant (tel. 24421). Popular with locals; a mixed cuisine.

Elite Restaurant (tel. 22103). Swiss-type food.

Haii Abdoun
Mandaloun Restaurant (tel. 43564). Lebanese nightclub and restaurant with smart décor.

Commodore Hotel Restaurant (tel. 65186–8). Oriental hors d'oeuvres, Tunisian salads, steaks.

Delicatessen Restaurant (tel. 63516). Small bistro-type; steak and *mazza.*

University District
Sports City Club, University Street (tel. 39341). Local and European cuisine, at moderate prices.

Al-Waha Restaurant, behind University Hospital off Hashemiyah Street (tel. 843734). Jordanian cuisine.

The above is by no means a full list. The many new hotels under construction will have restaurants. There are also chicken take-aways. The *Royal Automobile Club* in Wadi Sir Road (tel. 44261) and the *Orthodox Club* in Jebel Abdoun (tel. 44491) accept individual non-members for dinner.

Dining out in Aqaba
Holiday Inn Hotel: Coral Restaurant, sea front (tel. 2426). Local and European cuisine.

Samiramis Restaurant, Palace Street. Small, with Oriental cuisine. Try *Kishki –* laban, chopped walnuts, etc.

Samiramis Restaurant, behind Post Office, Amman Road. The food is Oriental with pastries a speciality.

Aquarius Restaurant, Aquamarina Hotel, sea front. Mixed cuisine.

Palm Beach Hotel Restaurant, sea front. In simple surroundings, a good barbecue of kebabs, etc., is served.

Basman Garden Restaurant, located after Palm Beach Hotel, before the port. Huge waterfront restaurant. Seafood and chips.

These are some of the restaurants in Aqaba. There are others, some of which are attached to hotels, such as the al-Cazar, Miramar and Coral Beach hotels. There are also several nightclubs.

Useful Arabic Words and Phrases

For those who wish to try Arabic, the following are some of the more common phrases, questions and answers that visitors may find useful to know:

Good morning	sabeh el khair
(reply)	sabah el noor
Good evening	masa el khair
Good night	laileh sa'eedi;
	tisbah 'ala khair
Hello	marhaba
(reply)	marhabtain
Greetings	
(peace be with you)	as Salam 'alaikoom
(reply)	'alaikoom salam
Goodbye (the	
one departing)	b-khatirkum
(the one remaining)	ma'-salama; fi
	aman allah
How are you?	keef halak? keef halik? (f)
Well, thank God	mabsut(a) el
	hamdu lillah
Welcome	
(host says)	ahlan wa-sahlan
(reply)	ahlan bekum
Yes	na'am
No	la
I do not speak	ana ma bahki
Arabic	'arabi
Give me	'ateeni
Excuse me	mut'asik
Stop	waqqif
Stop, enough	bass
Slower please	'ala mahlak 'ala malik (f)
Slowly	shway, shway
Take me to the	
hotel	khudni 'al otel
Wait here	istenna hoon
Come here	la'a la hoon
I do not know	ma ba'raf
See	shoof
Never mind	ma'lash
Another time	marra tani
Once	marra
Twice	marratain
Everything	kull
All of us	kulna
Is it possible?	mumkin?
Please	min fadlak, min
	fadlik (f)

After you, I beg
you to (enter, eat take)   tfaddel, tfaddeli (f)
If God is willing   Inshallah
Thank you   shukran
                            mamnoonak
                            mamnoonik (f)
What is your name?   shu ismak? shu ismik (f)?
My name is ...   ismi ...
Do you speak
English   btihki ingleezi

Numbers

Nought	sifr	Six	sitti
One	wahad	Seven	saba'a
Two	thanayn	Eight	thamania
Three	thalatha	Nine	tis'a
Four	'arba'a	Ten	'ashara
Five	khamsi		

Souvenir and Craft Shops
Amman

Amman souvenirs & Gifts, Jebel Amman, 3rd Circle
Grand Palace Bazaar, Grand Palace Hotel, near al-Hussein Youth City
Caravan Bazaar, Sports City
Ambassador Bazaar, Ambassador Hotel, Shmeisani
Al-Khayyam Bazaar, Jebel El-Weibdeh
Oriental Souvenirs, Jebel Amman, 3rd Circle
Jordan Gifts Store, Jordan Inter-Continental Hotel, Jebel Amman
Artizana Souvenirs, Jebel Amman, 1st Circle
Jordan Gifts Bazaar, Prince Mohammed Street
Philadelphia Oriental, Philadelphia Hotel
The Arabi Store, Al-Hashimi Street
Srojie Oriental Souvenirs, King Talal Street
Tamim Fur, Ras El-Ein Street
House of Old Arts, Abdali Street
Tamim Rihany Exhibition, Rainbow Street
Folklore Souvenirs, Jebel El-Weibdeh
Rabbat Ammon Bazaar, Jebel El-Hussein
Beit Sahour Bazaar, Jebel El-Hussein
Shafik Helteh Bazaar, Gold Market
Tyche Souvenirs, Merryland Hotel, King Hussein Street
Tamimi Souvenirs, Holiday Inn Hotel Street
Siriani Exhibition, Roman Theatre Street
Arab Bazaar, Jebel El-Weibdeh
Holyland Store, Al-Husseini Mosque Square
Arafat Bazaar, King Talal Street
Tourist Bazaar, Grand Palace Hotel, near al-Hussein Youth City
Yasin Souvenirs, Ras El-Ein Street

Zoghol & Al-Ahmmad Souvenirs, Malhas Market
Abu-Abad Stores, Jebel Al-Nuzha
Hashem Bukhari Souvenirs, El-Bukhari Market
Hebron Souvenirs, Al-Mesdar Street
Mitwali Bros., Jebel El-Weibdeh
Jerusalem Exhibition, Jebel Amman, 1st Circle
Holy Land Products, Amman Airport
Bethlehem Store, Jebel Amman
Jordanian Souvenirs Bazaar, Jebel Amman, 3rd Circle
City Hotel Bazaar, City Hotel, Prince Mohammed Street
Orient Fair, Ras El-Ein Street
Al-Mihraj Souvenirs, Jebel El-Weibdeh
The Leather Shop, El-Hussein Ben Ali Street
Jericho Souvenirs, Tyche Hotel, Shmeisani
Zarouba, Holiday Inn Hotel, El-Hussein Ben Ali Street.

Aqaba
Aqaba Bazaar, New Market
Gulf Museum, Port Street
Sea and Oriental Souvenirs, Port Street
Gulf Store, New Market
Naif Bazaar, New Market
Petra Bazaar, New Market
Abdeen Bazaar, New Market
Al-Fakhri Souvenirs, Amman Street
Redwan Museum, Aqaba Hotel, harbour front
Mosalam & Abu Zeid Co., Holiday Inn Hotel, sea front
Tahir Abdeen Souvenirs, New Market

Travel Agents
Amman
Abha Tours, Holiday Inn Hotel (tel. 663100)
Abha Tours, Airport Circle (tel. 93642)
Adam Tours, Shmeisani (tel. 663226)
Afana Travel & Tourism, Alwehdat/Madaba Street (tel. 78939)
Air Tours Jordan, Al-Rainbow Street (tel. 30582)
Al-Aqsa Tours, Alwehdar/Madaba Street (tel. 73091)
Al-Arabi Tours, Jabal Amman/1st Circle (tel. 38295)
Al-Buraq Tours, Alwehdat/Madaba Street (tel. 78015)
Alfadi Travel & Tourism, Ministry of Interior/Circle (tel. 668452)
Al-Jazi Travel & Tourism, Jabel Alhussein/Alrazi Street (tel. 662111)
Al-Jazzazi Tourist Office, North Marka/Main Street (tel. 94965)
Al-Kailani Travel & Tourism, Jabal El Weibdeh (tel. 37805)
Al-Kaikani Travel & Tourism, Marka/Main Street (tel. 93272)
Al-Karamah, Jabal Alhussein (tel. 663246)
Al-Khashman Tourist Corp, Almahattah Road (tel. 33060)
Al-Neel, Saqf El-Ssail (tel. 36973)
Al-Rabah Tours, Shmeisani (tel. 668561)

Al-Wahah Tourist Agency, Al-Abdali (tel. 669737)
Amani Tours, Prince Moh'd Street (tel. 667517)
Amin Kawar & Sons For Travel & Tourism, Prince Moh'd Street (tel. 22324)
Amman Tourist Bureau, Jabal Amman/3rd Circle (tel. 44321)
Amman Travel & Tourist Agency, Abdali (tel. 39995)
Amra Tourist Agency, Jabal Amman, 5th Circle (tel. 813460)
Apollo Travel & Tourist Agency, Prince Moh'd Street (tel. 41083)
Aqaba Tourism, Jabal Amman/lst Circle (tel. 23607)
Arabian Tours, Jabal Alhussein (tel. 675806)
Arab International Tourist Co., Shmeisani (tel. 668182)
Asea Tourist Agency, Abdali/Starco Building (tel. 670155)
Atlas Travel & Tourist Agency, King Hussein Street (tel. 24262)
Attawfiq Tours, Abdali (tel. 38379)
Attaher Tourist Agency, King Faisal Street (tel. 22128)
Aviatourist Travel & Tourism, Prince Moh'd Street (tel. 24805)
Aviatourist Travel & Tourism, Jabal Amman/3rd Circle (tel. 38146)
Ayoub Caravan Tours, King Hussein Street (tel. 38836)
Azure Tourism, Shmeisani (tel. 669799)
Baker Travel Co., Jordan Intercontinental Hotel (tel. 41873)
Banna Travel & Tourism, Jabal Amman/Albuhtori Street (tel. 44763)
Bestours/United Tour & TR-T Co, Prince Moh'd Street (tel. 37171)
Bestours/United Tour & TR-RT Co., Shmeisani (tel. 669532)
Bisharat Tours Corp, Jordan Intercontinental Hotel (tel. 41350)
Bisharat Tours Corp, King Hussein Street (tel. 22883)
Bisharat Tours Corp, Weibdeh (tel. 37830)
Blue Bell Tours, Grand Palace Hotel (tel. 661913)
City Tours, King Hussein Street (tel. 668265)
Concord Travel & Tourism, King Hussein Street (tel. 23536)
Crown Tours, King Hussein Street (tel. 36919)
Dajani Travel & Tourism Agency, Abdali (tel. 662914)
Dakkak Travel & Tourist Agency, Ambassador Hotel (tel. 670289)
Daoud Travel & Tourism, King Hussein Street (tel. 39881)
Delta Tourism, Prince Moh'd Street (tel. 25562)
Eagle Travel & Tourism, Jabal Weibdeh (tel. 21946)
Eastern Tours, Terra Sancta Building (tel. 21775)
Eurabia Travel & Tourism, Prince Moh'd Street (tel. 38415)
Fadle Deebah Travel & Tourism, King Hussein Street (tel. 25646)
Flying Arrow, Jabal Al-Hussein (tel. 666023)
General Tours, King Hussein Street (tel. 24307)
Golden Star Tourism, Ras El-Ain Street (tel. 70565)
Golden Wings, King Hussein Street (tel. 38787)
Grand Travel & Tourism, King Hussein Street (tel. 30125)
Granada Tours, King Hussein Street (tel. 38419)
Guiding Star Agency, Prince Moh'd Street (tel. 42526)
Halabi Tourist Co, King Hussein Street (tel. 39540)
Hala Travel & Tourist Agency, Alwehdat/Madaba Street (tel. 77283)
Hanin Travel & Tourist Agency, King Hussein Street (tel. 37749)
Haya Travel & Tourism, King Hussein Street (tel. 664825)
Holy Land Tours, Jordan Intercontinental Hotel (tel. 41783)
International Holiday Planners, Prince Moh'd Street (tel. 43269)

International Traders, Shmeisani (tel. 661014)
International Traders (tel. 25072)
International Travel & Tourist Services Co.
Jerusalem Express Co., King Hussein Street (tel. 22151)
Jordan Express Co, Prince College Street (tel. 662722)
Jordan International, King Hussein Street (tel. 25981)
Jordan Noorco, Lweibdeh/Alhaouz Circle (tel. 22974)
Jordan Resources Co, King Hussein Street (tel. 36772)
Jordan-Saudi Travel & Tourist Co., King Hussein Street/Al-Abdali (tel. 666229)
Jordan Travel Co., King Hussein Street (tel. 25585)
Kamal Travel & Tourism, King Hussein Street/Al-Abdali (tel. 666522)
Karnak/Jordan Tourist & Trans. Co. Ltd, King Hussein Street (tel. 25174)
Karnak/Jordan Tourist & Trans. Co. Ltd, North Marka/Main Street (tel. 93309)
Karnak/Jordan Tourist & Trans. Co. Ltd, Shmeisani (tel. 663243)
Katouri Travel & Tourist Co, Jabal Amman/2nd Circle (tel. 38804)
Khouri Travel & Tourism, Jabal Al-Hussein (tel. 23430)
Khurma Tours, Al-Hashemi Street (tel. 39087)
Lawrence Tours, Grand Palace Hotel (tel. 664916)
Madani Tours, Jabal Al-Hussein (tel. 667138)
Middle East Travel & Tourism, Middle East Travel & Tourism, Middle East Hotel (tel. 667150)
Mushtaha Tourism, King Hussein Street (tel. 36410)
Mu'tah Tours, Marriott Hotel (tel. 660100)
National Tourist Office, King Hussein Street (tel. 36293)
National Tourism, Jabal Amman/3rd Circle (tel. 42670)
Na'was Tourist Agency, King Hussein Street (tel. 22184)
Na'was Tourist Agency, Shmeisani (tel. 665718)
Nazzal Tours, King Hussein Street (tel. 36038)
Near East Tourist Centre, Jordan Intercontinental Hotel (tel. 41906)
Near East Tourist Agency, Sport City Street (tel. 662518)
Orient Express, King Hussein Street (tel. 39050)
Orient Tours, King Hussein Street (tel. 25471)
Pan Arabian, Sport City (tel. 666702)
Pan Arabian, King Hussein Street (tel. 23806)
Pan Pacific Travel & Tourism, King Hussein Street (tel. 21688)
Petra Tours, King Hussein Street (tel. 37380)
Petra Tours, Shmeisani/Near Alcomodor Hotel (tel.667028)
Petridis Travel & Tourism, King Hussein Street (tel. 36123)
Philadelphia Travel & Tourism, King Hussein Street (tel. 30800)
Rainbow Tours, King Hussein Street (tel. 21656)
Rasha Internal Tourism, Prince Moh'd Street (tel. 21175)
River Jordan Travel & Tourism, Jabal Amman/2nd Circle
River Jordan Travel & Tourism, Saqf E'ssail Street (tel. 25564)
Royal Tours, Jordan Intercontinental Hotel (tel. 44266)
Rum for Tourism, Jabal Amman/5th Circle (tel. 814055)
Rum for Tourism, Air Port Circle (tel. 93309)
Saeb Nahas Travel & Tourism, King Hussein Street (tel. 30879)
Saeb Nahas Travel & Tourism, King Hussein Street (tel. 22826)
Sahara Tours, Al-Abadali (tel. 665091)
Salam Tours, King Hussein Street (tel. 665269)

Sami Travel & Tourism, North Marka/Main Street (tel. 92392)
Seikaly Travel & Tourism, Prince Moh'd Street (tel. 22147)
Shatt Al-Arab Travel & Tourism, King Hussein Street (tel. 672211)
Shepherd Tours, Tyche Hotel (tel. 661114)
Shilieh Travel & Tourism, King Hussein Street (tel. 30629)
Sky Ways T.T.T., King Hussein Street (tel. 39575)
Sky Ways T.T.T., Prince Moh'd Street (tel. 21602)
Sky Ways Travel & Tourism, King Hussein Street (tel. 37205)
Space Travel & Tourism, Shmeisani (tel. 668069)
Sunrise Travel & Tourist Agency, King Hussein Street (tel. 669127/8)
Sun Tours, King Hussein Street (tel. 21108)
Tajco Travel & Tourism, Prince Moh'd Street (tel. 22925)
Tajco Travel & Tourism, Marka (tel. 93072)
Tawfig Za'Tarah & Co, Prince Moh'd Street (tel. 42332)
Telestar, Jabal Al-Hussein (tel. 660213)
Terra Sancta Tourist Co, King Hussein Street (tel. 25203)
Thabat Tourist Office, Shmeisani (tel. 673990)
The Arab International Tourism, Shmeisani (tel. 667576)
Trans Univers Tourism, Elwehdat/Madaba Street (tel. 76067)
Tourist Service Office, Jabal Weibdeh (tel. 24355)
Tyche Travel & Tourism, Shmeisani (tel. 663150)
United Travel Agency, Jabal Amman/Zahran Street (tel. 41959)
Universal Travel & Tourism, King Hussein Street (tel. 36425)
Unitours, King Hussein Street (tel. 36944)
Visa Travel & Tourism, Jabal Amman 3rd Circle (tel. 44196)
Wazzan Travel & Tourism, King Hussein Street (tel. 23180)
World Tour Services, Prince Moh'd Street (tel. 21118)
Yaish Tourist Agency, King Hussein Street (tel. 30610)
Yarmouk Tourism, University Street/Sport City (tel. 672674)
Za'Atarah Tourist & Travel Agency, King Hussein Street (tel. 36011)
Zaid Tours Agency, King Hussein Street (tel. 25197)
Zaid Tours Agency, Abu-Tammam Street (tel. 44036)

Aqaba
Abha Tours, Amman Street (tel. 4304)
Amin Kawar & Sonstr & T, Amman Street (tel. 4218)
Aqua Marina Tours, Hotels Street (tel. 4333/6)
Bitar & Abu-El-Iz Travel & Tourism, Hotels Street (tel. 4909)
Eurapia Travel & Tourism, Amman Street (tel. 3562)
Grand Travel & Tourism, Al-Cornich Street (tel. 4851)
International Traders, Municipality Square (tel. 3757)
Jerusalem Express Travel Agency, Al-Cornich Street (tel. 4991)
Madani Travel & Tourism, Al-Mina Street (tel. 2103)
River Jordan Travel & Tourism, Al-Cornich Street (tel. 4910)
Sharary Tours, Hotels Street (tel. 5004)
Telstar Travel & Tourism, Al-Mina Street (tel. 5123)

Irbid
Akka Travel & Tourism Agency, Prince Nayef Street (tel.2733)
Al-Akhras Tourist Agency, Post Office Square (tel. 3440)
Al-Sharah Travel & Tourism, Prince Nayef Street (tel. 3123)

Al-Tal Travel & Tourist Agency, Baghdad Street (tel. 2416)
Beit El-Maqdes Travel & Tourism, Baghdad Street (tel. 2521)
Jerusalem Express Travel & Tourism, Wasfi E'tal Street (tel. 2169)
Lona Travel & Tourism, Baghdad Street (tel. 2500)
Star Travel & Tourist Agency, Al-Jameel Street (tel. 3029)
Tahat Travel & Tourist Agency, Al-Hoson Street (tel. 74303)
Yarmouk Tourism, Baghdad Street (tel. 2424)
Za'atarah Travel & Tourist Agency, Prince Nayef Street (tel. 3995)

Zarqa
Al Jaber Tours, King Tala Street (tel. 85671)
Balqis Tours, Army Street (tel. 81254)
Haddad Tours Agency, King Talal Street (tel. 81836)
Jerusalem Express Travel, King Talal Street (tel. 82516)
Karnak/Jordan Travel & Transport Co, Army Street (tel. 84437)
Malak Travel & Tourist Agency, King Talal Street (tel. 86121)
Najjar Tours Co, Army Street (tel. 86485)
Natour Travel & Tourism, King Talal Street (tel. 81717)
Tyche Travel & Tourism, King Talal Street (tel. 81313)
Za'atarah Tourist & Travel Agency, King Abdullah Street (tel. 83089)

AL-H4
Al-Kailani Travel & Tourism (tel. 118)
Tajco Travel & Tourism (tel. 120)
Shatt Al-Arab Travel & Tourism
Za'atarah Travel & Tourist Agency (tel. 97)

Sweileh
Almanar Travel & Tourism, Al-Salt Street (tel. 842166)
Alraed Travel & Tourism, King Abdullah Street (tel. 841059)

Elmafraq
Beit Elmaqdes, Main Street (tel. 39164)
Canar Travel & Tourist Agency, A. Abdieh Street (tel. 31957)
Canar Travel & Tourist Agency, Main Street, El-Russaifah (tel. 117)
Al-Kailani Travel & Tourism, Al-Azraq (tel. 9)
Ma'an Tourist Co, King Hussein Street (tel. 32930)
Ben Batota Travel & Tourism, Wadi E'sseer (tel. 815331)
Al-Tal Travel & Tourist Agency, El-Remtha (tel. 83165)
Jerusalem Express Travel Agency, Al-Baqah (tel. 842196)
Al-E'etimad Tourist Agency, Main Street, El-Mushairfah
Tyche Travel & Tourist Agency, AL-H5 (tel. 18)
Palestine Tours, Al-Hashemi Street (tel. 23963) Amman

Getting Around

By taxi People in Amman commute by private car and taxi. Taxis are identified by a green number plate. Private taxis have a yellow square on the front door and cost about 500 fils from jebel to jebel. Taxis are metered. An example of an outside taxi fare is Aqaba to Amman JD25. Taxis with a white square on the front door are known as 'service taxis', where five passengers share a cheap fixed cost according to the route. The main station for 'service-taxis' in downtown Amman is near Cinema al-Hussein in Saqf el-Seil near the Roman theatre, Abdali and al-Wendat. This means of travel which also operates an inter-city service is recommended for young travellers.

By hired car Renting a car ranges from JD2.500 for a small saloon car, plus 25 fils per kilometre. A valid international driving licence is required. Most credit cards are accepted. The following car hire companies operate from Amman:

Al-Dairi, Wadi Saqra Street (tel. 669970)
The Gulf, Ain Ghazal Road Sport City (tel. 660902)
Al-Remal, Abdali (tel. 39861)
Al-Selwadi, Police College Street (tel. 664245)
Al-Said Co, Shmeisani near Comodor Hotel (tel. 667439)
Al-Shakhsheer, Shmeisani Middle East Hotel (tel. 68958)
Al-Labadi, Jabel Amman Circle 6 (tel. 813554)
Al-Waha, Abdaly (tel. 668988)
Al-Arz, Tyche Hotel (tel. 661114)
Amir Jarrar, Starco Building (tel. 670498)
Amra, Amman Marriott Hotel (tel. 39198)
Amman, Shmeisani (tel. 666327)
Afana, Madaba Street (tel. 78939)
Bisharat Touring Car, Jordan Inter Con. Hotel (tel. 37830)
Bisharat Cgr, Jordan Inter Con. Hotel (tel. 41350)
Derani, Shmeisani (tel. 660601)
Farah, Prince Moh'd Street (tel. 673330)
Firas, Prince Moh'd Street (tel. 664137)
Hisham, Hisham Hotel (tel. 42720)
Golden Wings, King Hussein Street (tel. 38787)
General Services, Housing Bank Building (tel. 44007)
Jameel Haddad, Ras Al-Ain Street (tel. 71707)
Jorac, Jabel Amman near Jordan Hotel (tel. 44938)
National, Jabel Amman Shebard Hotel (tel. 39197)
Nebo, Alswafieh Street (tel. 816792)
Rabbath Ammon, Shmeisani (tel. 664239)
Rayan, Um Uzeina Hotel (tel. 816146)
Satellite, Abdali (tel. 25767)
Sawsan, Sport City (tel. 8987)
T.T.T., Amman Crown Hotel (tel. 78968)
Tyche, Jabel Amman Circle 1 (tel. 25700)
Tiger, Sport City (tel. 660902)
United Corp, Jabel Weibdeh Firas Wing (tel. 22103)
U drive Rent A Car, Shmeisani (tel. 669376)
Wassim, Comio Hotel (tel. 43515)
Kada, Ambassador Hotel (tel. 51986)
Natur Rent-A Car, Jabal Amman (tel. 19187)
Al-Dairi, Housing Bank Building (tel. 5761)
Al-Manara, Municipality Square (tel. 4666)
Jorac, Aquamarina Hotel (tel. 4333)
Kedreh, Municipality Square (tel. 48198)

Rum, Commercial Center (tel. 3581)
Save, Al Cazar Hotel (tel. 4133)

By bus Cheap public buses operate throughout Jordan. There is also the excellent JETT coach-service operating between Amman, Petra and Aqaba.

JETT also operates to Damascus, Baghdad and Ankara. A hostess travels on board the coach which is clean and comfortable. A service leaves Amman at 8.00, 10.00, 15.00 and 17.00 hours (and 7.00, 9.00, 15.00 and 17.00 hours in summer). Reservations must be made at the bus station in advance. Toilet facilities and a money exchange bureau are located on the border. A good bus service also operates between Amman and Irbid.

By train A steam-train operates between Amman and Damascus, a 7–9 hour journey costing from 700 fils (the road journey takes about 4 hours). Until the Hejaz Railway is repaired, there is no other train service in Jordan.

By air The only domestic air service is to Aqaba, with daily flights (except Tuesdays) on ALIA, flight time about one hour. Air tickets bought in Amman are cheaper than if bought outside Jordan. Air passengers note there is a tax on final departure from Amman.

Information for Business Visitors

Exchange Control There are strict exchange controls in Jordan and suppliers are warned to ensure that buyers hold valid import licences. Otherwise foreign currency will not be released and documentary credits cannot be obtained. Before submitting the amount due to a supplier, the local importer submits his import licence to a bank, requesting foreign exchange for transfer to the beneficiary. The Central Bank of Jordan requires that letters of credit in the name of beneficiaries in the United Kingdom must include a condition that air consignments travel on ALIA – The Royal Jordanian Airline.

Customs Tariff Duties are either *ad valorem*, or specific. Certain raw materials and machinery are customs exempt, with prior approval of the Ministry of Industry and Trade. The *ad valorem* duty payable is assessed on the price of goods at the place of shipment or purchase on the day of clearance in Jordan, plus additional costs for transport, insurance etc. There is a 20 per cent tax on alcoholic beverages. An additional tax of 10 per cent is payable on luxury items (electrical goods, cosmetics, carpets, films etc.). An import licence fee is levied on most imported goods at 4 per cent of the c. & f. value (cost and freight).

Import Licensing Goods for government use are on open general licence, other goods require specific licences, issued fairly freely and carrying an allocation of foreign exchange. Importers must first apply for a trade licence. An import licence is normally valid for 12 months. A renewal fee of 1 per cent of the value of the goods is charged.

Documentation Shipments must be covered by a commercial invoice (original, and as many copies as may be required). Goods for export must be certified by a Chamber of Commerce and also by the Jordanian Embassy. Outside London, certification by the Chamber of Commerce is sufficient. Certification is exempt on value less than JD30. Goods accompanied by non-certified invoices are subject to a fine amounting to 2 per cent of the c.i.f. value of the shipment (cost, insurance and freight). The original invoice and copies should be sent to the consignee, or to the Jordan bank which opened the letter of credit.

Samples Samples not exceeding JD5 in value may be taken in by a business visitor without duty provided they are submitted for inspection on departure. After 60 days in Jordan such samples become liable for duty. All other samples and advertising material are subject to duty.

Goods in Transit Free transit of goods is allowed provided they enter and leave through previously specified points.

Warehousing Goods may be left in the port up to 45 days. After this period they are subject to a fine of 25 per cent of the value. They may also be removed from the port at the expense and responsibility of the owner.

Agents Exporters are advised to find an agent rather than attempt to export direct. A good agent in Amman should be able to cover the whole country. Most government officials, professionals and merchants speak English. Agency appointment is governed by the Commercial Agents and Intermediaries Law No. 20 of 1974.

Correspondence and trade literature should be in English. Prices should normally be quoted c. & f. Aqaba (or Beirut, if requested). Jordanian merchants expect to be given 90–180 days' credit.

Jordan Free Zones

Port of Aqaba: Projected area: 2,000,000 square metres.

Now in operation, the free zone in Aqaba is ideally situated for both the local and regional markets. Located about 7 kilometres from the seaport and 4 kilometres from Aqaba Airport and served by a modern network of overland routes and a railway, it links the region with the three continents of Africa, Asia and Europe.

The zone includes transit sheds, open storage areas, warehouses, cold storage facilities and suitable sites for the manufacture, assembly, blending or packing of products to be marketed in the region. Qualified firms may use either the free zone's facilities or construct their own.

Zarqa: Projected area: 5.2 million square metres.

Presently under construction, this zone is located 30 kilometres north of Amman in the Zarqa region and will serve as an inland free zone facility, with easy access to the main highway that runs between Jordan and Iraq.

Jordan-Syria Border: Projected area: 8 million square metres.

Presently under planning, this free zone will be located at the Jordanian-Syrian border near the railway line that runs through Jordan to Syria. Under construction is a major four-lane highway that will cross the border at the free zone site.

Free Zone Incentives

Jordan's free zone regulations provide a number of benefits designed to attract more industrial, commercial, investment and service firms into its free zones. Among them are:

1. No rental fees for the first year on sites leased for more than ten years to import, export and transit trade projects, and for the first two years on sites leased for more than ten years to industrial enterprises.
2. Exemption of land, licence and construction taxes on buildings and installations erected by investors.
3. Exemption from customs fees and other duties on goods and equipment entering the free zones.
4. 100 per cent income tax exemption for a period of 12 years.
5. Repatriation of profits and capital.

Inducements for potential investors: To encourage both domestic and foreign long-term investment in Jordan proper, the Kingdom has provided generous incentives to new companies, or to major expansion of existing establishments, through its Encouragement of Investment Law.

Over 100 Companies (more than 90 per cent of those applying) in the first three years since passage of the law received swift project approvals to qualify for special benefits, which now include:

100 per cent exemption from income and social services taxes on net profits for six years. This is extended to nine years if the project is located outside the governorate of Amman, or is a public shareholding company.

100 per cent exemption from all customs duties and import fees on equipment and replacement parts used.

100 per cent exemption from property tax for five years. This is extended to seven years if the project is located outside the governorate of Amman or is operated by a public shareholding company.

Guaranteed repatriation of capital and the free transfer of interest and profits. Even non-approved projects have no problems converting dinars or transferring funds abroad.

Government-owned land outside the governorate of Amman may be granted free of charge to approved projects.

In addition to these inducements to long-term investment, liberal benefits are now available to foreign companies which locate their regional headquarters in Jordan. Under Jordan's new Foreign Companies Registration Law, such companies are entitled to a 100 per cent exemption on income and social services taxes on profits earned outside the country. Also, foreign managers and employees of such offices are similarly exempted from taxes on their salaries and other company-related income. Companies registered under this law are allowed to open non-resident accounts whereby currency can be transferred in and out of their accounts with no restrictions.

Useful Addresses
Government Ministries

	tel no.
The Royal Hashemite Court	37341
Prime Minister's Office, Jebel Amman	41211
Agriculture, P.O. Box 2099, Jebel Amman	39391
Awqaf and Islamic Affairs, Jebel Hussein	66141
Communications, Third Circle, Jebel Amman	24301
Culture, Tourism & Antiquities	42311
Defence, Abdali	22131
Education, P.O. Box 1646, Amman	669181
Finance and Customs, P.O. Box 85, King Hussein Street	36394
Foreign Affairs, P.O. Box 1577, Jebel Amman	44361
Health, P.O. Box 86, Jebel Hussein	665131
Industry and Trade, P.O. Box 2019, Abdali	63191
Information, P.O. Box 1854, Jebel Amman	41467/44258
Interior, Abd Al-Naser Roundabout, Jebel Hussein	663111/38849

Justice, Shmeisani	663103
Labour and Social Development	67394
Planning	44466
Youth	44392
Labour, Shmeisani	663186
Municipal and Rural Affairs and Environment 3rd Circle, Jebel Amman	41393
Occupied Territories	666172
Public Works	668481
Supply, PO Box 830, Abdali	667141
Tourism Authorities, PO Box 224, 3rd Circle, Jebel Amman	42311
Transport, PO Box 1929, 4th Circle, Jebel Amman	41461/41485

Diplomatic Missions to the Hashemite Kingdom of Jordan

Algerian Democratic Popular Republic, Jebel Amman, Third Circle	41271/2
Austrian Embassy	44750
Belgium, Toufic Ayoub Building, Jebel Amman	675683
People's Republic of Bulgaria, Jebel Weibdeh, Hafiz Ibrahim Street	818151
Canadian Embassy	666124
Republic of Chile, Jebel Amman, Mutanabi Street	661336
Czechoslovak Socialist Republic, Jebel Weibdeh, Al-Awsat, Civil Defence Street	665105/6
Danish Consulate	22324
E.E.C.	668191
Finnish Consulate	37117
Republic of France, Jebel Amman, Mutanabi Street	41273/4
Greece, Jebel Amman, Fifth Circle	672331
Federal Republic of Germany, Jebel Amman	41351/2
Haitian Consulate	23163
Hungarian Embassy	667966
Republic of India, Jebel Amman, First Circle	37262/37029/22098
Iran, Jebel Amman, Fourth Circle	41281/2
Republic of Iraq, Jebel Amman, First Circle	23175
Republic of Italy, El Khansa Street, Jebel Weibdeh	381985
Japan, Jebel Amman, Fourth Circle	672486
Republic of Korea, Jebel Amman – Street 8313	42268/9
Democratic People's Republic of Korea, Shmeisani, near the Professional Association Centre	666349
State of Kuwait, Abu Firas Street, Jebel Amman	675135/8
Republic of Lebanon, Jebel Amman, Second Circle	41381
Kingdom of Morocco, Jebel Amman, Fourth Circle	41451/2
Norwegian Consulate	37164
Sultanate of Oman, Shmeisani	61717
Islamic Republic of Pakistan, Jebel Weibdeh (Opposite Bisharat Church)	22787
People's Republic of Poland, Jebel Amman, First Circle	37153/4
Portuguese Consulate	42248
State of Qatar, Jebel Amman, Third Circle	44331/2
Socialist Republic of Romania, Shmeisani	663161

Kingdom of Saudi Arabia, Abu Bakr Street, Jebel Amman, First Circle   814154
Spain, Queen Zein Street, Jebel Amman   22140
Switzerland, Abu Feras Street, Jebel Amman   44416/7
Syrian Arab Republic, Jamal El Din Al-Afghani Street, Jebel Amman,
  Third Circle   41392/41935
Swedish Embassy   669177/9
Tunisian Embassy   674307
Republic of Turkey, Queen Zein Al Sharaf Street, Jebel Amman   41251/2
United Arab Emirates 2623   44369
United Nations Development Program in Jordan, Jebel Amman   41202/5
United Nations Relief and Works Agency for Palestine Refugees,
  Ibn El-Amid Street, Jebel Hussein   669194
Union of Soviet Socialist Republics, 28 Zahran Street, Jebel Amman,
  Third Circle   41158/41229
United Kingdom of Great Britain and Northern Ireland, Jebel Amman,
  Third Circle   41261/6
United States of America, Jebel Amman   44371/6
Arab Republic of Yemen, Al Mutasem Street, Second Circle, Jebel Amman
  42381/2
Socialist Federal Republic of Yugoslavia   39576
W.H.O.   674583

Banks in Jordan Central Bank of Jordan, Arab Bank Ltd., Arab Land Bank, Bank al-Mashrek SAL, Bank of Credit & Commerce International, Bank of Jordan Ltd., The British Bank of the Middle East, The Cairo Amman Bank Ltd., The Chase Manhattan Bank NA, Chase Manhattan Overseas Corporation, Citibank, Grindlays Bank Ltd., Jordan-Gulf Bank, Jordan Kuwait Bank, Jordan National Bank, Petra Bank, Oesterreichische Laenderbank, Rafidain Bank.

Airline Companies

Aeroflot   41510
Air Canada   30879
Air France   666055
Air Lanka   23536
Alia   30318/19 24131/35, 22856, 39424, 22310
Alitalia   25203
American Airways   669068
Arab Wings Charter Service   94484/91994
Balkan Airways   665909
British Airways   41430
Cathay Pacific   24363
Cyprus Airways   38787
Egypt Air   30011
Gulf Air   665311
Hungarian Airlines   39295
Iberia   25197

Iraqi Airways   23648
Japan Airways   30879
K.L.M.   22175
Korean Airlines   24805
Kuwait Air   30144
Libyan Arab Airlines   67320
Lufthansa   41305
M.E.A.   36104
Olympic   24363
Pan-Am   41959
Philippine Airlines   38433
PIA   25981
Polish Airlines   25981
Royal Thai   22324
Sabena   675888
SAS   22324
Saudia   39333
Singapore Airlines   23536
Somali Airlines   39540
Swiss Air   41906
Syrian Air   22147
Trans Mediterannean Airways   22324
Tunis Air   30879
Turkish Airlines   39575
Varig · 30011
Yemenia   24363
Yugoslav   37171
Amman Airport   91489/91498 (10 lines)
                91680/91686 (7 lines)

Visiting the West Bank

Jordanian money is not valid in the West Bank, but there are exchange facilities in the Israeli immigration and customs shed. Israeli money may be changed for Jordanian money at the same bank, for tourists who intend returning to Jordan.

Israeli immigration officials do not stamp passports, but provide and stamp a separate form.

In the event of delay crossing the bridge, travellers are advised to carry fruit and refreshments.

Luggage is given a rigorous search by Israeli officials. There is a compulsory porterage fee on all baggage.

Public telephones, toilets and a small café are located in the Israeli immigration shed. Buses and taxis are available outside. Check taxi-fare with an official before starting journey.

There is a compulsory departure tax on leaving Israel. Tax stamps are sold at any post office; the Central Post Office, East Jerusalem, is open from 8.30–18.00 hours.

Recognised Hotels in East Jerusalem and the West Bank

Jerusalem

Inter-Continental, Mount of Olives (tel. 282551) 5 star
Mount Scopus, Sheikh Jarrah (tel. 284891/2) 5 star
St. George International, Salaheddine (tel. 282571/5) 5 star
Ambassador, Sheikh Jarrah (tel. 282515) 4 star
American Colony, Nablus Road (tel. 282421–3) 4 star
Capitol, Salaheddine (tel. 282561) 4 star
National Palace, 4, Azzahra (tel. 282246–8) 4 star
Panorama, Hill of Gethsemane (tel. 284886–7) 4 star
Ritz, 8, Ibn Khaldoun Street (tel. 284853–4) 4 star
Commodore, Mount of Olives (tel. 284845) 3 star
Holy Land East, 6, Rashid Street (tel. 284841–2) 3 star
Jordan House, Nur Eldin Street (tel. 283430) 3 star
Palace, Mount of Olives (tel. 284981) 3 star
Pilgrims Palace, King Suleiman Street (tel. 284831) 3 star
Strand, Ibn Jubeir Street (tel. 282079) 3 star
Y.M.C.A., 29 Nablus Road (tel. 282375) 3 star
Y.W.C.A., Wadi Jose Street (tel. 282593) 3 star
Astoria, Mount of Olives (tel. 284965) 2 star

Bethlehem

Handal, Cinema Street (tel. 40)
Palace Hotel, near the Church of the Nativity, 2 star

Restaurants in the West Bank
East Jerusalem
National Palace Restaurant (tel. 282139). Excellent Oriental food and service, superb *mazza* and kebabs.

Sea Dolphin (tel. 282788). Excellent sea-food fresh from Gaza with a good variety of local wines; reasonably priced. Shrimps are recommended.

Hassan Effendi: (tel. 283559). Good Oriental food.

Oriental Restaurant: (tel. 284397). Middle East cuisine.

Sinbad Restaurant: (tel. 272052). Suitable for a quick lunch or dinner; also take-away.

Ommayad Restaurant: (tel. 283542)

Bedouin Tent: (tel. 284397)

Select Restaurant: (tel. 283325)

Maswadi Restaurant: (tel. 284048)

Golden Chicken: (tel. 282915)

Philadelphia: (tel. 289770)

Ramsis: (tel. 280194). In the heart of the Old City, 31 David Street.

Bethlehem
Jamer Restaurant, Caritas Street (tel. 742317). Cool: Oriental cuisine.

Jericho
al-Rawda Park (tel. 92-24555). Alfresco, good local cuisine.

Travel Agents and Car-hire Companies in East Jerusalem
Shepherds Tours & Travels (Tjaerborg Agent): P.O. Box 19560, Azzahra Street, Jerusalem (tel. 284121, telex 26114). All sightseeing and hotel reservations, office within walking distance of the National Palace and the Ritz Hotels in East Jerusalem.

Avis Car-Hire: International reservations (03) 336363 Telex 32181

Hertz Car-Hire: 27 Salaheddin Street (tel. 238415) both from $U.S.16 per day. 0.16 per kilometre, plus 0.09 over 120 kilometres. Special rate for unlimited kilometres $38.60. Minimum age: 23. No VAT is added if payment is made in foreign exchange. Valid licence is required.

Coach Hire: Mount of Olives Tourist Travel Ltd., P.O. Box 19949, Jerusalem (tel. 283023 or 281774)

Son et Lumière: There are performances in English on Thursdays and Sundays at 20.45 hours at David's Tower, near Jaffa Gate, Old City. Also in French at 22.00 hours every evening except Friday. There is an admission charge.

Bibliography

AAMIRY, M.A.	*Jerusalem, Arab Origin and Heritage*, Longman, London 1976
ABDULLAH, KING OF JORDAN	*My Memoirs Completed – al-Takmilah*, Longman, London 1976
AMERICAN WOMEN'S ASSOCIATION	*Welcome to Amman*, American Women's Association, 1976
BARANKI, D.C.	*The Road to Petra*, Nazzal & Sons, 1973
BOULANGER, ROBERT	*Jordanie*, Les Guides Bleus, Hachette, 1979
BRITISH OVERSEAS BOARD OF TRADE	*Hints to Exporters*, British Overseas Boards of Trade, 1979/80
BROWNING, IAIN	*Petra*, Chatto and Windus, London 1973
CARR, WINIFRED	*Hussein's Kingdom*, Frewin, 1966
DEPT. ANTIQUITIES, JORDAN	*The Archaeological Heritage of Jordan – Part I* Amman, 1973
DUGGAN, ALFRED	*The Story of the Crusades*, Faber and Faber, London 1963
DUNCAN, ALISTAIR	*The Noble Sanctuary*, Longman, London 1972
DUNCAN, ALISTAIR	*The Noble Heritage*, Longman, London 1974
FISTERE, ISOBEL AND JOHN	*Jordan, the Holy Land*, Middle East Export Press, Beirut 1965
FRANCISCAN FATHERS	*Guide to Jordan*, Franciscan Press, Jerusalem 1978
GLUBB, JOHN BAGOT	*Syria, Lebanon, Jordan*, Thames & Hudson, London 1967
GLUECK, NELSON	*The Other Side of the Jordan*, The American School of Oriental Research, Cambridge, Mass. 1940
HARDING, LANKASTER G.	*The Antiquities of Jordan*, Lutterworth Press, London 1976
HATEM, M. ABDEL-KADER	*Land of the Arabs*, Longman, London 1977
HASSAN BIN TALAL, CROWN PRINCE	*A Study on Jerusalem*, Longman, London 1979
JABER, GHARAIBEH, KHASAWHEH, HILL	*Bedouins of Jordan – A people in Transition*, Royal Society Press, 1978
ABU JAFA, MAHER	*Some Multiple-Use Problems Associated with the Establishment and Management of Azraq Desert National Park*
JARVIS, MAJOR C.S.	*Arab Command*, Hutchinson, London 1942
JOHNSTONE, CHARLES	*The Brink of the Jordan*, Hamish Hamilton, London 1972

Bibliography

JORDAN INFORMATION BUREAU	*Jordan Magazines*, Washington
LAWRENCE, T.E.	*Seven Pillars of Wisdom*, Penguin, London and New York, 1976
LION PUBLISHING	*The Lion Handbook to the Bible*, 1976
MANNIN, ETHEL	*Lance for the Arabs*, Hutchinson, London 1963
MANNIN, ETHEL	*The Lovely Land*, Hutchinson, London 1965
MOUNTFORT, GUY	*Portrait of a Desert*, Collins, London 1965
NASIR, SARI J.	*The Arabs and the English*, Longman, London 1976
NATIONAL GEOGRAPHICAL MAGAZINE	"Aqaba" December, 1946
NELSON, BRYAN	*Azraq: A Desert Oasis*, Allen House, University of Princetown 1975
NELSON, NINA	*Your Guide to Jordan*, Alvin Redman 1966
RANDALL, RHONA	*Jordan, The Holy Land*, Frederick Muller, 1968
RODEN, CLAUDIA	*A Book of Middle Eastern Food*, Penguin, London 1970
SHAHEER, JAMEELA	*Arab World Cook Book*, International Book shop Dubai 1973
SHOWKER, KAY	*Jordan and the Holy Land*, Fodor, David McKay, New York 1979
E. W. EGAN (ED.)	The Middle East – *The Arab States*, Sterling Publishing Cie., 1978
TREECE, HENRY	*The Crusaders*, Bodley Head, London 1962
WADDY, CHARIS	*The Muslim Mind*, Longman, London 1976
WEIR, SHELAGH	*The Bedouin*, Museum of Mankind, London 1966

Index

Biblical and other ancient places with modern names

see also list of Decapolis cities (page 8)